Facing Value Decisions:
Rationale-building for Teachers

Facing Value Decisions: Rationale-building for Teachers

Second Edition

James P. Shaver
William Strong

Utah State University

Teachers College, Columbia University
New York and London 1982

Published by Teachers College Press, 1234 Amsterdam Avenue, New York, NY 10027

Copyright © 1982 by Teachers College, Columbia University

First edition, © 1976, published by Wadsworth Publishing Co., Inc.

All rights reserved. No part of this publication may be reproduced or transmitted in any form or by any means, electronic or mechanical, including photocopy, or any information storage and retrieval system, without permission from the publisher.

Library of Congress Cataloging in Publication Data

Shaver, James P.
  Facing value decisions.

  Bibliography: p.
  Includes index.
  1. Moral education. 2. Values. I. Strong, William S. II. Title.
LC268.S46 1982   370.11'4   81–18235
ISBN 0–8077–2682–6   AACR2
ISBN 0–8077–2681-8 (pkb.)

Manufactured in the United States of America

87 86 85 84 83 82 1 2 3 4 5 6

Copyright page continued on page x

**This book is for our parents,
who loved and trusted us enough
to value our valuing**

Jim and Bill

CONTENTS

Foreword to the First Edition   xi
Preface   xiii

1 Do You Want to Deal with Values?   1

Values in the Classroom   1
The Extracurricular Curriculum   8
Frame of Reference   8
From Frame to Rationale   9
Our Intent   10
A Lesson for Anthony   11
Value Exploration 1   14
Shop Sketch   15

2 Values—What Are They?   17

Some Distinctions   17
Types of Values   20
Value Conflict   32
Recap   36
Value Exploration 2   36
The Experiment   38
Moral Values and the "Teacher-Counselor"   41
Esthetic Values Over Tea and Crumpets   42
Instrumental Values, Kids, and Potted Plants   43
Value Exploration 3   45

3 The Democratic Context 46

Defining Democracy	47
Human Dignity and Intelligence	51
Pluralism—A Sine Qua Non of Democracy	52
Conflict	55
Cohesion	56
The Creed and Cohesion	57
Potential Objections to the Creed in a Teaching Rationale	58
Recap	62
Mini-Democracy in Room 16	63
Devil's Advocate	64
Chicano Maverick	66
The Problem	67
Value Exploration 4	68
Equality—For Whom?	69

4 Schooling, Professionals, and Values 71

The Distinction Between Education and Schooling	71
The Authority-Agent/Professional-Client Paradox	74
Recap—And Beyond	82
Value Exploration 5	83
Inner Office Conference	84
Faculty Meeting	85
Brotherhood	87

5 Teaching in a Democratic Context: Esthetic and Instrumental Values 88

The School and Esthetics	89
Instrumental Values in the Classroom—The Need for Dialogue	95
Recap	100
Making School Weird	100
Inservice Workshop	102
Means and Ends	104
Value Exploration 6	106

6 Teaching in a Democratic Context: Moral Values — 107

Cognitive Aspects of Moral Values Education — 108
Affective Aspects of Moral Values Education:
   Inculcation and Dignity — 114
Teacher and School — 119
Recap—And Beyond — 124
Civil Disobedience — 126
Current Events — 128
Story Within a Story — 129
Value Exploration 7 — 131
Pep Assembly — 131
After School — 132
Value Exploration 8 — 134

7 Two Other Approaches to Moral Values — 135

Values Clarification — 135
Cognitive Development: Moral Stages — 144
Recap — 155
Jeremy and the Public Interview — 155
Value Exploration 9 — 157
Value Exploration 10 — 159
The Dilemma — 161

8 Epilogue: The Teacher as Philosopher — 163

A Lifelong Commitment — 165
Philosophy as Action — 165
Why Focus on Values, Not Attitudes? — 166
The Cultivation of Self-confrontation — 168

References — 173
Index — 181

Reprint Acknowledgments
(Continuation of Copyright Page)

Page 4, excerpt from "A Christmas Call to Conscience: Do You Hear the Animals Crying?" by Judith Schmidt, published in *Family Weekly*, December 23, 1973, copyright 1973 by Family Weekly, Inc. and used by permission of Family Weekly, Inc.

Page 9, excerpt from *The Nature of the Social Sciences* by Charles Beard, copyright 1934 Charles Scribner's Sons, renewal copyright 1962 William Beard, used by permission of Charles Scribner's Sons.

Page 34, excerpt from *An American Dilemma* by Gunnar Myrdal, copyright 1944 by Harper & Row, Publishers, Inc., used by permission of Harper & Row, Publishers, Inc.

Page 51, excerpt from "Supreme Court Hears Arguments in Minority Admissions Case" by Cheryl M. Fields, published in *The Chronicle of Higher Education*, March 4, 1974, used by permission of the publisher.

Page 62, excerpt from *Stride Toward Freedom* by Martin Luther King, Jr., copyright 1958 by Harper & Row, Publishers, Inc., used by permission of Harper & Row, Publishers, Inc.

Pages 72, 73, excerpts from "A Careful Guide to the School Squabble" by Neil Postman and Charles Weingartner, published in *Psychology Today*, October 1973, used by permission of Dell Publishing.

Page 78, excerpt from "Educational Accountability for a Humanistic Perspective" by Arthur W. Combs, *Educational Researcher*, September 1973, Vol. 2, No. 9, p. 20 (from column 3), used by permission of the American Educational Research Association.

Page 91, excerpt from "Films: Creative Chaos" by Paul D. Zimmerman, published in *Newsweek*, December 1973, copyright Newsweek, Inc. 1973, reprinted by permission.

Pages 91, 92, excerpts from "Pop: Messiah Coming?" by Maureen Orth, published in *Newsweek*, December 1973, copyright Newsweek, Inc. 1973, reprinted by permission.

Page 92, excerpt from "The Arts in America" by Jack Kroll, published in *Newsweek*, December 1973, copyright Newsweek, Inc. 1973, reprinted by permission.

Page 98, excerpt from *Crisis in the Classroom* by Charles E. Silberman, copyright 1970, used by permission of the publisher, Random House, and of the William Morris Agency.

Pages 116, 117, excerpts from "Educational Policies That Frustrate Character Development" by Diane Ravitch, published in *Character*, Vol. 1, No. 2, 1980, used by permission of the editor.

Pages 118, 119, excerpts from *The Prophet* by Kahlil Gibran, copyright 1923 by Kahlil Gibran, renewal copyright 1951 by Administrators C.T.A. of Kahlil Gibran estate, and Mary C. Gibran, published by Alfred A. Knopf, Inc., used by permission of the publisher.

Pages 136, 138, 139, excerpts from *Values and Teaching* by Louis E. Raths, Merrill Harmin, and Sidney Simon, copyright 1966 by Charles E. Merrill Books, Inc., used by permission of Charles E. Merrill Books, Inc.

Page 142, excerpt from *Towards Judgement* edited by Donald Hamingson of the University of East Anglia (England) Centre for Applied Research in Education, used by permission.

Page 153, excerpt from "The Moral Atmosphere of the School" by Lawrence Kohlberg, published by the Association for Supervision and Curriculum Development in *The Unstudied Curriculum* (N. Overly, editor), 1970, used by permission of the Association for Supervision and Curriculum Development.

Pages 169-170, excerpt from *The Foxfire Book* edited and with an Introduction by Brooks Eliot Wigginton, copyright © 1968, 1969, 1970, 1971, 1972 by The Foxfire Fund, Inc., reprinted by permission of Doubleday & Company, Inc.

FOREWORD TO THE FIRST EDITION

In recent years, "values education" has increasingly been a topic for professional discussion in educational journals, teacher inservice sessions, professional conferences, and college methods courses. Most of this discussion has focused on two areas: (1) the description and defense of various models designed to teach (or teach about) values and the process of valuing; and (2) descriptions of different techniques that a teacher might use to implement one or more of these models in the classroom. Rarely, however, has there been any sort of critical analysis of either models or techniques with regard to underlying ethical premises, and the degree to which either models or techniques are or are not consistent with such premises.

In filling this lack, Professors Shaver and Strong have produced a noteworthy book. They present the reader with their own rationale for values education and identify the ethical premises which underlie this rationale. And they argue persuasively that it is absolutely essential for the teacher to develop his or her own rationale—a rationale that is intellectually defensible yet emotionally satisfying; a rationale that is based on fundamental value assumptions carefully thought out and clearly articulated. Only in this way will the teacher have anything more than a whimsical basis for dealing with values in elementary and secondary school classrooms.

The attainment of this goal—helping and encouraging teachers to develop such a rationale—is one of the authors' central concerns. A second concern—and a major theme of the book—is to help teachers (or anyone else interested) to help students develop a rational foundation for their own values, and learn the skills they will always need to analyze and defend their values rationally. Ideas about ways to achieve both goals abound throughout the book. A particularly exciting feature is a set of value explorations and exercises in which the authors present a variety of activities, vignettes, and provocative questions to help the reader think about values and how to deal with them in the classroom.

This is not a book of methodology, however. Rather, it is intended, in the authors' words, "to start the reader thinking about the value-related assumptions from which he or she teaches or will teach." This intent has been met, and in a manner that is always provocative, at times amusing, and in places inspiring.

Read on, you're in for a rich experience.

Jack R. Fraenkel
Professor of Interdisciplinary Studies in Education,
San Francisco State University

PREFACE

This is a book written for teachers—prospective and practicing. It is not written for academicians, although we have, of course, been constantly aware of our university colleagues' glances over our shoulders. It was our intent to write a book that would be valuable in undergraduate courses—educational foundations, general methods, methods of teaching social studies or English—for prospective elementary and secondary school teachers, as well as in graduate courses and inservice programs for practicing teachers and supervisors. That intent has guided the preparation of the revised edition as it did the first edition.

We are concerned with concepts and distinctions that seem suited to value-related teaching decisions and therefore are usable by teachers. We are less concerned with fine intellectual distinctions than some of our university colleagues might wish—not because such distinctions are unimportant, but because we do not view them as functional for teachers in dealing with the day-to-day realities of classroom life.

It should be noted, too, that our discussion of values is not based solely on writings in the discipline of philosophy. It also owes much to work in political science, to an anthropological view of the role of values, and to research in the psychological aspects of valuing. In short, we are more concerned with values as cultural, political, and psychological phenomena than with the analytic distinctions with which philosophers grapple in searching for intellectual rigor, precision, and consistency.

This book is founded on the authors' faith in rationality. We believe that rationality in valuing is good, and that value-related teaching decisions will be better if made through an open, rational process. This commitment to rationality implies a warning: Be alert throughout to our biases. We have tried to lay out a rationale and its implications, pulling our assumptions into the open, partly as an illustrative exercise that may help you to explicate and scrutinize your own frame of reference. But these are subtle and complex matters. We urge you to subject what we say to continuous examination as you read, and to guard against unwarranted conclusions on our part.

We should also mention that this is *not* a book of methodology, though its vignettes depict teachers in action. It is intended to engage the reader in thinking about the value-related assumptions from which he or she teaches or will teach. It is full of implications about how to interact with students; but to draw them out and develop them was beyond our present scope. This book is intended to be heuristic in nature. To spell out all the methodological implications not only would have taken too much space, but also would have belied our faith in the ability of teachers to think for themselves.

The theoretical framework of this book is the outcome of several years of graduate work, public school teaching, participation in teacher training, curriculum development, and consultant work by the senior author. He first set out to write the book alone; but after much of the basic manuscript was on paper, he sought a collaborator. Someone was needed who could provide critical feedback and apply a literary flair to the writing of the vignettes and value explorations intended to involve the reader in considering and applying the substantive content of each chapter. The Shaver-Strong association has, we trust, created a more readable, applicable book. Our frequent discussions have also resulted in introspection and expansion for both of us—and the volume is much more than either of us could have produced alone.

In preparing this revised edition, we have had three objectives: (1) to improve readability and clarity; (2) to update both the examples used and the sources cited; and (3) to sharpen the conceptualization of values without becoming unduly academic and complicated. Editing changes have been made throughout. In addition, five vignettes have been added to increase the reader's involvement in thinking about and applying the approach to values which we propose. Two chapters have undergone major revision. Chapter 2 has been rewritten to augment the conceptual soundness of our value schema. Changes in Chapter 7 include a somewhat expanded description of the values clarification approach; an updating of our presentation of the cognitive moral development approach to reflect recent publications; and a revised assessment of both approaches to reflect better our own rationale as presented in the earlier chapters. Chapter 8 is an entirely new chapter. It pulls together our intentions and hopes in a way that seems necessary to end the book on the proper educational note.

Any endeavor of this sort rests on the contributions of people too numerous to name. However, the early intellectual prodding of Donald W. Oliver, one of the seminal thinkers in American education and a master teacher at Harvard, cannot go without mention and thanks. Jack Fraenkel, editor of the series of which the first edition was a part, made helpful criticisms, as did the following reviewers of that manuscript: Lawrence E. Metcalf, Jack L. Nelson, and Michael Scriven. Glen Casto's critique of the material on Piaget and Kohlberg in Chapter 7 was also very helpful.

The revised edition has benefited from comments by readers and users of the first one. Richard Knight provided helpful observations based on his use of the book with inservice teachers. Reviews by Ian Wright in the *Journal of Moral Education* (1979, Vol. 8), Stanley Wronski in *Social Education* (1976, Vol. 40), and Hersh, Miller, and Fielding in their *Models of Moral Education* raised significant points about our discussion of values in Chapter 2, as did Robison James's thoughtful correspondence. Ross Lehman's consideration of our values schema as he used the first edition as the basis for developing a preservice instructional program, "Examination of Values for Teachers" (doctoral dissertation, Utah State University, 1980), also raised questions which we have addressed. These contributions, as well as many unidentified ones from our practicing colleagues in elementary and secondary schools and from our university colleagues, are greatly appreciated. Of course, any errors in thought remain our own.

Special thanks are also due Billie Sue McNeil and Karen Casto for typing and other manuscript contributions "above and beyond" on the first edition, and Kathrynn Whitney on this revision.

One last note: You will find two kinds of inserts throughout the book. One kind consists of cartoons and quotations that illustrate or elaborate on points being made in the text. These are meant to be read with the text. We hope that they will stimulate your thinking on the issues being discussed. The second type of insert material refers you to vignettes and value explorations located at the end of each chapter. We suggest that you first skim each chapter to get a sense of its thrust. Then, on a second, careful reading, turn to the vignettes and value explorations as you come to the inserted references. They will help to illustrate the ideas in the text and assist you in applying them to your own teaching decisions.

Now on to the main body of the book. We only hope that you find your involvement in it nearly as exciting as we have found ours!

James P. Shaver
William Strong

Facing Value Decisions:
Rationale-building for Teachers

Chapter 1

DO YOU WANT TO DEAL WITH VALUES?

It has become fashionable in recent years to speak of the school's "hidden curriculum"—school experiences that result in unintended, unplanned, even unsuspected and undesired student learning. The "hidden" curriculum is typically contrasted with the "formal" curriculum—the experiences purposely set up to accomplish the intended, although often not explicitly stated, goals and objectives of the various curriculum areas. The hidden curriculum includes the unintended implications of content and of teaching behavior, as well as the many "noninstructional" encounters that students have with teachers and other school people. Much of the hidden curriculum has to do with values,[1] even in subject areas that are frequently considered "value free"—such as science and mathematics.

VALUES IN THE CLASSROOM

As an illustration of the above points, consider what teacher values are implied in the following situations:

- An English teacher makes a point of noting sexist language when correcting papers.

---

[1] We define a value as a principle or standard of worth. This definition will be developed more fully in Chapter 2.

- A home economics teacher uses a series of ethnic dinners to teach not only food preparation but also appreciation of widely diverse tastes and traditions.
- Badly overweight and in need of exercise, a health educator lectures students on the importance of fitness.
- A music teacher picks up sheet music so that her music classes can sing currently popular songs.
- One teacher's bulletin board remains unchanged throughout the semester while another's has a steady rotation of exemplary student work.
- A shop teacher insists that all students strictly follow safety precautions.
- Students are asked to tidy up their classroom before going to recess.
- Responding to interests, a math teacher spends ten hours after school each week so that students can work with microcomputers.
- A remedial reading teacher decides to order paperback popular novels instead of a published reading series.
- A social studies teacher threatens to assign extra homework unless students behave.
- Achievement in reading for each student is charted publicly at the back of the room.
- A memorandum from teacher to parents contains mistakes in spelling and punctuation.
- A shorthand teacher uses John T. Malloy's *Dress for Success* as the content for dictation drills.
- After training students in the basics of small group discussion, a middle school teacher arranges the desks in small, circled clusters rather than in rows.

Such a list could easily be extended, of course. In fact, you will find it easy to do so just by reading the newspaper. As we were putting the finishing touches on the second edition of this book, we found two more items in a single edition of our local newspaper.

The first item informed us that the American Civil Liberties Union had filed a complaint with a local school district because a teacher had invited a Right-to-Life spokesperson to give anti-abortion lectures to her junior high classes and to provide graphic anti-abortion reading materials to the students. According to the article, that practice was a violation of a district policy requiring balanced presentations. We learned also that the staff of the local Planned Parenthood Center had not been accorded the opportunity to make presentations—in fact, earlier invitations to Planned Parenthood had been retracted.

Two further points in the above news story are of interest: The first is that the value of "balance" (fairness) was acknowledged by the school superintendent to be a key principle that should be taken into account in making decisions about visiting speakers. The second is the clear implication that indoctrination has been the moral agenda of the teacher involved in this incident, and that her exclusive use of anti-abortion speakers had been going on for "years and years."

So much for general examples. We want to turn now to a specific curriculum area, one that is often assumed to be value-free—science—and explore value implications there in a bit more depth.

Values in the Sciences

Thumbing more deeply into our newspaper, we were confronted with another item having to do with values in the classroom. A headline read: "Court Suit Seeks Teaching of Creationism." Reading on, we learned that in California (as of March, 1981) the question of evolution is by no means decided—at least as far as the science curriculum is concerned. In fact, a group of Bible fundamentalists (the plaintiffs) contend that Darwin's theory of evolution is being taught as fact, constituting an infringement of freedom of religion, protected under the First Amendment. They want the biblical creationist view taught as well. The attorney for the State Board of Education argues that science takes a neutral position on religion and that to teach the creationist view would insert religion into the curriculum.

At stake in this case are the science curriculum guidelines for the State of California. Since textbook publishers shape their textbooks to gain adoptions in large, heavily populated states such as California, the results of such a case can reach far beyond California. The California court did decide that the official guidelines provide ample opportunity for the children of fundamentalists to disagree with the idea of evolution. But many observers predict that the California case is only a prelude to court fights in other states.

Our point, of course, is that science and the teaching of science are by no means "value free." As a less dramatic illustration, consider, for example, a biology class in which no assignments or class discussions have to do with ecological problems. Or, how about a chemistry class that does not deal with ways of assessing the condition of the environment—for example, by using lab techniques to measure air or water pollution levels? The decision not to address such matters in any one science class may be justifiable. But, if the relevance of science to societal issues[2] is avoided totally, what might be

---

[2] See Steiner and Hitchcock (1980) for an excellent overview of such issues.

conveyed to students about the values of the teacher and the school, and about the kinds of intellectual activities and goals they should value?

Even the methods used in teaching science may have important value implications. For example, students kill and dissect frogs in a biology class: What are they being taught about the value of life?[3]

... [B]ills have been proposed before legislatures, over the years, to legalize the use of live animals, including cats and dogs, in high school science experiments. One of the arguments has been that by experimenting on a dog or a cat, the child will assume a more impersonal and objective attitude toward animals. Never mind the fact that we will be teaching our children to repress emotions of empathy and compassion. One high school student was reportedly traumatized during a diabolical experiment conducted by the biology teacher dissecting a half-anesthetized screaming kitten in front of the class. One cannot help but wonder what psychological effect experiences like this will have on the developing child.

—Judith Schmidt. *Family Weekly*, December 23, 1973.

The methods and content of science bring values into the classroom in yet another way. The image of the scientist in his laboratory, working long hours and abstaining from the more usual and mundane pleasures of life as he follows his commitment to the search for truth, is part of the lore of twentieth-century America. As Bronowski (1965, pp. 99–100) has put it:

In practicing science, we accept from the outset an end which is laid down for us. The end of science is to discover what is true about the world. The activity of science is directed to seek the truth, and it is judged by that criterion. *We can practice science only if we value the truth.* (Italics ours.)

What is truth to the scientist? George Gaylord Simpson, a Professor of Vertebrate Paleontology at Harvard University, gave the following answer (1962, p. 11):

---

[3]The use of animals in science education experiments continues to be a source of controversy. For example, the adoption by two national science teachers' associations of guidelines banning classroom experiments that harm animals has provoked the ire of some educators (Sun, 1980). If you are concerned with the value issues involved, see George K. Russell's (1972) discussion in "Vivisection and the True Aims of Biological Education."

The concept of truth in science is ... quite special. It implies nothing eternal and absolute but only a high degree of confidence after adequate objective self-testing and self-correction.

So science has imbedded in it such values as objectivity and the willingness to change one's beliefs when faced with contradictory evidence. To the extent that science teaching is faithful to science, the hidden curriculum should reflect such values; indeed, one could expect them to be an intentional part of the formal curriculum. On the other hand, science is sometimes taught in a noninquiring, absolute way that belies these commitments—but implies others.

In addition, the scientist's pursuit of truth can have tremendous implications for and impact on the values of society. Can science be taught adequately if these reverberations are ignored? For example, the Copernican view of the universe—that the earth and humankind are *not* at the center of things—shocked a world whose theology was built on the opposite premise. Galileo's demonstration of the truth of the Copernican theory led to his condemnation for heresy. The fantastic destructiveness of nuclear power, unleashed by physical scientists seeking to understand natural phenomena, raised as never before the question: Should scientific research be done without consideration of the morality of possible applications? Research in biogenetics is raising the same sort of question.

Research in the social sciences is also likely to have tremendous value implications. Two recent examples come from sensitive areas—race (ethnocultural differences) and sex. Psychologist Arthur Jensen entered the first of these areas in his research. He wondered (Jensen, 1969) whether the available data supported the hypothesis of genetic differences in intelligence between blacks and whites. The reactions of blacks and whites indicated how value-laden that "scientific" question was. Jensen's reports were greeted with cries of "racist," and there were attempts to keep him from teaching on the University of California, Berkeley campus and from speaking at professional meetings.[4]

In the area of sex, the example of Alfred Kinsey, zoologist turned sexologist, illustrates how the commitment to search for empirical truth, combined with a particular scientific perspective, can have a controversial impact on personal and societal values. Kinsey's scientific training and early research in zoology were taxonomic in nature—that is, he was concerned with classifying animals into natural, related groups. For example, from his collection of over

---

[4]Those interested in this still-percolating controversy will want to check sources such as the following: Jensen (1969, 1973), Nichols (1978), Rice (1973), Scriven (1970).

four million gall wasps, he gathered and analyzed data to determine whether the categories being used by entomologists to classify insects were adequate. When Kinsey moved to the study of human sexual behavior, he brought with him the data-gathering approach of his zoological research. He collected enormous quantities of information in interviews with close to twenty thousand men and women. The results, published in two controversial volumes, *Sexual Behavior in the Human Male* (1948) and *Sexual Behavior in the Human Female* (1953), were blockbusters. Among other things, Kinsey said his data indicated that people's sexual behavior often bore little relation to the sexual mores of our society.

Although the approach taken by Kinsey and his associates was quantitative, it had important implications for society's values. To many people, Kinsey's findings suggested that society's sexual moral standards were a facade, a sham to cover up what really was going on. To some, the implication seemed clear: Let's not pretend that we disapprove of sexual relations before or outside of marriage when our behavior indicates otherwise. It has been argued that the Kinsey volumes were a major factor in liberalizing—or, as some would put it, loosening—the moral standards of the following decades.

Although Kinsey apparently viewed his works as purely scientific documents, others saw them as "highly tendentious," with "a distinct permissivist bias," projecting a "fundamentally materialistic notion of human sexuality" (Robinson, 1972, p. 100). This latter subject—the implied standards by which personal sexual experiences are to be judged—bothered some people as much as did the implied rejection of long-standing sexual mores.

Robinson (1972), in reviewing two biographies of Kinsey, commented:

> There was some justice in these [criticisms]. Kinsey never recognized that by asking certain questions rather than others he committed himself to a particular conception of sexual life, which while "objective" in the sense that it did not contradict the facts, was nonetheless partial. He tended to ask about physical acts, not about the internal states accompanying them, and he naturally found it easier to measure the quantity rather than the quality of acts (pp. 100, 102).[5]

Science teachers, then, must be aware that science content may have a potent hidden curriculum bearing on the value orientations of their students and the broader society. In addition, they must consider this basic question: Can science instruction be adequate if it does not deal explicitly with the value implications of scientific findings?

---

[5] The more recent biologically oriented research on sexual behavior by Masters and Johnson (e.g., 1966, 1970) has been criticized on similar grounds: that their physiological orientation implied that sex can appropriately be viewed objectively, without concern for interpersonal obligations and social constraints. For an excellent discussion of this controversy, see Hogan and Schroeder (1980).

What happens when a young, earnest teacher meets a bunch of three- and four-year-old kids for a lesson about drums? See "A Lesson for Anthony," page 11, for a glimpse of how the hidden curriculum can communicate values in a profound and powerful way.

Other Curriculum Areas

Similar questions need to be raised in areas other than science, of course. A math teacher scolds a student for not appreciating the beauty of geometry. The students who are counseled into courses that call for the practical application of math concepts, such as business math, all come from working-class backgrounds. What is being implied about the kinds of knowledge to be valued, or the kinds of people who are most valued?

The inevitability of dealing with values in the social studies curriculum may seem clear when teachers seek such goals as "good citizenship." But what about the social studies teacher who sees the job as teaching social science and history concepts that have been adapted and simplified so that the students can understand them? What if this instructor teaches about hypothesis testing and presents content on such topics as poverty, alcoholism and drug use, and mental illness, without raising related issues of social policy? What if he or she teaches a neat, academically sound account of the Civil War, its causes and results—but doesn't comment on the morality of slavery or on the behavior of whites and blacks during the Reconstruction period?

What are the implied value priorities? What value-related outcomes are likely in regard to: The importance of dealing with abstract ideas as compared to the nasty realities of societal controversy? The importance of confronting basic moral issues? And perhaps most important of all, the student's tendency to value the school in terms of its relevance to the world "out there," especially as this world touches on his or her own life?

In curriculum areas such as music, art, and literature the central place of values probably is even more immediately obvious. After all, the school's esthetic curriculum is concerned with the student's valuing of beauty, and, in that sense, values are expected to be an explicit part of the formal curriculum. But as one would expect, values enter through the hidden curriculum as well. The tendency of art and music teachers to assume that their sophisticated views of esthetics have intrinsic value will be discussed later. Among literature teachers there is a tendency to assume not only that students should analyze everything they read, but also that some particular style of literary criticism is *the* frame of reference from which every person should approach the reading of fiction. Even more important, attempts to change black dialect and the failure to use minority literature have value implications that every conscientious teacher must confront.

Do these ideas apply to your own area of teaching? Give Value Exploration 1, page 14, a try.

THE EXTRACURRICULAR CURRICULUM

The obvious point is that *no* curriculum is value free. Values and value implications are an inevitable part of instruction. But it is also important to remember that as each teacher interacts with students, in and out of the classroom, as part of the social and political system of the school, much "teaching" takes place.

A teacher scolds a tenth-grade boy and girl for walking down the hall with their arms around each other. A seventh-grade teacher teases two boys for not playing football at noon. An elementary teacher chastises her children for wearing muddy boots into the classroom or for not putting books back on the shelves neatly. In each instance, the teacher is saying something to the students about his or her own values and about what he or she believes the students' values ought to be.

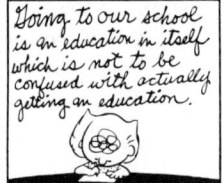

© 1973 United Feature Syndicate,

There is no use pretending that teachers can avoid such value-related decisions. We must act, and our values will be a major influence in determining how we treat students. The danger is in imagining that what we do can be "value free." Such thinking allows unexamined assumptions and biases to influence our behavior, and the impacts on our students will often be detrimental to the objectives that we consciously seek.

FRAME OF REFERENCE

The question, then, is not *whether* you will deal with values or *whether* your values will affect what you do. It is rather, *what* will you do about values, and *will you be aware* of the influence of your own values and make it as conscious and rational as possible? Charles Beard, a historian who wrote about the secondary school social studies curriculum in the 1930s, emphasized the importance of the latter point (Beard, 1934, p. 182):

> Every human being brought up in society inevitably has in mind a frame of social knowledge, ideas, and ideals—a more or less definite pattern of things deemed *necessary*, things deemed *possible*, and things deemed *desirable*; and to this frame or pattern, his thought and action will be more or less consciously referred. This frame may be large or small; it may embrace an immense store of knowledge or little knowledge; it may be well organized with respect to categories of social thought or confused and blurred in organization; and the ideal element in it may represent the highest or lowest aspirations of mankind. But frame there is in every human mind.
>
> ... Since all things known cannot be placed before children in the school room, there must and will be, inevitably, a selection, and the selection will be made with reference to some frame of knowledge and values, more or less consciously established in the mind of the selector.

For purposes of simplicity, we will use the term *frame of reference* to refer to what Beard calls "a frame of social knowledge, ideas, and ideals." In considering values and teaching decisions, it is crucial to underscore Beard's point that a frame of reference is not something that some people have and others don't. *Each* of us has a frame of reference; our values are a very important part of that frame; and *each person's* actions are influenced by his or her frame. A person who is unaware of that influence will unthinkingly apply and impose the elements, including the values, in his or her frame.

A big-shouldered shop teacher slams his fist into a shop table and summons Carlos Sanchez into his office. The boy's mouth goes dry with fear. See "Shop Sketch," page 15, for a check on Carlos's frame of reference as well as your own.

FROM FRAME TO RATIONALE

Many of the elements in one's frame of reference are unexplicated, unexamined assumptions. If your behavior as a teacher is to be as rational as possible, you need to bring your assumptions into the open, state them as clearly as possible, examine them for accuracy and consistency, and use them consciously as the basis for decisions about your instructional and other behavior toward students (for example, in the lunchroom or during hall duty). The product of this process of explicating and clarifying one's frame of reference we call a *rationale*. Defined more precisely, a rationale is the statement and explication of the basic principles upon which your school behavior (both in the formal classroom setting and during the other encounters within the school's social and political system) is based.

The development of an explicit rationale for teaching, as distinct from a largely implicit frame of reference, is essential but not easy. Among the areas needing clarification are your assumptions about society and the school's relationship to it, about the nature of children and how they learn, about the nature of values. The critical examination of your unconscious and frequently cherished assumptions in these areas is not something that you will accomplish overnight, or even during an undergraduate course or an inservice training program. In fact, you are not likely ever to arrive at a completely explicated and polished rationale.

A rationale, like the person who is attempting to develop it, evolves and is always in the process of becoming. Your rationale may become more explicit, more comprehensive, more logical in the interrelationship of its parts, clearer in its implications for your behavior as a teacher. But it ought never to be considered final, for that would imply that you have stopped changing and growing.

One important reason for developing a rationale is to avoid the unthinking imposition of your beliefs on your students. Equally important from a pragmatic point of view is the need for a systematic, well-grounded basis from which to explain, even defend, your instructional behavior to administrators and parents. In English and social studies, for example, teachers challenged for raising controversial issues in their classrooms have gotten into trouble because their justification was not much deeper than "Controversy is good." Certainly, in a democratic society a more profound and persuasive justification can be developed.

When schooling touches on values, parents are particularly likely to react emotionally. For that reason, any teacher who decides to deal with values explicitly (recognizing, of course, that no teacher can avoid dealing with values implicitly) ought to have a conscious rationale as a foundation for his or her approach. Communication of this rationale to other teachers, to the principal, and even to the superintendent, may help to insure that vital support will be available if needed. Moreover, going through the process of discussing your rationale with other school people may help you to discuss with parents your position on values, take into account their concerns, and convince them of the soundness of your approach.

OUR INTENT

The school's role vis-à-vis values has become a frequent topic of concern in recent years. While some commentators have lamented a lack of student commitment to important values and parents have objected to some value education programs (see Chapter 7), the Gallup poll on education has indicated that a strong majority of the public would like the school to deal with moral values (Gallup, 1980, p. 39). In the discussions of the school and values which go on, one often hears statements that reflect one of the following polar positions:

- Teachers have no business dealing with values. The school's role is to teach skills—in reading, writing, and arithmetic, and in vocational areas. The values of youth are the business of home and church.
- The school is an instrument of society. Teachers must, therefore, be deeply involved in shaping the values of young people—from instilling important personal values, such as honesty, to inculcating values of fundamental importance, such as patriotism. If they do otherwise, teachers are derelict in their duty.

As a teacher, you should be clear where you stand in regard to such statements. Our intent is to help you achieve that clarity. We hope to make you more aware of your value-related decisions as a teacher, to engage you in building a rationale for dealing with values, and to provide you with some ideas that will help you to develop an explicit basis for handling values. Of the many matters that are important in constructing such a rationale, none is more basic than reflection on the nature of values. And we turn to that next.

A Lesson for Anthony[6]

Problem. *As you read the following play, based on a real-life event, identify the "hidden" curriculum. Ask yourself: What assumptions about children and schooling does the teacher seem to be making?*

Scene: A day nursery. Crowded into the room are children, teachers, play equipment, books, a set of drums. The children are noisy and talkative, obviously excited about this special event. Their fingers reach out to touch the shiny enameled finish of the drums, the taut skins, and the crisp circles of brass. The teacher, Mr. Barker, is a young man with an earnest face. He is nervous, but he smiles in a teacherly way as he stands up, rubbing the edges of his mouth. They have been talking about the names of the drums.

---

[6]Many of the vignettes in this book are adapted from material field-tested with prospective teachers (Strong, 1973).

Mr. Barker: Hey, that's good, you guys. We got all the names now. Bass, snare, cymbals, right? Now the bass, you see, it's carried up front—like in a parade. And the snare—well, you see those in the dance bands, right? Every dance band has snares to give the *rhythm*. Can you say that word? Rhythm. *(Mr. Barker pauses to frown at some children who are getting restless.)*

Mike: Hey, I wanna hit it! *(He reaches for one of the drumsticks.)*

Mr. Barker: Whoa, young man. Just a minute now. Can you say *rhythm?*

Mike: Uhhhh. *(He looks puzzled.)* Riv-vum.

Mr. Barker: No, no. The word is RHYTHM.

Trudy: Ribbon, ribbon! *(She is making faces at another girl.)*

Mike: Uhhh, riv-vum; riv-vum.

Mr. Barker: Ri-thum.

Mike: Ri—Uhmmm.

Mr. Barker: You almost have it. Ri-thum. That's what the snares do in the dance band. One, two three, four—one, two, three . . . *(He begins to clap his hands, and the students quickly catch the beat; they clap along for about ten seconds.)* Okay, okay. That's enough, gang. Hold it down. *(Most youngsters are still clapping.)* Hey, that's about *enough.* QUIET! *(The noise drops off.)* Okay. Now we're going to march, so who wants to be the leader?

Anthony: Me, me! *(He is waving his hand.)*

Mr. Barker: Good, Anthony. You're the leader. You get out in the middle there; and everybody line up, right behind Anthony! *(The teacher's smile seems tighter, more restrained.)*

Anthony: I gonna be a leader. *(He scrambles up and races to the middle of the room; all of the children crowd around him in a confused knot of jabbering and noise. They are excited.)*

Mike: Hey, I hit the drum now? *(He is pulling at Mr. Barker's shirt.)*

Mr. Barker: Quiet, now. QUIET! Mike, you get out there to march. C'mon now, hurry up—and don't *hang.* *(The frown is back.)* LINE UP! Let's go now! Carol, get in line. *(The confusion continues for about thirty seconds, but finally some semblance of a line begins to form behind Anthony as well as around him. Everybody is talking.)* QUIET, now. SETTLE DOWN!

Jerry: I gonna march, march, march—*(He is out of line.)*

Debbie: We start now? Start it, Anthony.

Mr. Barker: Quiet down, you kids! You'll have to be quiet or we don't march. Marsha, Pam—you two get back in line and hush up. *(He has moved out*

# DO YOU WANT TO DEAL WITH VALUES?	13

toward the middle of the room, hunching his shoulders together aggressively.)

Victor: One, two, three, four . . .

Mike: Can I hit the drum? Teacher? Can . . .

Mr. Barker: Okay. Now, Anthony, you know which foot is your *left?*

Anthony: Uh-huh. *(He lifts his left foot and stands teetering on his right. A big grin creases his freckled face. He is obviously proud that he knows his left foot from his right.)*

Mr. Barker: Beautiful, Anthony. Really good. Now I want everybody to do just like Anthony here, right? Left foot up. Got that? Left foot. *(The children watch Anthony and switch from left to right to left. It is hard because some of them are facing the other way. The room resembles a training ground for unsteady young storks.)*

Debbie: We gonna start?

Mr. Barker: Real good. Hold up that left foot now, 'cause when we march we always start with the left foot first. *(Children are starting to topple back and forth, and Mr. Barker frowns again.)* Left foot, not your right. This is real important so we can all keep in step with the drum. Got that, Anthony?

Anthony: Uh-huh. *(Still standing on his right foot, his left in the air, Anthony blinks affirmatively. He is concentrating. His tongue curls over his front lip.)*

Jeff: My leg hurts. *(He has put his left foot down.)*

Judy: March, march, march—

Mr. Barker: Okay, everybody; let's get ready! *(He rushes back to the bass drum and squares himself for the swing; then he begins pounding the drum with big booming strokes.)* Go, Anthony!

Anthony: MARCH! *(Anthony begins HOPPING on his right leg across the tile floor in time to the bass drum. His tongue is still between his teeth. Several kids start hopping after him. Others look puzzled. Finally they all start hopping.)*

Mr. Barker: (The drum stops pounding, and Mr. Barker moves out toward Anthony, arms flailing a criss-crossing motion in front of him as his head wags an angry "no.") NO! NO! NO! ANTHONY! *(His face is fierce.)* I SAID MARCH!

A hush falls over the room at this outburst, and Anthony walks to the furthest corner, away from the drums. He sits down on the floor near the coat racks and pulls his knees up, putting his head down in a kind of fetal gathering in of himself. Mr. Barker is shaking his head. He and the other adults in the room cannot coax Anthony to get up and participate in the new march. They finally give up and Mr. Barker lines up the children again. This time Victor is the leader. The children begin marching as the lights go down slowly, a single spot lingering at Anthony's feet. The children's bodies become shadows. A bass drum thumps softly in the background, fading into silence as the light goes out.

Follow-up. *What do you think Anthony has learned about music class? About music? About teachers? About school?*

One of the readers of this manuscript commented, "I wonder if we shouldn't ask what Shaver and Strong's values are, in putting this poor guy Barker in the pillory." We think that's an excellent suggestion. Each of the narratives on the following pages should be examined for our hidden value assumptions.

Value Exploration 1

Take a single subject or skill area that you know something about and see if you can ferret out the value implications of different ways of teaching it. Contrasting one approach with another may help you in your analysis. For example, you might consider what values are implied by:

1A	a basal reading program (one that has a strictly controlled vocabulary)	1B	a language-experience approach (one that uses the vocabulary already possessed by students)
2A	a social studies program in which students are tested primarily on their recall of facts and concepts from history and/or the social sciences	2B	a social studies program in which tests frequently ask students to interpret ongoing social-political controversies using generalizations and concepts from history and/or the social sciences
3A	a math program in which students learn concepts by manipulating physical objects	3B	a math program in which students largely drill on basic operations
4A	writing assignments drawn from a "sourcebook" of proven topics	4B	writing assignments drawn from students' personal experience and interests
5A	a P.E. program that emphasizes team sports (football, basketball, etc.)	5B	a P.E. program that emphasizes individual sports (tennis, swimming, etc.)

Shop Sketch

Problem. *What do Carlos's reactions tell you about his frame of reference? How would you describe Mr. O'Hara's assumptions about teaching?*

Outside, the sky is clearing off.

Lon O'Hara, shop teacher and assistant football coach, grins to himself as he thinks about the crunch of pads and flesh tonight under the Friday night fieldlights. He slams his sledgelike fist into one of the oak drawing tables as he makes his way toward the drill press where two boys are working.

He is six feet, two inches tall—220 pounds of wedge-shaped muscle. His shoulders are thick knots beneath his white shop coat. He has red, curly hair and a red beard that needs trimming; his eyes burn like blue ice.

The boys look up, eyes white behind their goggles.

"Carlos," he says. "You come with me."

The boy swallows and looks at his friend. Lon O'Hara is striding toward his office, shoulders bunched beneath the coat. The boy peels off his goggles and hurries to catch up. The door squishes closed behind them. The teacher's face is thoughtful, silent.

"Yes sir?"

Lon O'Hara stares at him.

The buzz and snap of the arc welder are barely audible.

"How old are you, Carlos?"

"Fifteen."

"This is your first year here, I take it."

The boy nods.

"I thought so. Well, Carlos, I'll put it to you straight. You have made the O'Hara list." He opens his gradebook to a marked section and stares at it. "This is where I keep the list, Carlos."

The boy eyes the gradebook for a moment, working his mouth into a dry question. "Uh, what kind of list? I ain't done nothin'." His hands are jammed into his jeans.

"You're wrong, Carlos. Everybody who gets on the O'Hara list has done *some*thing." O'Hara flexes his shoulders, and the coat seams strain. "I know everything going on out there."

A crash echoes in from the shop, and Carlos begins picking at his front teeth. His eyes are black, narrowing as they focus on his tennis shoes.

"You've been doing a terrific job out there, Carlos. I like your work—what I've seen so far. You've got real potential."

Carlos lifts his eyebrows; his weight shifts.

"Not just anybody gets on my list, Carlos."

O'Hara stretches across his desk and pulls a tattered paperback book from a large stack. He thumbs the cover.

"Here's something I thought you might be interested in. Metal sculpture, you know?" He begins flipping pages. "You like that sort of thing?"

The boy shrugs as a small grin forms at the corners of his mouth.

"I thought you might," O'Hara says. "I noticed those drawings on your notebook." He pauses. "Maybe you'd like to take this home over the weekend."

Follow-up. *Think about Carlos's original reaction to his "summons" from Mr. O'Hara. What values does he assume are guiding the teacher's behavior?*

What curriculum values does Mr. O'Hara express as he hands Carlos the book on metal sculpture?

Get together with some friends and talk about situations where a teacher's implicit values affected your behavior, either positively or negatively.

Chapter 2

VALUES—
WHAT ARE THEY?

Perhaps we have put it off too long already, but if our deliberations are to be productive, we must define the term *value*. There are many theories of valuation, and value is defined in many different ways.[1] There is no sense pretending that any one definition is *the* right one. But several years of curriculum work (Oliver & Shaver, 1974; Shaver & Berlak, 1968; Shaver & Larkins, 1973a, 1973b) suggest that the following definition is a useful one: *Values* are our standards and principles for judging worth. They are the criteria by which we judge "things" (people, objects, ideas, actions, and situations) to be good, worthwhile, desirable; or, on the other hand, bad, worthless, despicable; or, of course, somewhere in between these extremes. We may apply our values consciously. Or they may function unconsciously, as part of the influence of our frames of reference, without our being aware of the standards implied by our decisions.

SOME DISTINCTIONS

It is important to distinguish between *values* and *value judgments*. The latter are assertions we make based on our values. A teacher who says, "Duke, you should get to class on time," is making a value judgment. What is the value

---

[1] For a comprehensive bibliography on the theory of value, see Rescher (1969, pp. 149–186).

(the criterion) that leads to that judgment? It may be *punctuality*. It may be *classroom order* (a student coming in tardy disrupts the class). It may be *respect* (coming in tardy implies a lack of respect for the teacher or the school) or, at a somewhat different level, *self-worth* (the tardy student is a threat to the teacher's conception of her own self-worth).

Statements that appear to be directives or factual claims often are implicit value judgments. For example, a teacher directive as simple as "Open your textbooks" contains implicit value judgments such as "Everyone in class should be doing the same thing."

Our implicit and explicit value judgments are typically based on unstated values that can, and should, be explicated in the interests of clarity and consistency. Such self-analyses may move us to modify a value to be consistent with what we are saying and/or doing; or, we may modify our assertions or our behavior to make them consistent with our values.

Do the distinctions between factual claims or directives, value judgments, and values make sense to you? Value Exploration 2, page 36, provides the opportunity to put these distinctions to work and run a self-check on your understanding.

Values—Affective or Cognitive?

In answering the question: What are values? it is also important to consider the distinction that is often made between affective objectives—those emphasizing feelings and emotion (Krathwohl, Bloom, & Masia, 1964, p. 7)—and cognitive objectives—those dealing with knowledge and with intellectual abilities and skills (Bloom, 1956, p. 7). Whether you see values as one or the other, or as a combination of both, can have serious implications for your teaching.

Many educators see values as falling exclusively into the affective domain—that is, as involving only feelings and emotion. For some, values as affective objectives take on a mystic aura—they are private inner feelings with which one hesitates to interfere. Many teachers have been led to throw up their hands in despair (or perhaps, in some cases, relief!) and say, "Oh, values are only feelings. Therefore, we ought not deal with them in the classroom."

We maintain that although values do embody and convey feeling, they are much more than emotions. Values and valuing clearly fall into the cognitive domain because standards are concepts, and valuing involves intellectual abilities and skills (Bloom, 1956, p. 7). Values have intellectual meaning that can be defined and clarified. And values can be compared, related to one another, and consciously applied as criteria.

For example, honesty is a value by which we frequently judge the actions of ourselves and others. The term "honesty" does evoke feelings. For most people, "honest" behavior calls forth a positive emotive reaction, and we have negative feelings toward people or actions that we consider "dishonest." But each of us, although we may not have taken the time and effort to define it precisely, also has a *concept* of honesty. With some thought, you could undoubtedly describe right now what you mean by "honest"—for example, what kinds of behavior you would consider to be honest or dishonest.

So values are both cognitive and affective—an important point to keep in mind. Whether or not you view values in this way is critical, because it will influence how *you* deal with values as a teacher. Will you be concerned with more than how your students feel about things? Will you also treat values as concepts and valuing as an intellectual process that can be rigorous?

Values—What They Aren't

It is common to hear educators use the terms *values* and *attitudes* interchangeably, as if they were synonymous. Often discussion will reveal that the person has not stopped to consider in what ways *value* and *attitude* might refer to different concepts. Just as instructional decision making can be more precise if values are distinguished from value judgments, so our thinking can be sharpened by distinguishing values from attitudes.

An *attitude*, as commonly defined by psychologists, is a number of interrelated beliefs and feelings focused on some object. The "object" may be a set of actions (e.g., welfare legislation), people (such as blacks or whites), situations (presidential elections), or things (American automobiles). Or it may be an individual action, person, situation, or thing. We have attitudes *toward*—for example, toward long hair or a particular student who has long hair, or toward black Americans or a particular student who is black. Our attitudes encompass and are affected by a number of factors, including our factual beliefs[2] and our values. Each of us has thousands of attitudes. The number is limited only by our range of experience and the number of objects about which we have feelings and beliefs.

Values, on the other hand, as standards of worth, are a more fundamental aspect of our frames of reference. They underlie our attitudes and are fewer in number. One psychologist (Rokeach, 1973) who has done considerable research into attitudes and values estimates that while each of us has thousands of attitudes, we are likely to have only several dozen values.

In one sense, then, attitudes and value judgments are similar in that both

---

[2]*Factual beliefs* are beliefs about what the world *is* like, *has been* like, *can be* like, or *will be* like.

are based consciously or unconsciously on one's values as well as on factual assumptions. In deciding what you, as a teacher, should do in regard to values, it is important to be clear in your mind whether you are concerned with value judgments, attitudes, or the underlying value and factual beliefs. For instance, do you simply want students to conform to your value judgments about classroom behavior, or do you want them to understand (and perhaps share) the values that underlie those judgments? Or, are you interested in changing your students' attitudes toward black Americans or classical music, or in helping them to clarify their own values and strive for consistency between value and attitude?

Which type of objective you seek will not only influence how you teach, but will also raise different questions of justification. For example, you may find yourself in rough territory when you try to convince parents that you should be shaping their children's attitudes toward minority groups. But it may be less difficult to persuade parents that your role should include helping students to clarify their values and use them as conscious criteria against which to match attitudes and value judgments.

In the opening chapter of *Hard Times,* Charles Dickens presents Mr. Thomas Gradgrind, owner of a British private school. Here, in Gradgrind's own words, is the essence of his pedagogical value system:

> Teach these boys and girls nothing but Facts. Facts alone are wanted in life. Plant nothing else, and root out everything else. You can only form minds of reasoning animals upon Facts: nothing else will ever be of any service to them. This is the principle on which I bring up my own children, and this is the principle on which I bring up these children. Stick to the Facts, Sir!

Should we "stick to the facts"? What happens when a teacher decides that "planting facts" is *not* the primary goal of education? See "The Experiment," page 38, for a glimpse of both the cognitive and affective aspects of values in action.

TYPES OF VALUES

Your decisions about what to do about values as a teacher must take into account different types of values with which you will be dealing. Values can be viewed from many different perspectives. Some people, for example, find it helpful to categorize values in terms of the spheres of activity in which they are applied—for example, political, economic, religious, or social. Categorizing values in that way is meaningful for social scientists' studies of value

VALUES—WHAT ARE THEY?

systems. But the categories do not seem particularly relevant to the analysis of value-related decisions for the formal or the hidden curriculum.

A more productive set of categories for educators, we believe, makes primary distinctions between *moral* and *nonmoral* values, on the one hand, and *intrinsic* and *instrumental* values on the other. That is, a value will be moral or nonmoral; at the same time, it will also be intrinsic or instrumental. Moral values also fall at different *levels* of importance—from *personal* to *basic*. And, nonmoral values are of two types—*esthetic* or *performance*. This schema is presented graphically in Chart 1. Following are brief discussions of the types of values.

Moral Values

Many of our decisions as teachers involve judgments about whether aims or actions are right or wrong, good or bad. Such decisions we call *ethical* decisions. And the standards or principles by which persons judge the rightness or goodness of aims or actions are called *moral* values.

	Intrinsic	Instrumental	
Moral			Personal — Basic
Nonmoral — Esthetic			
Nonmoral — Performance			

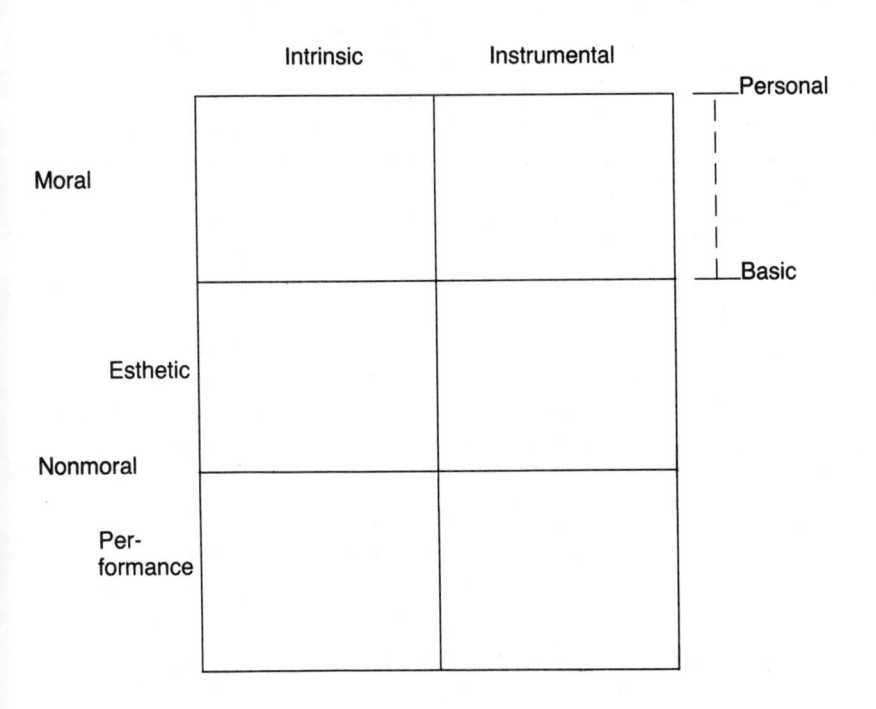

Chart 1. A Schema for Classifying Values

A husband argues that he shouldn't be pressured into going to a cocktail party because he prefers to spend the evening alone. A person's behavior on finding a lost purse is evaluated according to the "honesty" of his response. Someone opposes capital punishment in the name of the sanctity of human life. In each case, an ethical decision is being made: That is, each decision has an impact on the lives of other persons and could take on a serious tone for those involved. And in each case, a moral value—solitude, honesty, right to life—is used to judge behavior or policy.

Levels of moral values. These three examples illustrate an important point about moral values: They vary widely in their importance and applicability.

Personal moral values[3] are those used in making daily life decisions. People seldom believe that they should impose these values on other people or use them generally to judge others' behavior. We consider them to be moral values because *people use them to justify* their own *behavior toward others*.

Solitude is such a value. It is likely to take on considerable significance when it conflicts with the values of other persons—for example, if one's spouse values being at social gatherings. No one is likely to deny a person's right to solitude—even a husband or wife who is irritated because the spouse insists on staying home rather than going out to a party. But neither is anyone—not even the recalcitrant party goer—likely to argue that the right to solitude is basic to human existence, applicable to all persons as a universal value.[4]

Just the opposite is true of a value such as the sanctity of human life. When a society rejects that value—when Jews are herded to concentration camps for mass slaughter, black Americans are lynched for real or imagined intrusions into white sanctuaries, or innocent Vietnamese civilians are napalmed in their villages—human existence loses much of its meaning. Values such as this, deemed essential to human life, are often called *basic* values. In a democratic society, our basic values include commitments to such ideals as equal protection of the law, equal opportunity, freedom of speech, and religious freedom.

Between the extremes of *personal values*—such as solitude—and *basic*

---

[3]In the first edition, we used the term *personal preferences* here. But in the philosophical values literature, "personal preferences" are thought of as personal tastes—e.g., "I like chocolate ice cream." To avoid that confusion, we have switched words. The lack of established terminology to refer to levels of moral values is interesting in its own right. Linguists suggest that our language reflects our world view; or, conversely, our thinking is enhanced or restricted by the language available to us. The lack of value terminology, we believe, reflects and contributes to the lack of careful thought about values in our society.

[4]Note that we are talking about "solitude" (being alone), not "the right to privacy" (freedom from unwarranted invasion of one's personal life by government officials or other persons).

VALUES—WHAT ARE THEY?

solitude · cleanliness · hard work · cooperation · honesty · patriotism · freedom of speech · sanctity of life

| Personal Moral Values | | Basic Societal Values |

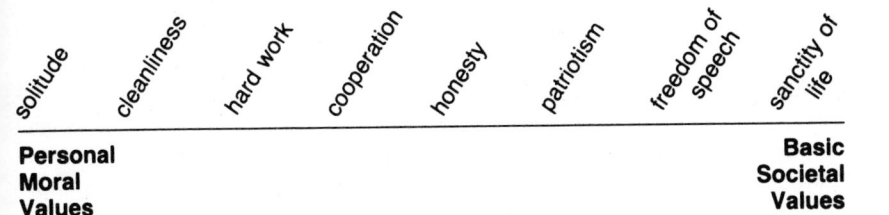

Figure 1. A Continuum of Moral Values

values—such as sanctity of life—there is a wide range of moral values differing in importance and in breadth of applicability. In fact, it can be helpful to think about moral values as ranging along a continuum from personal to basic societal values.[5] Figure 1 represents an example of such a continuum with a few values placed on it.

Where moral values are placed on such a continuum will differ from individual to individual and vary over time. For example, some people who read the first edition of this book objected to our categorization of honesty as a middle-level value. They argued that honesty, in the sense of "trustworthiness," is basic to our political process, even if usually taken for granted except during a debacle such as Watergate. Their point is that if people cannot trust one another in the majority of their relationships, life would be pretty meaningless. We agree, and only note two things: (1) our own constitutional system, as well as our criminal law system, is set up to circumscribe lack of trustworthiness; (2) the comments indicate again the difficulty of stating a consensus position on values in our society.

At any one time, people will disagree over the importance and general applicability of moral values. To some people, cleanliness is a personal moral value—an important consideration in one's relations with others in his or her personal life, but not a standard by which to judge the goodness or badness of those who are not personal intimates. To others, cleanliness is clearly at least at the middle of their moral values continuum. They believe it is important for people to be clean and judge even those they don't know by that standard. Some even treat cleanliness as a basic value during moments of unreflective emotional reaction ("They're like beasts, living in filth like that!").

---

[5]There are, of course, other continua along which moral values can be conceptualized. Maslow's (1970) famous hierarchy of self-actualization values is an example. However, we have purposely chosen a continuum with basic societal values at one end as particularly appropriate to the consideration of value-related decision in schools. The chapters that follow will, we trust, help to make clear our reasons for that choice.

Values in regard to sexual matters also are an excellent illustration of differences in placement on the continuum. Some people believe that sexual behavior in private is a matter of choice between consenting adults. Consequently, values in regard to adult sex fall at the personal end of the continuum for them. Others who believe that sexual standards are a matter of social concern endorse laws to punish certain types of behavior; they see sexual values as at least middle-level on the continuum. And then some people believe that standards of sexual behavior are fundamental. For example, when commune living, including the interchange of sex partners, was first reported in the media, many of these people condemned such arrangements as subhuman.

Moral values also change places on the continuum over time. Nowadays, for example, many people consider a full education to be a basic right of every citizen in a democracy, a value that would have astounded our colonial ancestors. Similarly, that one has a right to shelter and food if disabled or otherwise unable to work is a belief that has developed since the 1930s.

The point is that moral values do differ in importance and in breadth of applicability. Whether one is dealing with personal or basic moral values, or with values that fall somewhere between, is an important consideration in making teaching decisions. We will return to it in Chapter 3.

The time: 4:10 P.M. The place: A high school classroom. What happens when a first-year teacher subtly communicates to youngsters that it's "okay" to come in and talk? See "Moral Values and the 'Teacher-Counselor,'" page 41.

Nonmoral Values

Moral values are not the only standards of worth we use in teaching. Our decisions often deal with, and are affected by, both esthetic and performance values. Both are important in their own right. But, as we shall emphasize, both are also of consequence because they so easily take on moralistic shadings.

Esthetic values. Esthetic values are those standards by which we judge beauty. ("Beauty" is used here in its broadest sense—including, for example, a book, play, or painting which "beautifully" portrays a sordid, depressing bit of life.) Esthetics pertain to nature, to art, to music, and to literature, as well as to personal appearance, cookery (the culinary art), and manual skills (the vocational arts). Those parts of the school curriculum directly concerned with esthetics require explicit consideration of esthetic values.

The connoisseur or specialist in an esthetic field such as art often develops a complex and subtle system of standards for judging beauty. But each of us constantly makes esthetic judgments. Moreover, each of us also tends to allow his or her esthetic values (in regard, for example, to types of music or hair styles) to take on serious, moralistic tones. Not only is it frequently difficult, for example, for those who like the symphony to understand how "those kids" can like rock (and vice versa), but we tend to feel that there is something morally wrong with those who do not share our esthetic values. And the more divergent the esthetic values, the stronger the feeling of moral alienation is likely to be. For example, slight variations in hair styles don't bother most people; but when a male goes so far as to let his hair grow down to his shoulders, and then adds a beard (perhaps unkempt to boot!) and grubby clothes—well!! It's hard for some people to believe that such a man can have decent moral standards. They may even consider him a threat to the whole moral structure of a democratic society!

© 1974 United Feature Syndicate, Inc.

Prejudice based on unthinking esthetic reactions is common to all of us. For those who teach esthetic curricula such as music, art, and literature, it is particularly important to remember that the position of esthete too easily degenerates into snobbery. But all of us need to be attuned to our esthetic values as they influence, for example, our judgments about students' hair and dress. In short, esthetic values may be the focus of the formal curriculum or they may exert subtle and important influences as part of the hidden curriculum to which we expose students.

Esthetics has a social-political dimension, too. Esthetic products reflect the milieu of the artist. Also, it is assumed that esthetic works can have nonesthetic effects—that is, they may affect the morality of those who view them. In the Soviet Union and Communist China, materialistic art is promoted and abstract art condemned as debased; plays and movies are to support the Revolution and venerate heroes. In our country, nudity, the use of "street language," and gratuitous violence are often attacked.

Attempts to censor art raise ethical questions quite different from disagreement over the esthetic merit of a particular work. Censorship issues arise in schools as well as in the broader society. They may involve such matters as the selection of music for student dances, restrictions on reading selections for literature classes, books banned from the library, or the propriety of certain types of painting (e.g., nude figures) in art classes.

Esthetic values even affect classroom routine, as Patty (in the Peanuts cartoon) seems to understand clearly. A conversation at a PTA meeting, "Esthetic Values over Tea and Crumpets," page 42, raises questions about esthetics and grading of the type you are likely to face as a teacher.

Performance values. The second category of nonmoral values consists of the standards we use to judge whether a person or thing performs adequately some specified function (see Frankena, 1973, pp. 9–11). For example, the function of a watch is to tell time. A person might say, "That is a good watch," meaning that it keeps time accurately. Accuracy is the performance value, although its specific definition will vary from person to person.

Many of the standards we use as teachers are ostensibly performance values. Perhaps this is no clearer than in physical education and coaching. Here are fairly clear standards for judging performance in terms of speed, accuracy, and dexterity. But all teachers give grades for performance on tests and other exercises. The criteria (performance values) for different grades can be spelled out—and should be as guidelines for reliable grading and as guidance to students. The same holds true for discipline standards.

With objects (such as a watch or a textbook), it is usually clear that performance values are not moral standards. That is not true when judgments are made about the extent to which people are performing their functions. Here "good," "bad," or other evaluative words almost inevitably have moral overtones.[6] Performance cannot be meaningfully separated from obligation. "He is a good teacher" not only suggests that the teacher is functioning effectively (e.g., his lectures meet standards of clarity and organization), but implies that the person is proper in an ethical sense as well. The teacher is not only fulfilling a function, but meeting a moral responsibility to society and to individual students as well.

Performance values take on moral meaning when we apply them to students, too. "A good student is one who is punctual" sounds very much like, "A good watch is one that keeps time accurately." However, students are not

---

[6]It is worth noting that performance and esthetic judgments also often overlap. Function frequently has esthetic qualities. For example, many persons include in their definition of a "beautiful" watch one which keeps time with great exactness. See "Esthetic Values over Tea and Crumpets," page 42, for an instance of a teaching value which may be either an esthetic or a performance standard, or both.

mechanical contraptions. And their punctuality, or lack of it, is not only assumed to be reasonably within their control but also to have an effect on their own well-being and that of others. Punctuality, therefore, while having the appearance of a performance value, actually is used as an ethical standard to judge whether student behavior is morally correct. It is always important to inquire into the moral overtones of what are seemingly performance values set up to judge whether your pupils are functioning effectively in their roles.

Teachers and other school personnel may be particularly susceptible to subtle negative moral judgments based on performance standards when their students come from socio-economic or ethnic backgrounds different from their own. For example, some educators have objected to the use of the terms "culturally deprived" and "compensatory education" to refer to students and school programs for them. The use of such words, they argue, reflects ethnocentricity and social snobbishness. And "culturally different" should not automatically be taken to mean "deprived" or "defective":

> The "cultural deprivation" model is basically a defect model—children who are "culturally deprived" are seen as defective and their homes and communities are seen as defective. It is unfortunate that those who subscribe to "cultural deprivation" generally seem to be unaware of the effects that such beliefs have upon the students who are supposedly "deprived." The dislike of the different . . ., implicitly evident in most facets of the school, obviously has detrimental effects upon the school experience of a minority group child whose family's life style varies from that valued in the school. Dialect, dress, and behavior are integral parts of each person; they cannot simply be abandoned. (Clement & Johnson, 1973, pp. 24–25)

> Social-class differences will produce a discrepancy because the school values and rewards behaviors the "lower-class" child has not learned, but it does not recognize skills and abilities that are vital to his survival in his own environment. For example, some children from "lower-class" families may have learned to care for themselves and younger brothers and sisters; they may have learned to defend or fight for their rights and interests; they may have learned to share and cooperate; and they may have learned to live with hazards of city streets or to roam over the countryside. None of these skills turns up on measures of school aptitude or intelligence. . . . The fact that a child is learning to care for himself or to protect his rights, instead of learning colors, shapes, and forms or "correct" English, does not mean he is intellectually deprived. It simply means that he is learning different behaviors, some of which are probably more valuable to him in his life situations than those the school values. . . . [T]he school should recognize that children from different backgrounds bring different strengths to school. The school should also learn to respond to a child without attaching negative values to what he has or has not learned before he comes to school. (Nimnicht, Johnson, & Johnson, 1973, pp. 41–42)

Although the terms "cultural deprivation" and "compensatory education" are not often heard anymore, the underlying problems remain: a lack of attention to whether some performance standards are inappropriate for students from non-Anglo, non-middle-class backgrounds; and the tendency to make negative moral evaluations of those who do not meet our performance standards. Both call for attention to democratic values such as diversity and respect for the individual in building and applying your teaching rationale.

Intrinsic Values

Moral and nonmoral values that are important in and of themselves—i.e., sought for their own sake—we choose to call *intrinsic* values. Writers also refer to such standards or principles as "end values" (e.g., Rescher, 1969) or as "terminal values" (Rokeach, 1973).[7] We prefer not to use either term because each implies to us that the values so labeled can be attained, and that persons who attain the values (who reach the end) may then settle into a peaceful state of bliss. Both terms have a sense of finality to them which runs counter to the perspective we wish to encourage: that our values constantly shift in conception and are never fully realized, in part because they conflict with one another.

Moral values are often intrinsic—sought for their own sake. As an example, physical comfort—as satisfied by good food, decent clothes, and adequate shelter—seems intrinsically reasonable to most people. Similarly, many standards of conduct, from courtesy toward teachers and fellow students to respect for human life, are rarely thought to need justification.

Nonmoral values, too, are often regarded as ends in themselves. Beauty is a salient example. The justification for teaching music, art, and other esthetic subjects is that the appreciation of beauty is by itself an important human attribute. Physical education suggests a performance value—a finely functioning body—that is also intrinsically appealing to many, aside from the esthetic aspects of physical fitness.

Many of our values, however, are means to ends. We turn to those next.

Instrumental Values

Many of our values are standards set in order to achieve other standards. A principal might object to hair length or casual dress on the ground that it is

---

[7]Rokeach (1973, p. 7) defines terminal values as "beliefs concerning desirable end-states of existence." He also defines instrumental values, which we shall discuss shortly, as "beliefs concerning desirable modes of conduct." These definitions tend to blur the distinction between *values* (principles or standards of worth) and *value judgments* based on values (and on facts as well, of course), which we believe is important because it focuses attention on the standards or principles (i.e., the values) *by which* a mode of conduct or end-state of existence is judged to be desirable.

intrinsically offensive to her own esthetic tastes. She is, however, more likely to argue that allowing extreme fashions will interfere with the learning atmosphere of the school. Based on that same instrumental line of argument, a teacher may insist on a quiet classroom to enhance learning. Another teacher may argue for new paint for her classroom on the ground that if the room is attractive, the students will study better. Values such as these—which are not important in and of themselves, but because they help to attain other ends— we call *instrumental* values.

It is not always easy to decide whether a value is an instrumental one. In fact, such values often take on importance in and of themselves. Teachers may consider students "bad," for example, if they talk without permission in the classroom—not stopping to ask themselves whether the talking actually obstructed reaching the end (learning) for which the no-talking rule was established in the first place. Or a teacher who first valued an attractively painted classroom as conducive to student learning may come to insist on new paint just because he or she does not like a room that does not have a fresh decor.

It is important to raise questions not only about the end values we seek in the classroom (e.g., Is knowledge for its own sake an acceptable goal?), but also about the appropriateness of the instrumental values we set up. It is especially vital that you constantly ask yourself whether you are overlooking the purpose of the instrumental values you have established for your interactions with students in and out of the classroom. Have you unthinkingly allowed these values to become ends in themselves? Or are you maintaining them as tools to be judged by how well they help you to achieve your teaching goals?

It is helpful also to distinguish between *values* and *valued objects*. The latter are also used instrumentally. For example, teachers may use grades to motivate students to work harder, and parents may use automobile privileges to pressure a youngster to do something they deem desirable, such as getting good grades. When an object is used instrumentally, it is often productive to ask what values underlie its use, and then to examine these values. Thus the values that lead teachers and parents to use grades and automobiles as they do may include achievement, working to capacity, educational opportunity, or job opportunities. And the values that lead some students to try for good grades, and thus make grades effective instrumentally, might include status (though this is sometimes negatively related to grades), respect from others, and self-respect. The values that make the lure of an automobile effective instrumentally could include status, mobility, and freedom (e.g., to be able to choose where to go on dates).

"Look at my plants there," Mrs. Ashcroft said. "Without the care I provide for them, they simply wouldn't survive. It's the same for youngsters."

Are students like potted plants—dependent for growth on the ministrations of teacher-gardeners? How much order should a teacher impose on students? See "Instrumental Values, Kids, and Potted Plants," page 43.

Relationships

The discussion to this point has stressed several points about values: They can be thought of as falling into two sets of categories—moral and nonmoral; it is helpful to think of moral values as ranging from personal to basic; there are two types of nonmoral values, esthetic and performance; and moral and nonmoral values may be instrumental or intrinsic in nature. These ways of looking at values were summarized in Chart 1 (page 21). Deciding where to place particular teaching values in Chart 1 can be an important step in rationale-building because it calls for further clarification of the nature of your commitments. Categorizing your values can, then, help to ensure that your treatment of students is not based on unwarranted value assumptions. Your efforts at categorization are also likely to reveal that where any value falls in the schema depends on the way *you* use it in your thinking, and that the categorizations are not always neat and clear-cut.

Where, for example, would you classify a value such as "quietness," a standard a teacher might use to judge his or her students? We would regard it as a moral value if it is used to judge whether students' behavior is proper; otherwise it would be considered a performance value. Although we recognize that some teachers might view quietness as an end in itself (an intrinsic value), it is more likely to be considered an instrumental value, adopted to enhance learning. As to its level as a moral value, it is not likely that anyone would argue that quietness is a basic societal value. It is not a personal value when used to judge the behavior of students and its application is important to people other than the teacher and the students—for example, other teachers, the principal, and parents. Quietness would, then, fall toward the "personal" end of the continuum.

In thinking about how to regard values, it is essential to recognize that they are not inherently intrinsic or instrumental. It depends upon how they are thought of by the person or persons involved. Consider, for example, the spouse who says he or she prefers solitude to a social gathering. Solitude may be valued in itself, or solitude may be a means to another end. The person may be thinking, "I've got a tough day at the office tomorrow [and efficiency there is a higher level value]. I'll be more on the ball for work if I spend this evening alone."

The same holds true with basic moral values. They too are thought of both as intrinsic and as instrumental. Take, for example, equality of opportunity.

Some people argue that it is an important intrinsic societal goal. Others argue that supporting equality of opportunity (for example, through promoting a law outlawing racial or sexual discrimination in renting or selling housing) is important because it enhances another, higher value—human dignity. And some would say that equality of opportunity is important in itself *and* because, if supported, human dignity is heightened.

Remember, too, that instrumental moral values can range from personal to basic, just as intrinsic ones can. In fact, instrumental values are sometimes considered to be more important and more widely applicable than intrinsic values. A person who views solitude as important in itself (i.e., as an intrinsic value), but also sees equality of opportunity as instrumental to human dignity, might give up his or her solitude (for example, by participating in public demonstrations) to promote equality of opportunity. Teachers often may make similar decisions, sacrificing their own intrinsic values for values that will promote student growth. A biology teacher who gives up her solitude for a Saturday field trip to help students gather specimens is an example.

Another relationship, already noted in our earlier discussions, bears particular attention. Values initially set up as instrumental often take on importance as ends, and esthetic and performance values frequently take on moralistic overtones. One reason for classifying values is that it forces us to ask questions such as: Have I unwittingly let my instrumental values become ends, or have I let my esthetic or performance values become moral ones?

There is another relationship between esthetic and moral values that needs to be emphasized. Esthetic values are a matter of personal taste. Like other values they can be explicated, examined, clarified. But ultimately they are personal because beauty depends upon the individual's internal reaction. No external source, no matter how complex or sophisticated its judgmental scheme, is a more valid judge than you are of what is beautiful to you.[8]

---

[8]That this point of view is not very popular among esthetes goes without saying. Arguing against such a position, Harry Broudy (1972, p. 103) wrote:

> The problem of standards in arts, as far as education is concerned, is solved in the same way as it is solved in other fields of instruction. For the induction of the young, the judgment of the experts, the connoisseurs . . . is the only viable criterion. Authenticity of standards consists not in their originality or uniqueness. They are not authentic *simply* because they are mine but, rather, because I accept and introject them via the same sort of perception, analysis, and reflection as is used by the experts.

Broudy bases his claim for expert over personal standards in art on what we believe to be a fallacious leap from the intellectual discipline of science and scientific standards of truth to the "critical tradition in the arts" and standards for beauty (pp. 95–103). Broudy's frequent references to persons "cultivated" in the arts is reminiscent of the tendency, in years past, to consider people who liked classical art forms as being "cultured." His biases against "popular art" are particularly evident in a section (pp. 110–114) headed "Serious and Popular Art." (Our query: Can't popular art be serious?)

On the other hand, *because moral values are used to justify and judge ethical decisions which have impact on other people, moral standards are never merely matters of personal taste*. They concern those affected, and are legitimately subject to scrutiny by them. We will argue in Chapters 3 and 6 that, especially in making decisions about public policy, people expect one another to apply the basic values of our democratic society, even though the making of a decision must be a personal matter.

VALUE CONFLICT

One further point about the nature of our values. Europeans frequently note that, on the whole, Americans are not only moralists but rationalists as well.[9] That is, we try to justify our actions in terms of moral values at the highest possible level, and we are bothered if our decisions show signs of irrationality.

Americans see inconsistency as a sign of irrationality, and intellectual consistency—at least surface, public consistency—is valued by our culture. Politicians are criticized for shifting positions; parents worry if they change their minds in coping with their children from one situation to the next; teachers are jarred when they are accused of treating students differently.

It is ironic, in the light of this commitment to consistency, that our value systems are inherently inconsistent. Solitude may be important to a man when a cocktail party is involved . . . but what if a buddy calls to invite him to a poker party? Honesty is important . . . but what if a woman's boyfriend or husband asks if she likes his new haircut—and she doesn't! In each case, countervailing values are likely to prevail. The sanctity of human life is basic . . . but how about people who support capital punishment? Have they no basic values on their side? How about the security of the community or even the right to exact retribution? We rarely recognize our value conflicts, but it is critical to do so if our decisions about how to treat values in the hidden and formal curricula are to be realistic.

One way in which our value systems lack consistency is that, over time, the relative importance of values shifts. A few years ago, those who argued that the sanctity of life should prevail over capital punishment were clearly in the minority. They may still be today. But court rulings during the 1970s restricted the use of capital punishment, suggesting that the sanctity of life was taking on greater weight in the capital punishment controversy.

Changes in values over time can cause much consternation, especially as one grows older and, perhaps, more conservative. Conflicts over changes in

---

[9]See, for example, Swedish sociologist Gunnar Myrdal (1944, pp. xlvi–xlvii).

value orientation frequently become obvious as part of the abrasiveness of the so-called "generation gap." The "gap" illustrates that value commitments change, for individuals and for the society, over time. It also illustrates the notion of *interpersonal* value conflict—that is, value conflicts that occur between individuals. Recall the capital punishment controversy again. One person argues in terms of the sanctity of human life, another in terms of the security of the community or the right to retribution. There is a conflict between the values being emphasized by the antagonists.

Note also, however, that a good deal of the consternation caused by shifts in value emphasis is due not to interpersonal value conflict (between, for example, parents and children), but to *intrapersonal* conflict—between different values held by one individual. Each of us is likely to value solitude and socializing, honesty and compassion, life and security. And awareness of our commitment to conflicting values, especially when brought to our attention as we try to make a decision about appropriate behavior, is likely to make us uncomfortable.

How do we handle intrapersonal value conflict? The psychological manipulations (usually unconscious) that we use to avoid or reduce discomfort are commonly discussed in psychology texts. One is compartmentalization. We avoid the distress of inconsistency by maintaining neat, tight compartments in our minds. We may compartmentalize situations (a person who wouldn't steal money out of a cash register might steal towels from a motel, and not see any relationship between the two acts). We may compartmentalize values, which in essence means leaving one or more in the shadows of our mind (for example, by supporting an open housing law because it would enhance equality of opportunity, but neglecting to attend to the violation of property rights that might also occur).

Other psychological manipulations include discounting the importance of one of the conflicting elements ("Taking towels isn't really *that* big a deal!" *or* reducing the importance of the source of dissonance ("What does a young twirp [or a bearded creep] like that know, anyhow?").

Of course, a person can also try to recognize his inconsistencies and handle them rationally. The careful explication of your frame of reference in building a rationale for dealing with values as a teacher calls for the explicit recognition of inconsistencies and the rational resolution of them. Note, too, that as you consider what "values education" ought to be in your classrooms, an important consideration should be how to help students to recognize and handle rationally their own value conflicts. Discussions of "emergent" values, focusing on changes in values over time, have been fairly common in recent educational literature. But little consideration has been given to the phenomenon of intrapersonal value conflict. It is critical that educators pay attention to value conflict of this type.

The decisions teachers make often involve value conflicts. Value Exploration 3, page 45, gives you the opportunity to reflect on the conflicts raised when a teacher is confronted by choices among moral values.

Is Value Conflict Normal?

A keystone in an adequate conception of values is the recognition that value conflict is normal; it is not a sign of malformation, but an inevitable fact of life. This point was dramatically illustrated on the societal level by the title Gunnar Myrdal (1944) and his colleagues chose for their epic study of what was then referred to as "the Negro problem" in America. The title, *An American Dilemma*, epitomizes the consternation of a moralistic, rationalistic nation whose treatment of a large segment of its population did not (and still does not) square with its basic moral values. In Myrdal's words:

> ... [O]ur problem is the moral dilemma of the American—the conflict between his moral valuations on various levels of consciousness and generality. The "American Dilemma," referred to in the title of this book, is the ever-raging conflict between, on the one hand, the valuations preserved on the general plane which we shall call the "American Creed," where the American thinks, talks, and acts under the influence of high national and Christian precepts, and, on the other hand, the valuations on specific planes of individual and group living, where personal and local interests; economic, social and sexual jealousies; considerations of community prestige and conformity; group prejudice against particular persons or types of people; and all sorts of miscellaneous wants, impulses, and habits dominate his outlook (p. xlvii).

A man says he believes in equality of opportunity as a basic value; yet he hires no blacks in his factory or gives them only menial jobs (less likely to happen now with equal employment opportunity laws). Does this mean that equality of opportunity is *not* one of his values?

We often say that we can tell what a person values by how he acts. This is true. But the converse—that we can tell by the same acts what he does *not* value—is not true. The employer may value equality of opportunity, but he also has more specific values—the right to run his business as he pleases, the approbation of his neighbors. The pressures of his immediate environment will often make these relatively specific values more salient than a general value such as equality of opportunity, and the businessman acts in ways that belie his commitment to equality. But that does not mean that equality is not one of his values, any more than a man's decision to play poker means he doesn't value solitude, or his wife's decision not to tell him that his new haircut is dreadful means that she does not value honesty. In the immediate situation, one value takes precedence over another. Of course, if a person declared that he valued equality of opportunity but *never* acted in ways consistent with that value, we would begin to doubt his commitment.

Myrdal emphasized the conflict between "moral valuations on various levels of consciousness and generality." In particular, he stressed the conflict between values on "the general plane" and the "specific planes of individual and group living." But it is essential to remember that as we attempt to apply our values to specific situations, conflict also occurs between values on the same level of generality—between personal values, between middle-level values, and between the basic values that are so fundamental to our conception of democracy and to which we have such strong commitments that Myrdal referred to them as the *American Creed*.

Value conflicts occur not only between moral values, but between nonmoral values as well. One esthetic value may conflict with another (for example, the soft sound of Henry Mancini versus the more strident sound of The Grateful Dead in many homes); performance values, too, may conflict, as when the enthusiasm expected of "good" students leads to noisy outbursts that run counter to the restraint also expected of their performance.

And, of course, esthetic values may conflict with moral ones: The "esthetically pleasing" solution of urban renewal projects for slum areas has come into direct confrontation with moral values involved in displacing low-income, often elderly residents. In schools, dress standards may conflict with "the natural right to 'liberty' " as well as "such basic values as the preservation of maximum individual choice, protection of minority sentiments, and appreciation for divergent lifestyles," according to the Alaska Supreme Court in a 1972 ruling rejecting hair standards at a Fairbanks junior high school.

This last example illustrates an important point: When there is a conflict between a moral and a nonmoral value, other things being equal, the moral value will usually carry the day.[10] Likewise, a moral value toward the middle of the continuum will prevail over one at the personal end, and a basic value will prevail over a middle-level one. This tendency to view the more general values as more compelling is implicit in our definition of levels of values. It

---

[10]"Other things being equal" is an important qualifier. Recall that on page 34, we pointed out that we sometimes give into the pressures of the immediate situation and act in accordance with lower-level rather than basic moral values. In addition, this statement assumes an *awareness* of the higher value and its relevance to the situation. If the individual has compartmentalized (see page 33) and so doesn't see that the higher value is pertinent, he or she is less likely to act in accordance with it. Awareness of the higher value is even likely to counteract immediate pressures. This is one reason why attention to values in schooling is potentially so important. By making students more aware of basic moral values and how they relate to decisions, there is a good chance that we can improve the caliber of moral judgments by decreasing the impact of parochial pressures in contrast with basic democratic considerations. Myrdal (1944, pp. 1029–1030) suggested that the educational influences of mobility, the mass media, and schooling would have that effect on our society.

undoubtedly explains the inclination of persons to unwittingly convert nonmoral values to moral status. When we approve or condemn an action, we want to be on the strongest possible ground.

RECAP

This chapter has discussed the nature of values. The term *value* was defined and distinguished from the terms *value judgment* and *attitude*. It was emphasized that values have both intellectual and emotional components. Categories of values—moral and nonmoral; intrinsic and instrumental—were elaborated, and it was proposed that moral values can be profitably thought of as falling along a continuum which ranges from personal standards to basic societal principles. We also emphasized the inevitability of value conflict, both interpersonal and intrapersonal. The importance of the notion of intrapersonal conflict—its certainty in our culture and the uncomfortable psychological state caused by the recognition of value dissonance—was also stressed.

To build a rationale for dealing with values, the teacher must understand each of these distinctions and points. We have noted some of the ways in which they affect teaching decisions. But to a large extent this chapter on the nature of values has been laying the groundwork for the more specific discussion of values in the schools of a democratic society. We turn to the context of democracy in Chapter 3.

Value Exploration 2

A. If a teacher makes the following *factual claims* or *directives,* what might be the implicit *value judgments*?

Factual Claims or Directives	Implicit Value Judgment(s)
1. "This class is not putting forth the necessary effort to pass the exam."	*You students should work harder. Passing the exam is important. . . .*
2. "Let's brainstorm the question Judy has raised in her report."	*Judy's question is worth brainstorming. Discussion is good. . . .*
3. "If you have something to say, please raise your hand rather than just talking out!"	

VALUES—WHAT ARE THEY? 37

4. "This paper, though potentially interesting, is not well organized."

5. "Donna is a creative and independent thinker who can handle advanced work."

6. "Give your honest reactions to this unit; that is, specify what you liked and disliked most."

7. "I see from my records that you've handed in only half the worksheets."

8. "Hurry up and get those textbooks open or I'll give a pop quiz!"

9. "Rick, I'm interested in your point of view here. Perhaps you might relate your thoughts to Linda's."

10. "These kids are so apathetic! I'm pulling my hair out trying to motivate them!"

B   If a teacher makes the following *value judgments*—either implicitly or explicitly—what might be the underlying *value* (or values)?

Value Judgment	Value(s)
1. Students should ask questions rather than simply absorb information.	*Involvement. Personal relevance.* . . .
2. Evaluation of student performance should be related to course objectives.	*Fairness. Rationality in instruction.* . . .
3. A teacher should attempt whenever possible to individualize instruction so that each student experiences success.	

4. Youngsters who do not complete their homework should not be allowed to go to recess.

5. Each student should design his own course of study and means of evaluation.

6. Test grades should be posted on the bulletin board to motivate slower students and acknowledge the achievement of faster ones.

7. Students should be grouped according to ability.

8. Students should *not* be grouped according to ability.

9. Courses that deal with the concerns and heritage of minority groups should be added to the curriculum.

10. Our school should attempt to do more innovative things, such as modular scheduling and team teaching.

The Experiment

Problem. *Identify the values that you think are being taught in the following situation.*

"So what do you think's going to happen?" Mr. Tiller asks with a trace of squint.

The room is bright as he lifts the glinting beaker, eyes it with purpose, and begins to tilt the pale acid, as if to answer his own question. Then he hesitates—

"Any ideas? What's your hypothesis based on the information you've got so far?"

The class is crowding around the demonstration table. "The tease," he thinks. "The trick is to set the hook." He puts the beaker down for a moment. He nods to a lanky fellow at the edge of the circle, mouthing an admonition to "hold it down" to some others. "One at a time," he says. The boy's face

VALUES—WHAT ARE THEY? 39

is smug and owly as he adjusts wire-framed glasses across the bridge of a freckled beak.

"I say it'll make carbon dioxide."

"How come?"

Hands are waving in Mr. Tiller's face.

"Uh, just the reaction," the boy shrugs. "I think it'll give off water and carbon dioxide."

"Uh-huh," Tiller nods in a noncommittal way. "How many agree with Allen?" A few hands go up; others are coming down.

"I think it's carbon dioxide *or* carbon monoxide," a hulking pigeon-browed girl is whining. "You can get either one. I mean, like it *depends,* you know?" Her eyes, spaced wide, are a blue glaze.

"Depends on what?" Mr. Tiller smiles.

"On the reaction," the girl sighs. "You can get either one."

The parabola of this circumlocution causes Mr. Tiller to blink. "I'm afraid I don't follow, Janice. What we've got to think of, you see, are principles of combining that might account for your theory. See if there's anything in the elements we're dealing with that would generate carbon monoxide or dioxide, okay?

"Any other theories?" Mr. Tiller asks.

"Nitrogen," one girl says.

"Hydrogen," a boy grins.

"Mr. Tiller nods in a patient way. "Uh-huh. Tell me about the hydrogen theory, Curtis." He eyes the beaker again.

"Well, you mix the acid and the metal, see—"

"Oxygen," a girl offers.

The boy with the hydrogen theory thinks he is off the hook and lounges off to the right. Mr. Tiller picks up the beaker again. It is early in the year, and he rolls up the sleeve of his lab coat, baring his left arm. The students watch him finger a spattering of thin white scars.

"Here's what happens when you think chemistry is just messing around with chemicals," he says. "You see, I learned that it's probably a pretty good idea to do the experiments in your head before you do it in lab."

"Hey, *shrapnel,*" one of the clowns guffaws.

"Of course, eyes don't heal like this," Mr. Tiller counters. "So maybe we'd better think through our theories a little more, okay?" Somewhere down the hall students are laughing and banging lockers.

"You see, science isn't just a guessing game," Mr. Tiller continues. "It's a way of behaving—a whole set of attitudes, if you know what I mean. It's a way of asking questions and making theories and gathering data to confirm or deny whatever your hunch is. Every theory has a *why* behind it."

A hand is up. "So what kind of gas does it make, Mr. Tiller?"

"Use your head on it, Cindy. Think it through."

"Uh, I'm sorry. I guess I need some help to get it."

"Well, maybe this will help," Mr. Tiller grins. He passes around a mimeographed sheet on which the apparatus for the experiment and the problem equation are laid out; then he nods to the boy with the hydrogen theory.

"Why don't you take it from here, Curtis? Go to work on that equation if you can."

In a moment or two their attention has been directed to the homework problem which no one has done, and students are arguing back and forth about how the equation will work. Mr. Tiller moderates and listens, asking a question now and then or clarifying the muddle with a point of information.

It seems incredible to him that having this kind of fun with a bunch of adolescents can actually be accepted as professional and a way of making a living. It is too *easy,* he thinks. All he does is listen for those places where kids have trouble understanding the topic under study; this is where his teaching or reteaching begins. The main problem is helping them get over the fear of making mistakes.

A small, wild-haired boy off to Mr. Tiller's right is wrinkling his nose like a nearsighted mole. His name is Gunther and he's had nothing to say since the beginning of the semester. He is now fidgeting and staring at the beaker of acid.

"Any questions?" Mr. Tiller asks.

"Yeah," Gunther says. "We're going to bubble off some gas through water, right? But how do we *know* that the gas is what we think it is? I mean, it *could* be something else, if you follow what I'm saying. Everybody's just going on *faith* that this equation works like we've said it does and that the stuff Mr. Tiller's got is what he *says* it is." He narrows his eyes. "I mean, it seems to me we ought to be able to imagine some kind of experiment to *test* whatever we get coming off."

To Mr. Tiller, Gunther is talking science. He is crossing the line that distinguishes the experimental mind from the ordinary one. Here's a kid who'll be fun to have around for a semester.

"Hmmmmmmm," Mr. Tiller murmurs.

"Uh, if it's hydrogen it ought to burn," one of the quiet girls says. "There may be some other tests, I don't know."

"Let's talk about that for just a moment," Mr. Tiller says. He is having a good time as he watches notebooks click open. With luck, he suspects that they may even get to the experiment before the period is over.

Follow-up. *What values does Mr. Tiller seem to have in mind? Can you distinguish the cognitive and affective elements? Is he doing a good job of teaching values?*

Moral Values and the "Teacher-Counselor"

Problem. *What moral values should guide the teacher's behavior?*

It's inevitable. Different teachers attract different kinds of youngsters. And for some reason I seem to attract the shy ones. Maybe it's because I'm rather quiet myself and can understand how it is when you'd rather not talk up in front of a group or share your problems and feelings with just anyone.

In any case, I was in the habit of staying around after school—and I tried to communicate to my students that they were welcome to drop by any time. No big thing, really. I was just there—correcting papers and planning and talking to whoever wanted to talk. I think they can tell if you're there to listen or if you're just waiting for a ride. So I tried to be around, and I tried to listen.

I had perhaps half a dozen regular visitors to my after-school "class," plus occasional "strays." Sometimes they'd come to do homework, sometimes to chat, sometimes to look at the magazine rack, sometimes to horse around—and sometimes to harass me. It was really sort of nice. But a little scary, you know? Sometimes kids will lay some pretty heavy stuff on you if you let them see you're interested in them as human beings.

I was just about ready to go home the afternoon Ilene came by. She's a quiet little sophomore—sensitive, pretty, a beautiful smile. We were gossiping about nothing in particular, and I remember I had just asked her about the plaid jumper she was wearing because I was interested in getting the pattern from a fabric shop on the way home. There was a slight pause as if she were catching her breath. I just waited without saying anything and smiled at her. That was all it took, I guess, because she looked at me and then put her head down on the desk top and began sobbing.

She was two months pregnant. And she was scared because she was only fifteen years old, and her boyfriend was just seventeen. She knew that her parents were going to "go through the roof" if they found out. I suggested that "if" would probably have to be changed to "when." It was then that I found out that she and the boy were talking about running away—which, in her opinion, was better than facing up to her folks.

Since I didn't know exactly what to do, I said something about talking to the Girls' Counselor. Ilene just started to cry again, harder this time. Her parents and the other kids would find out for sure, she said, and if that happened, she'd run away by herself, especially if I betrayed her. That really put me on the spot. Then she wanted to know if I knew where she could get an abortion. I'll have to admit I didn't know what to say for a moment.

Follow-up. *What would you do? List the short-range and long-range alternatives that you can think of. Then list the moral values that would justify the alternatives you've identified. Check your lists against those of others.*

| A. Short-range Alternatives | Values Supported | B. Long-range Alternatives | Values Supported |

Esthetic Values Over Tea and Crumpets

Problem. *Whose views on esthetics and grading do you share?*

"Excuse me? Do you have a moment to chat?"

Mrs. Lawrence was smiling as I gathered a small cake into my napkin and tried to balance a shaky tea cup.

"Of course," I said.

In a few moments we were seated across from one another at one of the cafeteria tables. Mrs. Lawrence was a slender, personable woman in her late twenties—attractive, intelligent, and vice-president of the PTA. She was also the mother of Todd Lawrence, a gabby, undisciplined youngster who sometimes gave me fits. Todd wasn't a "bad" child—I knew that—but he *was* physically and mentally immature.

"It's about Todd's work," Mrs. Lawrence said. "From your comments on his coloring work and penmanship exercises, I take it that he's not doing very well."

"Well, Todd *is* having some problems," I admitted. "In the area of neatness and following directions he seems to have a little more difficulty than most students. I think we just have to be patient with him."

"I'm glad to hear you say that," Mrs. Lawrence said. "That's *precisely* my feeling. I know that Todd isn't an angel and I know that he's not as coordinated as he might be. What I've had some trouble understanding, though, is why you should criticize the *form* of his work the way you have—I mean, with 'happy faces' and 'sad faces.'"

"Well, I'm simply trying to get Todd to do his best," I said. "Even though he may be immature, he needs to learn what's expected of him. If he gets the idea that sloppy work is acceptable, he'll have problems all the way through school." I tasted the crumbly, warm cake.

Mrs. Lawrence tried to smile, but her mouth was tight. "I'd feel better," she said, "if you wouldn't put those 'sad faces' on Todd's papers—even if he *does* go outside the lines."

My stomach knotted slightly. "I see." I touched my napkin to my lips.

"After all, we *do* have to be patient with him, don't we?"

"Yes, I think we do," I said. "But tell me: Don't you agree that good handwriting, neatness, and attractive looking papers are worthwhile things for Todd to work at?"

"Frankly, I'm not so sure." Mrs. Lawrence answered after a pause. "When we focus all our attention on neatness—on penmanship and margins and staying in the lines—we forget what the child is actually *saying* in his composition or drawing. Perhaps his coloring work isn't so good in your eyes, but *I* think it's very creative at times. In fact, I'd like to see Todd *experiment* with color—to go outside the lines whenever he feels like it. I'd like to see him make his letters in whatever way comes natural to him."

"We have to have a certain amount of discipline," I said. "Naturalness may be good, but. . . ."

"But do we have to make the children into conformists?" Mrs. Lawrence asked.

> **Follow-up.** *Continue the dialog in your mind. Try to answer Mrs. Lawrence's question. Deal directly with the possible moral overtones of the teacher's insistence on neatness.*
>
> *Find another person who has also read the conversation up to the point where it stops. Role-play the situation to see where it takes each of you in an exploration of your esthetic values. Then switch roles.*
>
> *In your opinion, is it fair for teachers to give grades on esthetic criteria such as form, neatness, and penmanship? If so, under what circumstances? Should esthetic criteria be separated from other criteria—for example, the "content" of an in-class essay?*
>
> *Is neatness always an esthetic value? Might it be a performance value? Some people enjoy "beautiful" handwriting as an end in itself (an intrinsic value). To others, neatness in handwriting is an instrumental performance value: It is important to learn to write neatly in order to do well in school and/or get a good job after one's schooling is completed. Read through "Esthetic Values over Tea and Crumpets" again and reconstruct the conversation as it might have gone had the teacher clearly been thinking of neatness as an instrumental performance standard. Again, role-play the situation as a way of exploring the ethical implications of imposing performance values.*

Instrumental Values, Kids, and Potted Plants

Problem. *How much "order" is necessary to have a productive classroom?*

I guess I had the first ominous twinge about student teaching on the morning I met my cooperating teacher. She was a tall, heavy-set woman in her late forties, and she was busily at work lining up desks along the gray and white tile lines. The students had just been dismissed for lunch.

"These kids," she sighed. "Sometimes I think they're nothing but *wild animals.* Just *look* at this mess they leave!"

I blinked and tried to find the mess. What I saw were even rows of desks and books neatly shelved. Mrs. Ashcroft's potted plants were lined like sentries along the window ledge, flanked by two printed signs that read "Do Not Touch." She picked up a scrap of paper and shelved a dictionary. "*There,*" she said. "That's better."

I soon discovered that Mrs. Ashcroft's universe was one where everything—and everyone—had its place. Her gradebook, her desk, her time schedule—all were laid out with care and precision. Each student knew the schedule of activities and understood that this schedule was fixed, unchanging; each knew the specific place for various kinds of assignments, the deadlines, the procedures for makeup work, and the penalties for failing to observe manuscript conventions; each knew that the program of study moved straight through the text, lesson by lesson, and that questions not pertinent to the current reading upset Mrs. Ashcroft.

About a week after I had that first twinge of uneasiness, Mrs. Ashcroft and I had a talk about my ideas for student teaching. I had submitted a unit plan to her, and we were going over it.

"About this group work," she said. "I think you'll find that youngsters take advantage of that kind of situation. They need a very definite structure, you see. And I think you'll find that they do better and *like* it better if they move along at the same rate. That makes things easier to manage, too."

I chose my words with care. "Well, I'm hoping to provide some structure *in* the groups," I said. "Each group will have a chairman, and. . . ."

"That's good in theory," Mrs. Ashcroft interrupted. "But it's difficult to maintain a good work atmosphere with a lot of confusion. These youngsters definitely need a sense of order—they need things laid out for them. If you let the students start going off in all directions, you have chaos and discipline problems. Your job is to control and *teach* these youngsters, not run a circus."

"I definitely don't want a circus," I murmured. "What I want is to promote involvement. I know that some groups will need to have things laid out for them, but I'm also hoping that some youngsters will get involved and do more than just enough to get by."

Mrs. Ashcroft shook her head. A small sigh escaped between her teeth as she looked at the plants again. "I don't see how you expect to keep track of all this," she said. "You'll have kids all over the room, working on different levels."

"I'm willing to give it a try." I winked, testing a grin on her.

Mrs. Ashcroft didn't smile back. "And because you can't plan this kind of program out in advance," she added, "it's bound to be disorganized and chaotic. I'm afraid it will be a bad experience for the students."

Silence.

"I know that all the details haven't been nailed down," I admitted. "It just seems to me that the students will be more likely to learn if they have a say in *some* of the directions we take."

Mrs. Ashcroft turned to the window ledge. "After all, you don't ask the plants whether they *need* water. It's your job—your responsibility—to provide what they need."

I closed my planning book and looked Mrs. Ashcroft in the eye. "We certainly see things differently," I said.

Follow-up. *What instrumental values seem to govern Mrs. Ashcroft's point of view? What are the instrumental values of the student teacher? Are the instrumental values performance, esthetic, or moral?*

Assume that you are the student teacher in this situation. What would you be inclined to do? Argue? Attempt to effect a compromise? Give up? Role-play the conversation with a friend to sort out your instrumental values and resolve the conflict.

Value Exploration 3

Turn again to "Moral Values and the 'Teacher-Counselor' " (page 41). Think about your answers to the "Follow-up." Which short- and long-range alternatives would you choose? Which values would you be supporting?

Would you have made the same choice four years ago? Might you make a different choice ten years from now?

Would your parents have made the same choice? If not, what value (or values) would they emphasize? Or think of some other significant person in your life who might disagree with your choice of alternatives. What different value or values would that person probably want to support?

Look at the values that support the alternatives you did not choose. Are any of these values unimportant to you? Are you sure that these values are not as significant to you as the ones that support the short- and long-range alternatives you chose?

Finally, think of another situation, perhaps one in which you were personally involved as a student, in which a teacher made an important ethical judgment that affected you. (Perhaps it was a judgment involving grades or discipline, or even something that happened out of school.) Identify the interpersonal value conflicts (perhaps between you and the teacher, or between the teacher and someone else, such as the principal or your parents). Then identify the intrapersonal value conflicts that could have occurred for you and for the teacher.

Chapter **3**

THE DEMOCRATIC CONTEXT

What, you might ask, is a book that purports to be about values and teaching in general doing with a chapter on democracy? After all, social studies teachers take responsibility for citizenship education, don't they? So, aren't they the only ones who need to be concerned with the meaning of democracy?

Social studies teachers are particularly concerned with preparing students to be "good" citizens. But most teachers, regardless of their teaching area, profess some interest in citizenship as an educational goal. Training for citizenship, or at least for proper deportment, is usually considered to be a function of the total school.

But a teacher has other reasons to contemplate the meaning of democracy. The school, as a formal educational institution, is a creature of the society it serves. And teachers, in turn, are agents of that society.[1] For that reason, it is vital that each teacher have a clear conception of democracy as a critical part of an adequate rationale for dealing with values in the school. Your conception of democracy will influence your decisions about what values to treat and how to treat them, as well as help or hinder you in justifying your decisions to parents and administrators.

What follows is a sketching of some value-related assumptions about the

---

[1]That is, of the *society*, not of the *establishment*. A major premise of this book is that each teacher needs to be clear about his or her role as an agent of a *democratic society*, not of whatever economic, racial, ethnic, and/or religious group is currently in power.

society which employs us to teach. Read and criticize. Above all, ask whether the view of democracy laid out here coincides with your own, and if not, which perspective provides the more adequate framework for deciding what you as a teacher should do about values.

DEFINING DEMOCRACY

We assume that most people will agree that our society is a democracy—at least in intent, if not always in actuality. Democracy is commonly defined as a society which is governed by the majority. The Greek *demokratia* and the New England town meeting are often cited as examples, with an ideal of direct participation by the citizen in mind. But ideals and reality frequently differ. In neither the Greek *demokratia* nor the New England town meeting did all of the citizens have the will or the opportunity to participate. In each case unelected representatives made the decisions.

Our modern form of government, called a *republic*, is a response to the obvious impossibility of bringing large masses of people together to make laws. It fits the majority rule definition of democracy by providing elections as the mechanism whereby a majority of concerned citizens can select governmental representatives and subject them to periodic review. When votes are taken in legislative and judicial bodies, decisions are also by majority rule.

This popular definition of democracy—that is, democracy as majority rule—is the source of many complaints about "undemocratic" actions by the government. People find fault, for example, with court decisions that limit prayer in the classroom because "the majority wants prayer, and in a democracy, the will of the majority should be followed."

But what if a national plebiscite were held on the question: "Should all Mormons be executed?"—and a distinct majority voted "yes"?[2] Would we say that this was clearly a democratic decision, that the government should execute Mormons because it was mandated to do so by a majority vote? Undoubtedly not!

As a matter of fact, even taking such a vote would be considered an unthinkable heresy to the democratic faith. There would be an immediate outcry, and not only from the group threatened with extinction. Clearly, democracy involves more than majority rule. Protection of the rights of individuals and minorities is also essential. (Ironically, many people who argue vociferously for prayer in the schools on the basis of majority rule—even though some minorities claim that such prayer violates their right to religious

---

[2]Substitute the name of any religious, ethnic, or other minority group that is more meaningful, i.e., evokes more emotional reaction, for you.

freedom—would be strident in opposing the persecution of a religious minority, especially one to which they belonged. This is a good example of value conflict and the shifting of value emphasis as the pinching shoe shifts feet.)

But why majority rule, and why protect minority rights? An adequate answer is one that justifies and integrates majority rule and minority rights in a definition of democracy. One plausible approach to such a definition is suggested by the responses that could be anticipated to the somewhat facetious suggestion above that a vote be taken on genocide. "It would be inhumane." "You just don't treat humans that way." Implicit in such reactions is an ideal of human-ness—that being human is of itself important and demands respect. This belief that each individual has worth and deserves consideration because he is human—and equal to anyone else in that sense, if not in wealth, intellect, or physical prowess—is, we believe, central to democracy.[3] Its essence is captured in the phrase *human dignity*. It is this central democratic value from which the values of majority rule and minority rights are derived and to which they contribute.

Majority rule, for example, is not just a chance occurrence in the development of democratic political institutions. It directly reflects an emphasis upon equality which is inherent in the ideal of individual dignity. When the votes of those who have equal dignity are being weighed, the scale shifts according to the number of votes on each side, not according to *who* cast them.

The emphasis placed by the ideal of human dignity upon the worth of each individual also provides the basis for individual and minority rights in a democracy. The right to life, liberty, and the pursuit of happiness, to freedom from despotic government, to freedom of speech, press, and religion, to due process of law, and to equal protection of the law—these rights, as spelled out in our fundamental political documents, are values essential to the definition of human dignity in this society. And so are others, such as the right to shelter and to freedom from hunger, added during the Great Depression. That is, it is commonly accepted that protection of these values—the principles of the American Creed—enhances the dignity of individuals in our society.

It is important to note that the basic democratic rights are moral values. They are principles or standards by which we judge the morality of individual, collective, and governmental actions. But when we think of democratic values, we must go beyond rights. Such values as domestic tranquility (law and order; a reasonably stable existence) and responsibility (often overlooked

---

[3]Michael Scriven (1966) uses the notion of equal rights, in the sense of equal consideration, as the basis for a democratic ethic. His work suggests another way to construe the democratic context for schooling. However, it should be noted that Scriven's ideal of equality and the ideal of human dignity, as defined here, are closely related (see, for example, Oliver & Shaver, 1974, pp. 46–48).

by young people who see their rights violated but are not ready to take full responsibility for their own actions and well-being) are also extensions of, and essential to, human dignity.

> The classroom crackles with tension. A rebel youngster has challenged you. "We voted on this thing. I thought we had majority rule!" Do the ideas in this chapter apply to the classroom? See "Mini-Democracy in Room 16," page 63.

Basic Instrumental Values

As we mentioned earlier, the values in the democratic ethos—the American Creed—are basic moral values which are important ends in themselves. That is, they are intrinsic values. But they also function as instrumental values[4] in two related ways: (1) values such as due process of law, especially as interpreted by the courts, provide procedural guidelines for government officials; (2) preserving each of the values in the Creed helps to maintain the broader concept of dignity.

Let's consider the value of freedom of speech to illustrate these two functions. Court interpretations of the meaning of freedom of speech provide standards for officials who must make such decisions as whether to allow the use of loudspeakers on cars for political announcements, or whether to issue permits for various types of rallies. Also, when the policies and actions of government officials, and private citizens, are judged by, and forced toward, the criterion of free speech, it is more difficult for public officials or private citizens to deny human dignity in other matters. In an environment of free speech, which includes protection for people who speak out against the government or against popular private positions, violations of other basic values are less likely. Freedom of speech (and press) makes it probable both that such violations will be made known and that proposed or present policies will be openly debated in terms of the values they may violate.

Here's what Franklin D. Roosevelt, 32nd President of the United States said about the importance of a free press:

> "Freedom of conscience, of education, of speech, of assembly are among the very foundations of democracy and all of them would be nullified should freedom of the press ever be successfully challenged."

---

[4] See Chapter 2, pages 28–30.

And so for all of the basic democratic values: Each is an important end in itself in our society; and each helps to define and maintain the conception of dignity that is so central to a democracy. But, as we emphasized in Chapter 2, the basic values in the Creed conflict with one another by their very nature.

Application of particular values to concrete situations reveals the incompatibilities. Conflicts occur between individual and minority rights (as between freedom of association and equal protection of the law, in cases of racial segregation). Conflicts occur between individual or minority rights and societal values such as majority rule (as in the classroom prayer dispute) and domestic stability—values that are also rooted in the ideal of dignity.[5]

This inherent conflict means that we cannot fully attain all of the basic values at any one time. As we move toward full attainment of one, we inevitably will have to compromise another. Hence the major continuing policy question that underlies so much political and social controversy: What blend of the conflicting basic values should we support in order to achieve optimal dignity for every member of our society? Thinking about values in this fashion will help you to avoid treating basic values in a way that leads students to have unrealistic expectations. That may help to counteract the cynicism of students who see unfulfilled ideals and conclude that this lack of fulfillment reflects only the evil in people.

Last week, for the first time, the Supreme Court publicly grappled with the sensitive, divisive issue of preferential admissions policies for minority-group college students. . . .

The case was brought by Marco DeFunis, Jr., a white student who claimed that the University of Washington unconstitutionally discriminated against him by refusing him admission to law school while accepting 36 minority-group students with lower academic qualifications. . . .

The case was a conflict between two cherished popular notions—the idea that minorities discriminated against in the past should have special help to overcome the effects of past inferior treatment and the notion that everyone should be judged on his own merits.

---

[5]It is worth noting that the conflict between majority rule and individual-minority rights is built into our governmental system. Two branches of the government—the executive and legislative—rest on electoral bases that force them to reflect (or to try to give the impression of reflecting) the democratic concern for majority rule. One branch, the judiciary, was established to protect the individual and minority rights that are also fundamental to our conception of democracy. That is a basic reason why judges are not elected. The United States Supreme Court in particular, with its function of ultimate review of constitutional questions, finds itself dealing with disputes involving the basic rights of individuals and minorities. When it fulfills its obligation and on occasion rules against the "majority," the Court finds itself subjected to criticism that often

[DeFunis' attorney argued that] "The failure to consider all applicants on an equal basis was a denial of the equal protection of the laws . . . [and that the University] . . . had demonstrated no 'overriding public interest' in . . . admitting some minority students with 'lower grades and qualifications'. . . ."
—Cheryl M. Fields, *The Chronicle of Higher Education,* March 4, 1974.

Can you state the values underlying the two "popular notions" mentioned above? Are "equal protection of the law" and "public interest" basic values?

HUMAN DIGNITY AND INTELLIGENCE

Autonomy and intelligence are at the essence of human dignity. However, the democratic ideal is not that of an individual completely free to do as he or she wishes. Nor is it that of an unfeeling, unemotional, totally rational being. Rather, the ideal of human dignity implies that each person has the right to self-fulfillment, to make the major decisions about his or her own destiny, and that emotion and commitment will be tempered by intelligent reflection in the decision-making process.

A democratic society is not only committed to intelligence and to the right to choose as essential ingredients of humanness, but to the belief that intellectual abilities can be improved, even if they cannot be perfected. The public generally assumes that the improvement of decision-making capabilities lies within the school's legitimate domain.

Clearly, parents accept formalized thinking skills—such as in mathematics—as within the school's instructional prerogatives. Problems arise when teachers attempt to move beyond the boundaries of formal subject matter into the cultivation of thinking for everyday life. As John Dewey (1916, p. 148) noted, thinking involves risk. When you encourage students to think, the end product cannot be guaranteed, and it may deviate substantially from what parents would like. Trying to improve the thinking skills of young people in order to enhance their dignity can therefore be dangerous.

---

reaches an incredibly vituperative level. (Dahl, 1958, has suggested that there is no evidence to prove that the Supreme Court has frequently gone against the wishes of the majority. Instead, extremely vocal minorities cry out so loudly that it sounds as though a majority has been affronted.) By the very nature of their attacks—vilifying the Court for acting contrary to what they assume the wishes of the majority to be—the critics frequently evidence an unfortunate shallowness of understanding of the relationship of the courts to the democratic ethos, and of the conflicting nature of our basic values. (For a more detailed discussion of the democratic role of the courts, see Shaver, 1978.)

It's 7:10 A.M. You're leisurely sipping orange juice and scanning the "Letters to the Editor" in the morning newspaper. You're hoping to find some juicy items for class discussion. Then, suddenly, you're trembling with a sick feeling—a mixture of anger and fear. See "Devil's Advocate," page 64, for more details.

School people who seriously attempt to assist students in applying their intelligence outside narrow academic limits are often severely criticized. This ironic state of affairs becomes comprehensible if we add to the notion of value conflict a consideration of the nature of a pluralistic society. Understanding how values and pluralism are interrelated in building a rationale can help you avoid being trapped and penalized by the paradoxes of the society you serve as a teacher.

PLURALISM—A SINE QUA NON OF DEMOCRACY

In some national and local communities there are strong, frequently conscious, efforts to subjugate individual differences to one predominant doctrine, whether political (as in the Soviet Union or China) or religious (as in Utah). Such communities demand uniformity on doctrinal issues, especially as interpreted and propounded by political or religious authorities. The result is often considerable homogeneity—at least on the surface for public view. This is especially true when there is little influx of new ideas because dissemination is controlled by the authorities or because few new people join the community.

It makes sense to describe such societies as monolithic, especially when they are contrasted with pluralistic societies. While the monolithic society attempts to make its members feel that their affiliation with one dominant group should be *the* determining influence on their lives, the pluralistic society encourages, or at least openly tolerates, a multiplicity of groups. Members of the society see this pluralism as a positive attribute. They accept the diversity of ideas that are expressed as a result, and they protect the expression of these ideas (even if with misgivings at times).

This diversity can be difficult to accept when the ideas expressed are viewed as radical, as was the case with early opposition to U.S. involvement in Vietnam. For that reason, institutionalized protections, such as our commitment to freedom of speech and our judicial system, are vital. Most important, however, is the democratic commitment to a process of rational consent in decision making. It provides the context for expression of opinion, for exercise of persuasion and reason, and finally for abiding by decisions reached via legitimate procedures.

Teachers would often be well advised to consider whether they treat unconventional students in ways consistent with human dignity and the assumed benefits of pluralism. School people also need to reflect on the validity of students' complaints (which the courts have agreed to on occasion) that our schools do not adequately protect the expression of divergence, and thus lose the benefits of pluralism for education.

What is so great about pluralism? To begin with, diversity is interesting—it is boring to be surrounded by people who are all alike. But avoiding dreary monotony is hardly the basic justification for pluralism. On the contrary, the assumed benefits of a pluralistic society are fundamental to democracy; and, as noted above, pluralism and basic values such as freedom of speech and press go hand in hand.

The pressure of diverse views in the community and the provision of the means to express them serve fundamental functions. In many situations, latent problems, overlooked by people with similar outlooks on life, are identified by the person whose outlook is different. When a newcomer raises questions about the treatment of minority groups in a community which "has no minority problem," or a student challenges long-standing procedures in your classroom, the consternation that is created may be unwelcome—but it often throws the decision-making process into motion. Moreover, once problems are posed, diversity of opinion makes it likely that a broad range of options will be available from which to work out solutions. Diversity, and controversy based on diversity, can even be the catalyst for a rejuvenation of commitments. Clashes with those of unlike mind can force people to reconsider the meanings of their values and the reasonableness of their priorities—as college students proved in the late 1960s.

. . . If there is no struggle, there is no progress. Those who profess to favor freedom, and yet depreciate agitation, are men who want crops without plowing up the ground. They want rain without thunder and lightning. They want the ocean without the awful roar of its many waters. . . .

—Frederick Douglass

These contributions to the decision-making process, and not just dissent for its own sake, were undoubtedly what Supreme Court Justice William O.

Douglas had in mind when he commented: "I don't know of any salvation for society except through eccentrics, misfits, dissenters, people who protest."

Without a variety of openly expressed views, decision making is meaningless, an empty exercise. In monolithic societies, regardless of the form it takes, decision making is a sham because the problems to be dealt with, and frequently the decisions to be made, are prescribed before the process begins. For that reason, pluralism is a *sine qua non* of democracy. Real opportunities for decision making are an essential aspect of the core concept of human dignity.

This emphasis on the contribution of divergent points of view may seem to be a belaboring of the obvious. But the concept of pluralism should be central to your decisions as you interact with students in noninstructional situations and to your decisions about how to deal with values in the formal curriculum. People often fail to appreciate the importance of pluralism and diversity when they are faced with specific situations. The results of the National Assessment of Educational Progress (1970) illustrate this and confirm the findings of other polls. When knowledge and attitudes related to citizenship education were assessed, the freedom to express unpopular opinions was the "least understood or valued" of the Constitutional rights (pp. 28–29, 35). People were asked whether three statements should be allowed on radio or television. One statement said that Russia was better than the United States; one that some races of people are better than others; and one that it is not necessary to believe in God. The results suggest how difficult it is for people to support the expression of ideas they disagree with: 94 percent of the thirteen-year-olds, 78 percent of the seventeen-year-olds, and 68 percent of the adults answered No. And of those who said the statements should be allowed, only 3 percent, 17 percent, and 24 percent respectively cited the civic value of freedom of speech as a reason (pp. 28–29, 34–35). Such findings, which are not unique, merit attention whenever school people consider whether schools are fulfilling their obligations to a democratic society.

The United States is a multi-cultural society of considerable diversity, containing various ethnic groups, social-class subcultures, rural and urban subcultures, and a distinctive youth subculture, all of which vary in characteristics (i.e., emphases in language, thought, behavior, and values). The educational system, however, is largely mono-cultural; teaching proceeds within the cultural and linquistic framework of the dominant group. . . .

Instead of the "melting pot" objective of blending divergent groups into a single homogeneous mass, the objective should be to develop a "tossed salad" of different cultures and life styles, enhancing the values and uniqueness of each culture, so that, taken together, they become complementary. In other words, the objective should be to prepare people to live in a pluralistic society. This goal obviously goes beyond merely dealing with language differences or making minor accommodations in the system.

—D. C. Clement, P. A. Johnson, Glen Nimnicht, and James Johnson. *Beyond "Compensatory Education,"* 1973.

Recognition of the significance of pluralism may help you to appreciate the point of view of minority group parents who object to what they call the "white, middle-class" orientation of our schools. You may also be better able to comprehend the dilemma posed by, on the one hand, the historical role of the public schools in building a sense of political community (see Butts, 1978) and, on the other hand, recent minority group demands that schools emphasize the distinctiveness and contributions of different subcultures and life styles. But if your rationale is to be adequate, it must take into account the paradoxical role of values in promoting both conflict and cohesion in a pluralistic society.

Money. There's nothing like it to bring out differences in human values. Read "Chicano Maverick," page 66, to see how $88.50 raises a real problem—as well as an opportunity for value clarification.

CONFLICT

Pluralism is not all honey and cream. Diversity creates societal stresses, as has been obvious in recent years. And the divisive forces in a society have their impact on the schools that serve it. Pluralism means, for example, that school people are confronted with competing points of view about the proper role of the school. Under these conditions, it is not easy for a teacher to determine what his or her mandate is in regard to the teaching of values. This is especially true when you are aware of the inevitable influence of your own frame of reference, and want to make decisions that are more than affirmations of the prejudices and biases of the particular groups to which you happen to belong. A valid conception of the role of basic values in our democratic society can do much to bolster your confidence in those decisions.

In Chapter 2 we discussed the inevitability of value conflict—both between the values held by any one person (*intra*personal conflict) and the values emphasized by different persons (*inter*personal conflict). In a pluralistic society, interpersonal value conflict occurs because persons from different backgrounds and, therefore, different frames of reference will choose to advocate different basic values as they try to influence public policy.

Controversy is also the result of vagueness in the descriptive meanings of our basic values. There is rarely consensus on the definitions of our value terms. Consequently, when a value is applied as a criterion for judging a specific situation or policy (for example, in deciding whether classroom prayer violates freedom of religion), the descriptive meaning of the value term must be explicated. Otherwise, it is impossible to decide rationally whether the behavior or policy in question fits or violates the value criterion.

The ways in which people define value terms are a function of the different experiences and, consequently, the different frames of reference that are encouraged in a pluralistic society. As value terms are defined specifically, differences in the way people construe the terms become apparent. Controversy is the result, then, of differences in value emphasis *and* definition that are heightened by our commitment to pluralism.

In 1962, the U.S. Supreme Court[6] declared (in *Engle v. Vitale*) that having students say prayers in public school classrooms violated the First Amendment prohibition against the establishment of religion by government. Some saw this decision as an important contribution because it reinforced the separation of church and state. Others saw it as a denial of personal religious freedom and of the school's obligation to promote morality. Strong controversy continues over the 1962 prayer decision, and over a 1963 decision (*Schempp v. School District of Abbington Township*) barring Bible reading and recitation of the Lord's Prayer during opening exercises as unconstitutional.

Obviously, whether a person views school prayer and Bible reading as falling within or outside the realm of freedom of religion—and thus as either justified or unjustified—depends on the person's frame of reference. The differences in experience that lead people to disagree over such vital questions are an interesting area for speculation, but one that is outside the scope of this book. What is relevant here is a recognition that such disagreements are inevitable and legitimate in a pluralistic society. Therefore, you will need to reckon with them in your decisions about the formal and hidden curricula, as well as when you deal with parents.

COHESION

When people differ over the descriptive meaning of values and over which values to emphasize at any particular point in time, conflicts result. These

---

[6]Note that the courts have been given the ultimate responsibility for providing authoritative definitions of disputed legal-value terms. Again, the nature of the task assigned them has embroiled the courts in heated controversy and opened them to vituperative attack.

conflicts are so obvious and so pervasive that they lead some people to conclude that there really is no such thing as an American Creed—no set of basic values to which all Americans tend to be committed. These people are correct in one important sense: *There probably is no one set of values which has the same descriptive meaning for all Americans.*

Yet, in another vital sense, the challengers are wrong. That is, *at the affective, emotional, level there is a commonality of commitment to a set of values that allows us to speak of an American Creed.* The very vagueness in descriptive meaning that underlies so much controversy allows the widely divergent groups in our society to hold common affective commitments to the basic values. Individuals across the nation can and do have common "good" feelings about values such as freedom of religion—the "rights of Americans"—even though they assign these values different descriptive meanings and different priorities.

We have noted that when people attempt to translate the basic values into social policies, or use them to judge specific actions, the disparities in descriptive meaning become obvious. It is important to note that, even then, persons who oppose a policy or action that others support in the name of a basic value rarely reject the value itself. Rather, they either argue that the value has been misdefined or they use other basic values to support their own position. For example, those who opposed the Supreme Court's decisions on prayer and Bible reading in public schools did not argue that the First Amendment restriction on government establishment of religion was wrong. Rather, they argued that opening prayers and Bible reading did not fall within the meaning of "establishment of religion." They also contended that the decisions violated other basic values, such as majority rule (polls indicate that a majority of Americans favor prayer in the public schools), freedom of religion (those who wanted to pray were being denied the right to do so), and local control (limited federal authority, with the emphasis on decision making by those directly affected by the decisions).

THE CREED AND COHESION

The contention that there is an American Creed that carries a common emotional meaning is no trivial matter. People who travel throughout our country are frequently impressed by the vast geographic territory and the tremendous subcultural differences. They find it remarkable that somehow, despite all these differences and divisive forces, the nation holds together.

What is the binding force? Is there something beyond the pervasive concern with economic welfare—middle-class materialism and financial security—which links the variety of subgroups in this society? Gunnar Myrdal

(1944) concluded, "It is difficult to avoid the judgment that this 'American Creed' is the cement in the structure of this great and disparate nation" (p. 3).[7]

Common emotive commitments are critical to the cohesiveness of any society. Anthropologists pinpoint the nonintellectual nature of this aspect of culture when they refer to it as "projective reality."[8] It is a framework that the society's members take for granted as a context for thought, discussion, and action. In that sense, the American Creed is important in much the same way as a religious faith—not because its truth has been verified scientifically, but because it is accepted as part of the "natural" order of things.

The "cement" of a creed is especially vital to a pluralistic society with its emphasis on diversity and personal freedom. The emotive force of the ideals in the Creed provides a context for interaction that is often implicit, sometimes explicit, rarely questioned. It provides a common bond between, and a basis for confrontation and debate among, those with contending views.

Have you ever tried to have a reasonable, productive discussion geared toward solving a problem with someone who did not share your values—that is, not someone who emphasized values differently than you did, but who argued from a *different set* of values? Under those conditions, arguments about what is proper pass one another by without effect. To meet head-on, they must come from common value premises. Shared commitments are the basis for intelligent confrontation—even when the dispute involves which values are most important or how to translate them into policy and action.

"Everyone needs goals, something in life to strive for. You know, getting ahead, being someone. . . ."

Oh, do they? The lack of shared commitments can get in the way of classroom problem solving, too. See "The Problem," page 67.

POTENTIAL OBJECTIONS TO THE CREED IN A TEACHING RATIONALE

Awareness of the cohesive function of our society's basic values is a vital aspect of an adequate teaching rationale. However, there are two potential

---

[7]For an excellent discussion of the Creed and its historical roots, see Myrdal's (1944) Chapter 1, "What Ideals and the American Conscience." R. Freeman Butts has discussed the importance of basic values to our political community in both an historical (1978) and a contemporary (1980) context.

[8]This term is used by Donald Oliver (1960, p. 212) in a perceptive discussion of the dilemma of diversity and cohesion in a pluralistic society.

objections to this conception of a Creed. These objections need to be anticipated and dealt with.

The International Scene

If a conception of values is to provide an adequate basis for your teaching decisions, it must take into account the fundamental fact that the United States is part of a world community. The role of the nation-state in this era of high speed travel and communication is not yet clear. World government does not seem any closer to reality than it was at the end of World War II; yet there is a growing consciousness that if the world is to survive, we must not cut ourselves off physically, intellectually, or emotionally from people in other countries. This leads some people to reject out-of-hand any conception of an "American Creed" as being too nationalistic, too chauvinistic. They argue that if teachers include such a conception in their rationales, it will work against the goals of international education.

The paradox raised by such a protest is difficult to handle. The need for national cohesion, for a framework of mutual commitments from which people in our society can contend with one another, seems evident; yet so does the need for international understanding and compassion.

A starting point for dealing with this paradox is an explicit recognition that the Creed is not exclusively American, although adherence to it is an American phenomenon. The Creed's philosophical roots are many: the English culture, with its early emphasis on law and order, justice and equality; the Judeo-Christian heritage, especially its democratic notion of brotherhood in the sense that, rich or poor, we are common in the eyes of God; the European Age of Enlightenment, which sought the emancipation of human nature and highlighted the conflict between libertarianism and equalitarianism that continues to this day.

Commitment to the basic values in the Creed varies significantly from time to time and from country to country. The democratic tradition is more limited, for example, in Germany than in Scandinavia. And Americans seem to be more compelled than Europeans to defend their policies and actions in terms of basic ideals, wearing their values on their sleeves and constantly chastising themselves in political speeches and newspaper editorials for failing to live up to their ideals. One commentator (Myrdal, 1944, p. 4) has suggested that in contrast to other nations, "America is continuously struggling for its soul."

Despite these variations, however, the values in the Creed are clearly a Western phenomenon, not an American one. The major difference appears to be the moralistic fervor of Americans.

Is the Creed an exclusively Western phenomenon? Anthropologists May and Abraham Edel (1968, pp. 91 ff.) have suggested that concern for the worth and dignity of the individual is present in many societies and may approach the status of a universal value.

It might be tempting, but a mistake, to jump to the conclusion that the commitment to individual worth and dignity makes the Creed truly universal. The values in the Creed are predominantly Western in origin and orientation. Cultural differences between East and West—for example, the Chinese tendency to view time in a scope much broader than individual lives—should not be too easily discounted.

Still, the possibility that individual dignity in the Western sense is not a truly universal value should not prevent us from judging American international behavior—our own personal actions as well as our national policy—by the values in the Creed. Moreover, if individuals made conscious attempts to identify and clarify commonalities in moral values across cultures, centering on human worth and dignity, they might find the common context for international debates on policy that now seems frequently to be missing. Building such a context may be the essential first step in creating a viable basis for world government.

To explore this important point, with all its ramifications (the questionable current stature of the U.S.A. as an international moral leader; potential reactions against what some countries perceive as American evangelism; the chance that cultural differences may make it impossible even to approximate a common definition of dignity), is beyond the scope of this book. We only want to emphasize that the American Creed is *not* intrinsically ethnocentric.

Certainly, an adequate rationale for dealing with values as a teacher cannot ignore the international setting of our society. Our societal commitment to human dignity should be a conscious part of the frame of reference from which teachers make decisions about international-intercultural education. And teachers should also keep in mind the potential international-intercultural impacts (for example, on the ethnocentrism of students) of value-related teaching decisions.

Democratic values, the international scene, and your teaching call for considerable thought. Value Exploration 4, page 68, has some suggestions for reflection.

Minorities and the Creed

Another objection to the notion of an American Creed comes from the perspective of ethnic and other minorities. The indictment is often stated in the form of a reproach such as "How could anyone who knows how minority groups are treated in this society say there is an American Creed that emphasizes values like equality and freedom?"

Those who have suffered from racism or other forms of prejudice can hardly be faulted for being cynical about our society's commitment to basic democratic values. Yet in their cynicism they often confuse the failure to attain an ideal with the absence of the ideal. A person who strives to be honest may not always succeed. As already noted, his lapses do not mean that he does not value honesty. By the same token, if the society or individuals in it do not always act in conformity with the basic values in the Creed, this does not mean that the Creed (that is, a commitment to the basic values) does not exist.

There can be only one (I repeat: *Only one*) aim of a revolution by Negro Americans: That is the *enforcement of the Constitution of the United States.*

—Chester Himes. *Black on Black.* 1973.

For one thing, the basic ideals of our society are lofty, and by their very nature difficult to attain. Also, we have already stressed that because the values in the Creed conflict with one another, support or promotion of one will ordinarily come at the expense of another. Extensions of freedom of speech are likely to encroach on domestic tranquility; greater equality for some—the outcome of civil rights movements—results in limitations on the liberty of others. In no instance is any one value likely to be fully realized as the society struggles toward the ultimate ideal of dignity for all. Recognizing the conflicting nature of our basic values—which is not to deny that some people have been unjustifiably deprived of rights and opportunities taken for granted by the dominant white society—can be a powerful and valid antidote to the cynicism of youth and minorities alike.

In fact, the recent gains in rights for blacks, women, and the handicapped—belated as they have been in coming—illustrate the power of the Creed. The struggle for equality has indeed been a war within America's conscience. How else can one explain the overcoming of deep-seated prejudice except through the buffering effect of commitment to deeper values? The power of the Creed was recognized by black leaders such as Martin Luther King, Jr., who premised the nonviolent civil rights movement on the belief that if blacks could demonstrate their unequal situation and assert their demands for rights without violence, they would prick the conscience of the nation. And the peaceful sit-ins and marches and the televised confrontations with often brutal law enforcement officers did move the nation toward redressing the wrongs that blacks have suffered in this country. Policy and action were brought more in line with the commitment to equality inherent in the ideal of human dignity. Commitment to equality of opportunity has also provided the means for gains in women's rights and is the basis for the emerging civil rights movement on the part of handicapped persons (see Kleinfield, 1979; Bowe, 1980).

> The nonviolent resister must often express his protest through noncooperation or boycotts, but he realizes that these are not ends themselves; they are merely means to awaken a sense of moral shame in the opponent.
>
> —Martin Luther King, Jr. *Stride Toward Freedom,* 1964.

The relative emphasis placed on the various values in the Creed is continually changing. A fixed, clearly defined and ordered set of dogmas would be maladaptive in a dynamic society. Gains by minorities and value shifts in other fields, such as criminal justice, prove once again that the struggle toward dignity is never-ending. Judgments about whether policies and actions take the nation in the proper direction will be largely a function of each individual's frame of reference. But the Creed, with its cognitive vagueness and emotive solidarity, does provide a viable context for confrontations over fundamental issues as we adapt to tomorrow's realities.

> Equality of opportunity is a basic value in our society. "Get off it," says a black student. See "Equality—for Whom?", page 69.

RECAP

Each teacher in a democratic society ought to have a clear conception of the nature of that society and of the role played by its basic values. Human dignity and the basic values that define and protect it; the contributions of pluralism; the importance of emotive commitment to the American Creed; the vagueness in the descriptive meanings of the basic values in the Creed that underlies controversy, but allows change—these are all things that must be considered in developing a rationale adequate to the task of making and justifying value-related teaching decisions. Of particular importance is the recognition that the ideal of human dignity includes commitment to intelligence and to the belief that it can be improved.

Such considerations about society and the nature of values have profound implications for the school's formal and hidden curricula—for which you, as a teacher, must share responsibility. Next, we need to consider more specifically your role as a schooling agent for the society.

Mini-Democracy in Room 16

Problem. *What values are at stake in the following episode?*

One of the things I've always believed is that people learn responsibility by *being* responsible—not by being *made* to do what's "good" for them. I also believe that kids can make pretty good decisions for themselves if we'll just give them a chance to do so now and then.

That's why I decided to set up a kind of democratic Forum in my sixth-grade class. My basic idea was that the Forum would be a weekly meeting—a place where we could kick around problems, make up reasonable rules for our class, and decide how to handle kids who couldn't behave responsibly. The notion, in short, was that the Forum would be "Democracy in Action," and I hoped that it would help to offset some of the authoritarian, nondemocratic modes of working that the kids were used to.

I guess the first real challenge to my mini-democracy came about two weeks after school started. The class had decided that quietness was probably pretty important during study periods, but that there wasn't any real reason to prohibit visiting *after* they'd completed their assignments. I agreed to this. I mean, it seemed to make sense at the time.

What I didn't count on was that I'd have a five-year spread in reading abilities for those sixth graders—not an unusual situation, I found out later. Some kids were finished with their work in ten or fifteen minutes, while others labored for forty minutes or more. This meant that each day the classroom talk began with low, tolerable whispering and ended up in bedlam. The situation clearly discriminated against slow readers.

I brought up the problem in our weekly Forum meeting and informed the class that I had gotten a couple of complaints from the principal. Anne Green, one of the bright, very able youngsters, challenged me right away. "I thought you said we were going to have a democracy in here," she said.

"That's right," I countered. "But we've got a problem. And I think we need to deal with it."

"You mean, *you've* got a problem," Anne retorted. "We voted on this thing. I thought we had majority rule. Either you stick by what the majority wants or we go back to the old teacher-rule thing."

I could feel the blood flush my cheeks. "What about the kids who need a little more time to get their work done?"

"Send 'em out in the hall," Anne giggled. "I say we ought to do what's good for the rest of us!"

There was applause from Anne's grinning supporters. Then it got very quiet. The kids were waiting to see what I was going to do.

Follow-up. *Decide how you would probably handle this issue of majority rule versus minority rights. Find someone else in class and try role-playing the dialog between Anne and her teacher. See where it takes you in an exploration of values.*

The notion of human worth and dignity underlies both majority rule and minority rights. If students comprehend this point, it may help to resolve the conflict. Reread pages 47 to 50 for some ideas on how to handle Anne's position. (Hint: The analogy regarding a vote on genocide may make a powerful point from which you could examine the definition of democracy as majority rule.)

Devil's Advocate

Problem. *Can the technique of playing "devil's advocate" be defended on the basis of developing rationality?*

The whole thing started with a series of heated discussions we had in my fourth-period class—with me playing "devil's advocate" and really forcing the students to defend their ideas about American values. Specifically, as we were talking about America's place in the world community, I was challenging the notion that America should dictate political, economic, and military policy for other countries—as we have so often in the past.

Not long after I started working in this way, there came a series of gentle inquiries, first from my cooperating teacher, then from Principal Heinlein. The principal seemed a little uptight, and I assumed that maybe there had been a complaint. But I was sure that any flack from the parents would blow over in a day or two.

I wasn't prepared for a "Letter to the Editor" that showed up in the morning edition of our community newspaper—a fairly conservative publication. It went like this:

> As a parent and citizen, I believe it is my duty to inform the community that anti-Americanism is being taught at the high school. I believe America is the strongest and greatest democracy in the history of the world, and therefore feel people shouldn't always be tearing it down and criticizing it. It

is getting so that any patriotism or love for our way of life is an object for ridicule. I think every person has a right to their own opinion and that a student teacher shouldn't have power over students' ideas. It is a privilege for college students to practice teaching at the high school, and I for one don't think they should be abusing their responsibility to parents. And I don't think that students who disagree with a student teacher's negative ideas should be humiliated in front of the class and have their grade lowered.

Mrs. John Umbrillo

Well, when I saw this letter, I got pretty upset. Not only was the reference to me unmistakable—since I was the only student teacher in the high school—but Mickey Umbrillo was in my fourth-period class.

I was half panicked as I tried to figure out the communication breakdown between Mickey and me. His behavior in class was always marked by a sullen kind of quietness. His contributions were brief and tight-lipped—almost *parroted,* I sometimes thought. I had only challenged him two or three times on his ideas; but I did remember how on one occasion I had staged a mini-debate in class and asked him to participate. To say that Mickey had "not done well" would be the understatement of the year.

I didn't know what to do, so as soon as I got to school I asked my cooperating teacher for advice. She suggested that I talk with Mr. Heinlein right away to work out the next steps—the moves that would be best for the school, for Mickey and his parents, and for me as well. That's what I did.

Mr. Heinlein was really nice. He said that objections from parents weren't all that rare—that he got minor complaints every day, and that usually he handled them over the telephone. Sometimes, though, a problem was serious enough to deserve a parent-teacher-administrator conference. This, in his opinion, was one such problem.

"What I want you to do," he said, "is to make sure you've got a good rationale for dealing with values in the way you've been doing. In other words, I want you to explain your aims and methods in terms the Umbrillos can understand. Make it clear and to the point, okay? I'll back you up."

"I'll do my best," I said, swallowing my fear at the thought of such a conference.

Follow-up. *Mr. Heinlein apparently believes that if it's good for kids to defend their values, then it's good for student teachers to defend theirs, too. Do you agree with his strategy?*

Now imagine that you're the student teacher in the conference with Mr. Heinlein and Mrs. Umbrillo. What will you say by the way of rationale? Role-play this conference with two other people in class. If possible, tape-record the conversation for subsequent in-class analysis.

Chicano Maverick

Problem. *Identify the three distinct value positions in the following episode.*

Jerry Burton, treasurer of the Spanish Club, was winding up the financial report. The kids were all ears. "And so, after expenses, that leaves us $88.50." Jerry grinned. "Man, we can have a real blow-out!"

Applause erupted all around me. The idea of a Spanish Club party was meeting with enthusiastic approval—and making me wince inside. I had been hoping to convince the kids that some kind of club donation for filmstrips and records might be in order, especially since our district had just gone through two years of financial belt-tightening, with no expenditures for supplemental materials.

One of the students was already at the blackboard, chalking the word "MENU" in big, bold letters. Hands were up all over the room. Janet Pritchard, the club president, glanced quickly at me. She and I had already discussed the possibility of funneling a sizeable piece of the club budget into new teaching materials.

Janet called the meeting back to a semblance of order. "Let's discuss the treasurer's report." She smiled. "We need to consider *all* the alternatives on how the club funds might be spent."

There were three or four groans from the back of the room. "A party would be fun," Janet added, "but are there any other ideas?"

As if on cue, Sharon Martin raised her hand. Sharon was just a junior and had some pretty obvious aspirations to be Spanish Club president.

"I've been thinking," she said. "I wonder if the Club might make a real long-range contribution to things around here by doing something important. I mean, why couldn't we have a party and *still* do something for the Spanish program, too? Maybe buying some filmstrips or something—I don't know. I just think maybe we could do both."

Janet gave me a small quick wink, as she thanked Sharon for her suggestion. Was there any discussion, she asked. One of the girls in the corner wondered if we couldn't split the money in half. "That's a good thought," Janet murmured. "I kind of like that idea. It means that we're doing something for our club yet still having a party. How does that sound? Do you want to take a vote?"

The response wasn't exactly enthusiastic, but I could see that things were drifting my way. The club would purchase *some* supplemental stuff for my Spanish program.

"Uh, just a minute!" came a hoarse voice from one of the corners. "I think we ought to discuss this a little bit more."

All heads turned, including mine. Miguel Garcia, an angular young Hispanic student who had just recently transferred into our school, was running his fingers through his black hair. "Is this all you can think of?" he asked. "Having a party? Buying supplies for the teacher?"

His face was angry.

"Here we are, talking about this stuff, when right now there are kids in the ghettos of Mexico City going without food. How can you be so selfish? You study the Spanish language, but you don't care about the people. You want to buy filmstrips? Oh, beautiful! You watch filmstrips while hungry little kids cry themselves to sleep?"

The room was utterly quiet. Janet was inspecting her fingernails while the other kids fidgeted. Finally she looked up, eying me for help.

Follow-up. *Students like Miguel frequently torpedo the teacher's hidden agenda. Will you encourage maverick viewpoints even when the dissension runs counter to what you want?*

What would you do at this point in the discussion?

The Problem

Problem. *Check out the implied and explicit values of the two persons in the following dialogue. Is there any point where you get the feeling that lack of shared commitments is a serious obstacle to a joint handling of "the problem"?*

"Craig, this paper is terrible. A 'D' is a gift! And you still have eight out of ten assignments left to do—and there's only two weeks left in the term. . . ."

Silence, a long silence, was the only response to my spiel, half harangue, half plea. Not even a groan or a grimace.

Nearly nonplussed, but not defeated, I went on: "We both know you have the ability. The Iowa Test scores and the I.Q. scores in your file show that. And you do get good grades in *some* of your classes. . . ."

Again, silence, not hostile, no turning away or shrugging of the shoulders. Head high, sitting relaxed, Craig was more indifferent, even contemplative.

"Hey, look," he finally said. "You know there *is* a lot more to life than getting assignments done to get marks on a report card—like doing things that mean something to me, not because some teacher says, 'Do this and you'll be a success'—whatever that means."

"But, Craig." ("Careful," I thought. "No pleading. This kid's seventeen, too old for that.") "Everyone needs goals, something in life to strive for. You know ... getting ahead, being someone. An ideal of success that helps you over the rough spots. All classes, all assignments can't be pleasant. You can't always be 'turned on.' Life just isn't that way."

"Yeah, sure, not to you. You're like my parents. Be someone! Be something! What? Who the hell am I supposed to be, anyhow? How can I be anything but me? Listen, I'm not going to waste my days getting ready for what *might* happen. I'm not interested in books and in screwed-up, make-work assignments."

"Look, Craig, we've got a problem. And we've got to decide how to handle it. Right?"

"Yeah." The word sounded right but the face, friendly but disinterested, told me that *I* had the problem. Frustration! Hopelessness! How to get through?

"Craig, can we work out a schedule for handing in the assignments? Maybe if you worked here after school . . .?"

"Well, I'm pretty busy. . . ."

Follow-up. *What should this teacher say next? Do the teacher and Craig agree about the nature of "the problem"? About its importance? What do you think the odds are that they'll agree on how to handle it (as opposed to the teacher trying to force a solution)?*

Value Exploration 4

The section of this chapter that deals with the Creed and "The International Scene" may be subjected to various criticisms. One group of people may ask why we included the section at all. To them it will not seem relevant to a chapter on "The Democratic Context" for values education. Another group will object because the section is so brief. They will argue that in this day and age, all schooling must take place within an international, multicultural context, and that questions about the international implications of the Creed should not be passed over so lightly. Others may say it is presumptuous even to suggest that teachers ought to be concerned with engaging the "world community" in considering whether human worth and dignity is a universal value that could serve as the basis for debate. And to some, it may be an unthinkable heresy even to imply that world government is possible.

Your position on such issues will affect how you teach both your hidden and formal curricula. Some exploration of your thinking seems in order. First, write a brief statement (two or three pages) discussing your view on the world-wide application of the basic democratic values in the American Creed. You might consider such questions as: Should the American Creed apply to all people? Do other national value systems differ from the Creed? If so, how? Are Americans too ethnocentric, on the one hand, or too willing to give up national ideals under international pressures, on the other? Share your paper with others in your group. Discuss the basis for any differences and the possible impact of your ideas on the things you will do as a teacher.

Then think of teaching decisions you will have to make that have to do with American values in the international context. List several of these decisions and the value implications of each. You might want to begin by considering in this context the issues raised by "Chicano Maverick" (page 66). The following may also help you to get started:

Decision	Value Implications
Have students write to pen pals in other countries	Sharing of values is good. May help to implant American values. May lessen commitment to American values.
Read literature from other nations	Such reading may give additional meaning to American values. It may make the students question the ways in which we've applied our values abroad.
Have students participate in mock U.N. meetings	
Use Spanish Club funds to. . . .	

Equality—For Whom?

Problem. *Does this teacher respond appropriately to an in-class challenge to one of society's basic values, and to her authority?*

It was a warm spring afternoon, and the kids in my ninth-grade civics class were restless. We'd been talking about the merits of a democratic society versus other forms of government, but somehow things just weren't clicking. Spring fever seemed to be at work in my room.

"Now in a democratic society like ours," I said, "people believe in a common core of values. Equality of opportunity. Freedom of speech and . . ."

I was interrupted by an exasperated groan from Rebecca Taylor, one of the black students. "Equality of opportunity? You mean like in Detroit or Watts or Baltimore? Have you checked the unemployment numbers lately? How come there are three or four times as many blacks out of work as whites?"

"That's a complex issue," I responded. "The problem of unemployment has many causes . . ."

"Sure it does," Rebecca said hotly. "And the main one is that equal opportunity is a *joke.* Nobody takes it seriously. I mean, the statistics don't lie. If you're white, you've got a lot better chance for a job. Some folks are *more equal* than others."

"Well, employers do take into account differences in education for one thing . . ."

"*That's my point!*" Rebecca interrupted. "Look at the scores on achievement tests! Anybody who thinks minorities get an equal education has got to be blind or stupid—or both. The education system is wired from top to bottom, and so are the jobs. All the talk about equality of opportunity is just white propaganda to keep blacks and Chicanos dumb and happy."

"Are you finished?" I asked as calmly as possible. My throat felt tight. Rebecca looked at me. "I'm not sure."

"This *is* something we need to explore," I said. "It's very important."

"You just want to brainwash me."

"No, I want to *reason* with you and with the rest of the class," I said, sitting down on the corner of my desk. "But I don't want us shouting at each other. We have to *respect* what the other has to say. Fair enough?"

Rebecca hesitated for a long moment. "Fair enough."

Follow-up. *Put yourself in this teacher's place. What do you say next? Can you help the class to focus on the values that conflict with equality of opportunity?*

Would you concede the point that in the past gross inequities have existed in opportunities for minorities? How would you characterize the situation today? What would you say if Rebecca maintained that blacks and other minorities will never receive fair treatment in our society? Role-play the conversation with another person.

Chapter **4**

SCHOOLING, PROFESSIONALS, AND VALUES

The basic purpose for our discussion of values and democracy has been to illustrate some important considerations in examining one's frame of reference and building a rationale. We hope that being exposed to some of the results of our attempt to build a rationale for dealing with values as a teacher will stimulate you to engage in the same type of introspection and analysis.

Two other matters related to the teacher's complex, and often baffling, relationships with parents also need to be considered. One has to do with how much responsibility for students' learning you ought to accept. The second has to do explicitly with the teacher's role vis-à-vis parents and the community. The first we will label the distinction between education and schooling; the second, the authority-agent/professional-client paradox.

THE DISTINCTION BETWEEN EDUCATION AND SCHOOLING

In common parlance, education is often taken to be synonymous with learning. That is, when someone has an experience—such as getting caught cheating on an exam—which we hope has "taught him or her a lesson," we often speak of it as "getting an education." Stephens (1967, p. 20) noted in his provocative analysis of the school as an institution that "education can be as broad as life itself." Perhaps it would be more appropriate to say, "Education *is* life itself," for what is life but a continuous process of reacting and adapting to experiences—that is, learning? Clearly, much—some would argue most—of our education takes place outside of school, society's formal institution for education. Our parents, other adults, our siblings, our peers, and the other human and nonhuman elements in our environments, serve to educate us.

I never let my schoolin' interfere with my education.

—Mark Twain

Except in specialized skill areas such as mathematics, other people and institutions undoubtedly play a more significant educational role for most children than school does. This may be partly because formalizing education—structuring it so that it can be implemented at specified times and places and with assigned people—detracts from its naturalness, and therefore reduces its meaningfulness.

In theory, the most important purpose of school is to give an individual some assistance in educating himself. . . .

—Neil Postman and Charles Weingartner. *Psychology Today,* 1973.

Qualitatively, the school's opportunity for impact is frequently less than that of the many other influences on young people. And an individual teacher's opportunity for impact is also not as great *quantitatively* as one might think at first, given the number of hours that youth spend in school. The secondary teacher's contact with any one student is frequently limited to forty to sixty minutes in the classroom, plus unscheduled and usually fleeting encounters in the hallway and the lunchroom. The brief amount of time a student spends in each classroom does not afford much opportunity for educational impact. (Five hours a week is not much time, especially when one remembers that the teacher's personal contact with any one student is restricted by the number of students in the class.) Areas that can be specifically defined and taught for—the skills and the factual data so commonly the focus of classroom instruction—are most likely to be affected.

> ... [O]ne must make a distinction between education and school. Simply, education is a lifelong process of learning how to negotiate with the world. For "negotiate with," read: understand, accept, cope with, manipulate, triumph over, enjoy, be-one-with, or whatever is your fancy. The important part is that it is lifelong—it begins before you enter school, and ends when you do.
> —Neil Postman and Charles Weingartner. *Psychology Today,* 1973.

For the institution the picture is somewhat different, because of a potential accumulative effect. Students are engulfed in the physical and social settings of the school for several hours a day each week, for several months each year. What they learn through this extended, intensive interaction with the institution and the teachers, counselors, and administrators who are also entwined in it is frequently not at all what these people intend. But they do learn—about the institution, about the faculty and staff, about interaction with other students, about schooling as an activity.

In short, the hidden curriculum—that is, the pervasive approach to discipline, the approaches to "teaching" that are shared from one classroom to the next, the techniques of hallway-lunchroom-playground management—has a powerful educative influence. And school people ought to deal explicitly with the underlying assumptions.

Several related points bear emphasis, then: (1) Schooling is only one educational influence on youth. (2) The school as an institution may have considerable impact on students' values, but (3) the impact is often not congruent with the written or openly admitted educational objectives of the school. Although (4) the individual teacher has responsibility as part of the overall institution, (5) the opportunity for impact on values in formal classroom instruction *may* be less than he or she, or the general public, thinks.

You will need to consider all these points in building your own rationale for dealing with values as a teacher. Most laymen, when asked what they expect from the schools, probably think in terms of the results of formal classroom instruction. Educators cannot afford to be so restrictive in their views. Whether you are dealing with parents' expectations or with your own professional beliefs concerning what teachers *ought* to do about values and what they can *reasonably* expect to do, it is critical that you distinguish between schooling and education. As Postman and Weingartner (1973, p. 80) pointed out:

> ... Thus, "to be schooled" is not the same thing as "to be educated." This view should not be construed as either an apology for or an attack on schools.... By pointing out the limitations of an institution, we do away with the need to defend it against unreasonable demands, and we clear the way for a realistic appraisal of what it *can* do—and might do better.

One caution, however: The distinction between education and schooling should not be used as a rationalization. It would be all too easy to say, How can they expect *us* to accomplish *anything?* Instead, the distinction should be used as one basis for setting reasonable expectations, given the many powerful educational influences that operate on students.

In short, as you develop your rationale for dealing with values as a teacher, consider carefully the distinction between education and schooling. It has implications for what you *should* do about values because it suggests what you reasonably *can* expect to do. You should also consider carefully your obligations and responsibilities—as an agent of the society which employs you, and as a member of a profession.

How does the distinction between education and schooling apply to specific value-related teaching decisions? Value Exploration 5, page 83, will help you to decide.

THE AUTHORITY-AGENT/PROFESSIONAL-CLIENT PARADOX

A clear conception of your role as a teacher, firmly grounded in a democratic frame and clarified to the point that you can communicate it, will help when you move, either consciously or unconsciously, into the sensitive and potentially volatile area of values. As we emphasized earlier, you cannot avoid treating values as part of either the formal or the hidden curriculum. Later, we will argue that for a teacher not to deal with values explicitly is, in fact, a dereliction of duty.

This position raises the very serious question: How do you, as teacher, react and relate to parents' queries and demands in regard to what you teach children? Your relationship to parents can be particularly perplexing because as a teacher you are, in fact, caught between two potentially paradoxical roles. You are both an agent and a professional. Thus you must view parents as both authorities and clients.

At the beginning of Chapter 3, we alluded to the teacher as an agent of society and remarked on the complex and far-reaching implications of that role. An agent is a person empowered to act for someone else. In this sense, school people—teachers, administrators, counselors, and others—have been given the authority to carry out certain educational functions for the society. Each teacher represents the society in the classroom and during other school interactions. That is one reason why we discussed democracy so extensively in Chapter 3.

It may seem obvious that teachers function as societal agents. It is not always so obvious which educational duties they are to carry out. Nor are the processes always clear by which the society makes and communicates decisions about which functions to assign to its schooling agents.

Local school boards are one legitimate mechanism in the process. State legislatures are another (for example, states have laws requiring the teaching of certain subjects, such as United States history). So are state boards of education and departments of public instruction.

But how about citizen pressure groups? Or even more telling for the individual teacher, how about vocal parents who individually or in groups try to exert their influence directly on the teacher rather than on the formal decision makers? What should their impact be on your instructional decisions, especially your decisions about values? To whom must you or should you be responsive?

Professional versus Agent?

The preceding questions become even harder to answer when the teacher's role as societal agent is juxtaposed with his or her role as professional. An agent acts for others, responding to their demands, always striving to serve their best interests as they define them. A professional brings to his or her relationships with clients expertise in a specialized area, presumably backed by special knowledge and experience. A professional also operates within a frame of ethics shaped and policed by members of the profession. The professional frequently interacts with and does things to the client: The doctor treats his patient, the lawyer participates as an advisor in setting up a corporation.

Often the professional acts like an agent. For example, the attorney expresses his client's wishes in negotiating a contract or instituting court action. While agents are typically expected to act within the common moral expectations of the society (the authority-agent relationship is no excuse for illegal behavior), society's demand on the professional is greater. He or she is expected to conform to a professional ethic. Doctors are not to prescribe medicine just because their patients ask them to. An attorney would be professionally proper in refusing to file a suit if he thought it had no other purpose than harassment.

Of course, all professionals do not live up to the ethical standards of their profession, just as they are not all equally competent in specialized knowledge and behavior. On the other hand, professionals may argue that their professional ethics supersede common moral or legal restrictions. Some medical doctors have carried out euthanasia on what they believed to be professional grounds. Attorneys have felt justified in provoking contempt-of-court charges while defending their clients.

One common, workable distinction between "agent" and "professional," then, is that the agent relationship involves *one acting for another*, and the professional relationship involves *one interacting for and with another in a context broader than* that of the other's *self-interest*—even, according to some professionals, broader than the common community moral standards and the laws of the society.

Now, what is the point of all this? Remember that we are discussing what *you* should do about values as a teacher. An important element in the frame of reference from which you make such decisions will be your beliefs about the source of your authority. Will you see yourself exclusively as an agent, hired by the local school board, and responsible only to it? Or will you consider yourself responsible to the broader society and to a conception of democracy which goes beyond local views and constraints?

These questions might also be rephrased: Will you feel obligated to follow expressed or implied local self-interests in a limited authority-agent type of relationship? Or will you feel obligated to respond as a professional, bringing to the situation specialized knowledge and a set of professional ethics from which to approach and defend your decisions about values in the school?

These questions are not just matters for idle speculation. Although it is common to talk about the "teaching profession," we often act as if we were only agents. Teachers are often not sure what it means to be a professional—or even whether they are professionals.

A scribbled note in the mailbox. A hurried meeting with the principal just before school starts.

See "Inner Office Conference," page 84, to zero in on the professional/agent paradox—a dilemma in values.

Education, Law, and Medicine

One way to clarify your thinking about teaching as a profession and you as a professional is to contrast teaching with other professions, such as law and medicine. Such comparisons are fraught with latent difficulties because these professions differ in striking ways. But if one approaches the comparisons by paying careful attention to differences in circumstances as well as in professional goals and roles, rather than by trying to suggest that the analogies are perfect, the process can be instructive. As we look at some differences, keep in mind that our concern is what to do about values as a teacher.

BE PROFESSIONAL
JOIN THE
TEACHERS ASSOCIATION!
TEACHERS ARE "PROS"
LIKE DOCTORS,
LAWYERS, AND FOOT-
BALL PLAYERS.
THEY JUST MAKE
LESS MONEY

—Sign from cartoon by Don Allen and Halsey Taylor. *Media and Methods,* 1972.

It is significant that teachers, unlike what is usually the case for lawyers and doctors, are hired directly by a governmental agency, and receive fixed salaries rather than fees based on services. You may want to explore the potential implications of this situation. Does it lead to a "stay out of trouble with the public" approach to one's work, as contrasted with a view that you must perform so well that new clients will seek you out? Do the two situations provide different opportunities for independence? If so, do these affect the willingness of teachers to take strong professional stands, especially when they go counter to local public opinion? These are relevant concerns for values education.

Another important difference, one familiar to any teacher, is the aura of mystique that surrounds medicine and law—but not the teaching profession. This may be in part because of the technical language that doctors and attorneys use—derisively called "jargon" when used by educators. But there are other reasons. There *are* differences in length and intensity of training. Perhaps more important, people are not compelled to spend their childhood in daily contact with doctors and lawyers. Doctors and lawyers typically see their clients only at times of crisis. The forced and sustained contact with teachers can breed contempt at worst, and at the very least make people so familiar with what goes on in school that each person becomes a self-styled educational expert—something that rarely happens in medicine and law.

In addition, the costs of medical and legal services fall largely on the individual client. With "free" public education, individuals are not billed directly. (Note that when voters become conscious of education costs in local bond elections, many bond issues are defeated.) In our culture, we tend to judge worth in terms of monetary cost; and once something is paid for, we want to believe it was worth the cost. While doctors and attorneys may make more money because their services are worth more to the public, it is hard to avoid the conclusion that they often have more prestige simply *because* they make more money.

What does all of this have to do with values and a rationale for teaching? Because your field lacks mystique and prestige, it is especially important for you to develop a clear rationale from which to make teaching decisions. This will not only help to insure that your decisions will be sound and defensible, but it will build the type of professional relationship that allows you greater freedom of judgment, because your clients will be convinced of your expertise.

The antithesis of professional responsibility is mindlessness. Professional workers can and should be held responsible for being able to demonstrate some rational basis for whatever they do, be it research, logical thought, experience, consistency with theory or whatever.

—Arthur W. Combs. *Educational Researcher,* 1973.

Two other distinctions are particularly relevant. One is the distinction between dealing with illness and with normal growth. Both doctors and lawyers tend to deal with pathology. People commonly go to doctors when they are sick, to lawyers when they are in trouble or anticipate problems. Analogies, especially medical analogies, to the teaching profession are pernicious when they lead teachers to see their role as making students "well," rather than as participating in a process of normal, healthy development. In the area of values, for example, the former view might lead the teacher to seek out what is "wrong" with the students' commitments, rather than to help them build and clarify their own frames as part of a natural process of development and refinement.

A related difference has to do with what might be called guiding ideals. As professionals, doctors and lawyers are to guide their day-by-day activities by overriding commitments. The doctor is supposed to be committed to the preservation of life and the alleviation of suffering; the attorney, to the basic ideal of justice.

The attorney's ideal of justice is *one* basic element in the American Creed. However, the medical ideals of life and alleviation of suffering are not just imbedded in, they actually transcend, the democratic ethos of human worth and dignity that underlies the American Creed and its basic democratic values. Without life and reasonable freedom from the ravages of illness, human dignity is a meaningless concept. The ideals of both professions provide fairly clear prescriptions for ethical behavior, even if the professionals are not always clear about their meanings. (The education of doctors and lawyers, like that of teachers, has little in it to help them develop rationales for professional behavior.) Of course, the ideals are not always followed in the face of conflicting demands, even when their meaning is clear.

Unlike lawyers and doctors, the teacher has no one guiding ideal, except the vague ideal of human worth and dignity, by which to set a professionally ethical course. The school's concern is with the broad spectrum of life in a democracy, not with one sector (e.g., the medical or legal elements). For that reason, the ideals that provide the teacher's professional guidance must be as comprehensive as the society itself. And it is essential to consider the nature of a democratic society when one is developing a rationale for dealing with values as a teacher.

This is a basic point of intersection between the notions of the teacher as agent and the teacher as professional. To fulfill his or her professional role, the teacher must clearly understand the nature of the democratic society to which he or she is responsible. This understanding forms the basis of an ethic for deciding when to rise above the demands of local interests. And given the concept of the professional as one who interacts with clients rather than just resonding to their wishes, the teacher has an obligation to try to shape the expectations of his or her clients—that is, the students' parents and, more broadly, the community—to help insure that schooling does take place in a context of democratic commitment. Being able to show some special insights into the nature of a democratic society and its implications for schooling is one way to convince parents that you as a teacher bring special professional competencies to your position.

As a professional, how far should your concern with providing a democratic context for schooling extend beyond the classroom? See "Faculty Meeting," page 85, for a situation that raises that question.

Implications for Teaching and Values

Because teachers in public schools are clearly employed by the society to perform educational functions for it, it is to be assumed that they are committed to the basic democratic ethos—the basic values—of that society. A person who accepts a teaching position without that commitment has signed a contract under false pretenses—surely a sufficient reason for dismissal.

The school is not a legitimate place for subversion in the sense of encouraging or advocating the destruction of the values and basic governmental forms set up—with all their theoretical and practical limitations—to protect our evolving conception of human dignity. But what constitutes subversion needs to be weighed carefully, taking into account societal values and the attendant goals of schooling.

For example, how should a teacher treat the use of physical force to compel solutions to societal issues? Although violence can threaten the stability of the society and run counter to the basic commitment to a peaceful consent process, it is occasionally a justifiable alternative even in a democratic society. Private individuals protecting themselves or someone else against physical attack, the protection of property and life by the police, the protection of national security by our armed forces may each entail acceptable violence. and when no other avenue appears open to secure human rights from government itself, violent action may be defensible—as was argued in support of our own American Revolution. Dilemmas regarding the use of violence are therefore viable and fit subjects for classroom discussion. In fact, if teachers ignore that some people value violence as an end and that others view it as a legitimate means of protecting or furthering values, they will not contribute to a citizenry which can confront rationally the advocacy of violence under extreme economic or political conditions. And to students who view a violent world on television or experience physical force in their own lives, the avoidance of violence as an instructional topic is likely to provide further evidence that the school is out of touch with "reality." But to *advocate* violence as a form of political action clearly falls outside the proper role of a public school teacher responsible to a democratic society, and would be legitimate grounds for dismissal.

The classroom is not the appropriate place to advocate other political positions either. Some may protest that this stricture violates the teacher's freedom of speech, that it is the teacher's right as a citizen to express his or her views in the classroom. But that value is not involved here. The argument is not that a person should lose any of his or her rights as a citizen by becoming a teacher, but that teachers are not hired to carry out partisan political indoctrination. They must function as professionals in a pluralist society with many different subgroups, none of which has a right to dominate the schools. The teacher has no right to use the classroom as a platform for expounding his or her own political beliefs.

This does not mean that you should not express your own beliefs in the classroom or during out-of-class discussions with students. Students too often feel, legitimately, that the school and its staff are plastic, insulated and isolated from the real world as the students see and feel it. To be authentic as a teacher, you will need to express beliefs, especially when students seek your opinion. But this expression should be an educational act in the context of the values of a democratic society, not an act of political indoctrination. In this sense, the difference between the sustained and impassioned pressure of advocacy and the occasional, nonpolemic expression of one's opinion is critical.

― ― ― ― ― ― ― ― ― ― ― ― ― ― ― ― ―

"They *aren't* dumb," Carrie blurted out. "They're just as good as anybody! Maybe smarter! Lots of Negroes go to college and. . . ."

"Jungle-bunnies," Joey interrupted.

See "Brotherhood," page 87, to sort out your responsibilities in a tense, value-laden discussion.

— — — — — — — — — — — — — — — —

Of course, out-of-school activities are another matter. Teachers should not be restricted by school boards, or anyone else, from participating actively in politics and stating their views as citizens. In fact, they should be encouraged to do so. One difficulty in teaching democratic values that have to do with commitment and involvement is that teachers frequently abstain from active political involvement. Teachers tell students that they should become active, involved citizens as adults (How about active involvement *now* in the political system of the school?),[1] but all too often are not involved themselves, except in "safe" civic clubs such as the Lions or Kiwanis. Consequently, the students see teachers as hypocrites and gather further evidence that the school is an "unreal" place.

But political participation can be a double-edged sword, in terms of what students are told about teachers' values. Consider an event widely covered by the news media of one state in 1981. It was reported that thousands of angry teachers staged a demonstration at the state capitol to protest a proposed six percent increase in salaries—a figure almost seven percent short of what the teachers had proposed as necessary to meet inflation. According to the reports, one senator who tried to speak to the teachers drew boos and catcalls and finally left the speaker's platform when hecklers continually interrupted his attempt to explain why he voted for the six percent increase.

It is not likely that the protesting teachers would condone such behavior on the part of students in the schools where they teach. To the contrary, most would probably insist to their students that *reasoned discourse* and *respect for the views of others* are fundamental values in a democratic society. But what conclusions might student viewers of the news reports draw about teachers' values?

Back to Subversion.   In our society, there is not likely to be consensus on what is subversive—that is, corrupting. Moreover, parents tend to overestimate the teacher's power to influence their children's beliefs and feelings. So instruction that touches on values is particularly likely to generate heat. As a matter of fact, some parents will consider such instruction subversive even when your teaching activities are legitimate. And they may well be correct—in the sense that you will be helping students to think for themselves, and as a result they may reject their parents' value definitions and priorities.

---

[1] For some excellent proposals for engaging students in the study of the school as a political system, see Gillespie and Patrick (1974).

Parents—and other community members—often fail to distinguish between what is subversive in their eyes and what is subversive to a democratic society. The problem is compounded when parents (and teachers) confuse the parents' role as clients with their role as members of the authority-granting society. Parents who object to what is, or appears to be, happening to their children are not likely to consider first the nature of a democratic society and the school's function in such a society. Nor are they likely to recognize that demands based on their own personal interests and biases may not be compatible with the demands of the teacher's professional role. So it is critical that you as a teacher have a clear conception of the nature of values and the nature of democratic commitments, and that you recognize your professional obligations. It is also critical that you be able to explain those obligations to parents and other persons—in the form of a rationale that emphasizes value considerations in a democratic society.

Look again at "Inner Office Conference," page 84. How should Miss Dunning respond to a parent or to a land developer who visits her after school to object to her students' land use activities?

RECAP—AND BEYOND

The argument in this chapter is, then, that the teacher must be responsible to a conception of democracy—as attorneys are to be responsible to an ideal of justice and doctors are to be to the preservation of life and alleviation of suffering—and that this conception of democracy must supersede strident local interests and prejudices. The teacher is not the voters' servant or the servant of the pupils' parents. He or she is an agent of the society. But beyond that, each teacher is a professional with an obligation to promote educaton in the broad democratic context, not just to reflect the parents' or the voters' wishes.

We have argued that a teacher has no right to use the classroom for partisan politics. Yet each teacher does have an obligation to the basic values of society. Therefore the teacher must be willing to deal in the classroom with flagrant denials of these values in the local community. For example, to ignore the plight of racial or religious minorities in some communities would often be to deny one's professional commitment to an ethic based on democratic ideals.

It takes courage to deal openly with local situations that run counter to basic democratic values. Taking a stand on such issues can be not only uncomfortable, but sometimes very risky. Teachers are hired by local school boards, and local school boards are responsible, and responsive, to the local clientele—as they should be. But even professional teachers' organizations are becoming more aware that teachers have a right and an obligation to act in a context broader than that of the local community. For example, the NEA and the National Council for the Social Studies, among others, now have defense funds for teachers caught between local and professional demands.

The point is *not* that all control of the school program should be taken out of the hands of lay people and given over to professionals. It is, rather, that decisions about what the school should teach ought to be made in light of the school's role as an institution of a democratic society. By the same token, decisions about what constitutes reasonable behavior for a teacher should take into account the teacher's somewhat paradoxical responsibilities as both an agent and a professional. If you understand this point, you may be more willing as a teacher to assert yourself against unexamined local prejudices and their impact on the school. If you can communicate this point to parents, you may well make them more willing to tolerate, perhaps even to support you in, your exercise of professional responsibility.

As professionals, teachers and other school people have educational responsibilities that extend beyond teaching students, and beyond adult education in the usual sense. The school cannot be expected to reform the society that supports it. But school personnel should help their clients—parents as well as students—clarify and develop their views of society and the school's role in it.

Wouldn't it be excellent if adults brought to their interactions with teachers a perspective, a frame of reference, that included an understanding and an appreciation of the importance of pluralism, the inevitability of value conflict, and the implications of the democratic commitment to human dignity. That they so rarely do so is a major indictment of the schools. Next, we turn to some ways in which schooling might be made more consistent with democratic ideals, and therefore more likely to be a viable element in the student's life both during and after his time there.

Value Exploration 5

Many incidents, large and small, will arise because of your responsibility for values. In deciding what to do, you should take into account what you can reasonably expect to do. For each of the following situations, decide what the teacher's response should be. Discuss your decisions with others in your group. If you find yourself thinking about the implications of your decisions in terms of the various types of values (Chapter 2) and the teacher's commitment to human dignity (Chapter 3), so much the better! But try to focus especially on the reasonableness of the expectation for a teacher in the schooling context.

- A parent complains about her fourth-grade son's sloppy handwriting. She insists that part of the problem is that the school (and you as a teacher) have not taught him to value neatness.
- Two youths are caught shoplifting. The local newspaper comments on the lack of moral education in the school.
- A matron of the arts, a graduate of the local schools, condemns modern art and rock music as decadent forms of nonart that should not be allowed in the school. (Focus here on the school's responsibility for her attitudes toward esthetic values.)
- A recent graduate of your high school is convicted of first degree murder. A colleague comments, "We must all share in the blame for not teaching her to value life."
- A parent is disturbed that his daughter does not "value learning." He asks that you, as her teacher, try to have an impact.
- Two students are having a discussion in the hallway, which you overhear. They seem confused about whether individual freedom or majority rule is more important.

Now, with others in your group, think of other such situations and discuss the appropriate responses to them.

Inner Office Conference

Problem. *Identify the professional/agent paradox for Miss Dunning.*

The principal's hands were folded, his thumbs twiddling nervously. His frown deepened while Miss Dunning waited.

"Janet, you're putting me in a real spot here. The superintendent's called me twice on this thing."

"I'm sorry to hear that," Miss Dunning responded. "But my biology classes are into water sampling in a real way. If we call it off, it'll simply mean that we're capitulating to the lobbyists—the industrialists and land developers."

"But Janet—be reasonable!"

Miss Dunning smiled. "Mr. Maynard, I *am* being reasonable. Some of the factory owners and fast-buck developers have nearly *ruined* our streams. They've ignored what the wastes from their businesses are doing to our drinking water—and to our streams! It's just incredible! Why, the water-sampling project my students are doing is the first breath of *reason* this community's seen in the past twenty years! It's showing just what we're up against in terms of a community problem."

Mr. Maynard sighed elaborately. "Conducting a study is one thing," he said. "But I wonder if your students are really being *objective* about this."

Miss Dunning shrugged. "We're gathering samples on a regular basis.

SCHOOLING, PROFESSIONALS, AND VALUES

We're careful in our analyses, and in how we record and summarize them. I'd call that 'being objective.'"

"Now don't get me wrong, Janet," said Mr. Maynard. "I'm sure you have good intentions and all that. But aren't you inflicting your personal biases on the students? We all know you're very concerned about ecology. Isn't that your *real* motivation for doing this field work in water sampling?"

"No, I don't think so."

"The superintendent thinks you're on a muckraking campaign."

"Maybe there's a lot of muck to be raked." Miss Dunning smiled again. She chose her words with care. "But seriously, I really think the most important thing about biology is the process of inquiry. And you can't inquire in a vacuum. You have to have a problem you're trying to solve. And it just so happens we've got a beauty in this community—one that's far better than any in the lab manual, I assure you."

"I see," Mr. Maynard grimaced. "I suppose you're aware that the people you're irritating are very influential in this town?"

"I'm aware that some powerful interests would like to see us get back to our textbooks."

"And you won't reconsider?"

"No."

"Are you prepared to forego any chance of tenure in this district?"

Follow-up. *The battle lines are drawn. Can the teacher's position be rationally justified? Can it be legally justified if worst comes to worst and she is denied tenure?*

How would you answer the principal's final question?

Faculty Meeting

Problem. *What are the value conflicts in the following interchange?*

"We've got a crisis on our hands," Miss Wilson, the school principal, said to open the weekly early morning faculty meeting. "By now, you've undoubtedly seen the KKK letters and swastikas painted on the gym walls. And you've probably seen or heard about the harassment of Jewish students in the halls."

Mr. Sandler raised his hand. "Freedom of speech is one thing, but the destruction of property—we cannot condone that."

"I know," Miss Wilson said. "The police are investigating. What concerns me more than the damage, though, is what this represents. There's a potential for violence in this school, and I want to get to the root of the problem."

"It's no secret that the Klan has been getting stronger in this area," Mrs. Roberts said. "There have been cross burnings downstate."

"I've heard there's also a youth training camp," Mr. Phillips added. "Racist indoctrination plus paramilitary training."

Mrs. Weinstein spoke up. "It's no wonder that such a camp exists. with our school and community not taking a moral stand against such ideas. . . "

"Not taking a stand?" the principal interrupted. "Each year we've shown the 'Holocaust' TV series in social studies classes."

Mrs. Weinstein did not back down. "Anti-Semitism and racism are very deep-seated in our society—ready to be touched off. That's what the 'Holocaust' series has done in many parts of the country. Simply *showing* a program without going into depth, without helping students understand the human causes . . . "

"Now, just a minute," Mr. Phillips interrupted. "I've used the film, and I resent your implication."

"Okay. Let's keep calm," Miss Wilson intervened.

"I didn't mean that the way it sounded," Mrs. Weinstein apologized. "I'm sure the 'Holocaust' program was discussed. I was referring to the need for us—the faculty—to take a strong, clear position on such matters—to let students know that Klan or Nazi ideas about racial superiority are simply rubbish. We should come out *against* what these groups are promoting. We cannot remain silent. *Silence is moral cowardice.*"

Mr. Freeman, an articulate black teacher, voiced enthusiastic support for Mrs. Weinstein's position. Mr. Smiley was a little more tentative, saying that while he agreed in principle, he also felt that what students did after school or on weekends was their own responsibility and that the school could not dictate moral issues to the community.

"You're asking for indoctrination against a particular point of view—ideas espoused by the KKK and American Nazi Party. That sounds rather dangerous to me," Mr. Smiley concluded.

"A serious problem demands a serious response," Mrs. Weinstein rejoined. "We can't sit on the fence! The least we can do is expel the students responsible for the damage and the harassment."

"I agree," Mr. Turner murmured. "These young people need discipline. Too much freedom of speech just leads to problems."

"Well, I don't agree," Mr. Rosen said. "Nothing this faculty says or does will make any difference. And we'll just create problems for ourselves and the school if we take on the job of moral spokesman for the community."

It was then that the office secretary came in with a message for Miss Wilson. Someone had just reported that three students had come to school with Nazi armbands on their sleeves. Miss Wilson looked at the group.

Follow-up. *What advice would you give Miss Wilson? Should she follow Mrs. Weinstein's proposal and send the students home? Justify your stand using ideas presented in preceding chapters.*

Would you discuss the issues raised by the harassment of Jewish students in your classes? Role-play such a discussion with other readers of this book, emphasizing the school's societal responsibilities.

Brotherhood

Problem. *Is the teacher morally obligated to express personal values in the following episode?*

The filmstrip on "Brotherhood" clicked through the last frame, and I switched on the lights. Hands went up all over my fourth-grade room.

Timmy was out of his seat. "But my Dad says niggers just cause *trouble*. He don't *want* us playin' with no black kids! He says. . . . "

"Okay, Timmy, please *sit down*," I said. "We have to have an orderly discussion."

"I think they're lazy," Lucie mumbled.

"Dumb," Joey hissed.

I glanced around my all-white class of rural kids. Carrie was jerking her hand up and down.

"They *aren't* dumb," she blurted out. "They're just as good as anybody! Maybe smarter! Lots of Negroes go to college and. . . . "

"Jungle-bunnies!" Joey interrupted.

"That's about enough," I heard myself say firmly. "If we're going to have a discussion about the ideas in the filmstrip, we'll have no more of this name calling."

"But they *are* dumb," said Timmy.

Joey grinned. "They don't even talk good, so you can understand 'em. A lotta niggers, they can't even read or write. My uncle knows, 'cause he's had 'em working out to his farm."

"They are *not* dumb," Carrie repeated, her voice full of indignation. "They're probably smarter than you!"

"Hey, nigger-lover!" Joey drawled accusingly.

"Joey, that's *it!*" I nearly shouted. "No more name calling!"

Carrie had tears at the corners of her eyes.

The class was utterly still.

Follow-up. *How does this discussion make you feel? What do you believe about racial differences in intelligence?*

What would you say next if you were the teacher?

Should you be willing to allow some students to maintain unchallenged their belief that "niggers are dumb"? If not, explore with other readers of this book what you might do immediately or during the rest of the school year to deal with that issue.

Chapter 5

TEACHING IN A DEMOCRATIC CONTEXT: ESTHETIC AND INSTRUMENTAL VALUES

We have spent considerable time setting forth assumptions. Now we will examine some implications for your in-class and out-of-class contacts with students. The purpose is not to make prescriptions for you as a teacher, but to illustrate the importance of having an explicit rationale, set in the context of a democratic society, from which to deal with values. Of course, if some of the following ideas have an impact on your decisions and your behavior as a teacher, we will not be disappointed.

How to treat moral values as goals of instruction is a central issue in values education, and we turn to that topic in the next chapter. In this chapter, we address two value areas that are often overlooked in discussions of values education, but which have much to do with the view of democratic values that students pick up from their schooling. First, we will treat teachers' decisions in regard to esthetic values. Then, we will turn to a subset of instrumental values—those, whether nonmoral or moral, used by teachers for classroom management.

Both types of values will be considered from the perspective of the democratic ideal of human dignity, with its implication that human beings are thinking, intelligent beings with the right to control their own destinies. If you take this conception seriously, you cannot see the school's proper role as only, or even primarily, the imposition of values. The school is legitimately concerned with the improvement of intelligence. And a vital aspect of this concern must be to help students become clear about their own values and, perhaps more important, learn to apply their values consciously on their own. Helping your students to become aware of their values, to define and apply value terms, to be aware of conflicting commitments and their implications for action, and to develop conceptual frames that will enable them to do all this for themselves out of the classroom—these goals are consistent with our society's commitment to individual worth and dignity.

This basic position—that the teacher's role is to assist each student to develop a rational foundation for his or her values and to acquire the related analytic concepts to use after leaving school—is a fundamental theme of this book. But that theme has variations depending on the kind of values under consideration.

THE SCHOOL AND ESTHETICS

We have defined esthetic values as the standards people use to judge beauty. Beauty is an internal, personal experience. There is no ultimate basis for determining what should be considered beautiful, nor is there any compelling reason why a democratic society should inculcate any one set of standards for beauty. Consequently, in the context of human dignity, the school's proper role vis-à-vis esthetics is to provide opportunities—to *encourage*—but *not to impose*.

For the teacher of music, art, literature—or any other subject that has esthetic overtones, such as cooking, physical education, or vocational arts—the implications are clear. One goal should be to expose students to different esthetic experiences in order to give them opportunities to expand their interests. Another goal should be to introduce students to more sophisticated schemata for making esthetic judgments.

Teachers have many ways to open new vistas for their students and encourage the growth of refined esthetic standards. They can expose students to different periods of art. They can illustrate and explain composition and balance in paintings. They can play and discuss various types of music. They can have students listen to various musical instruments and discuss how the composer combines them to achieve his effects. But youngsters often do not respond the way teachers want them to, and the resulting frustration can pose a quandary: How can the teacher maintain his or her own esthetic commitments *and* a commitment to student dignity?

Part of the difficulty, of course, is that you have probably chosen to teach a subject because you are interested in it, or, even more challenging in terms of maintaining objectivity, because you love and feel a strong commitment to the content. When this is the case, it can be tough to remember that the purpose of instruction is not to make the students feel and think the way you do, but to help them develop their own potentials for enjoyment and satisfaction.

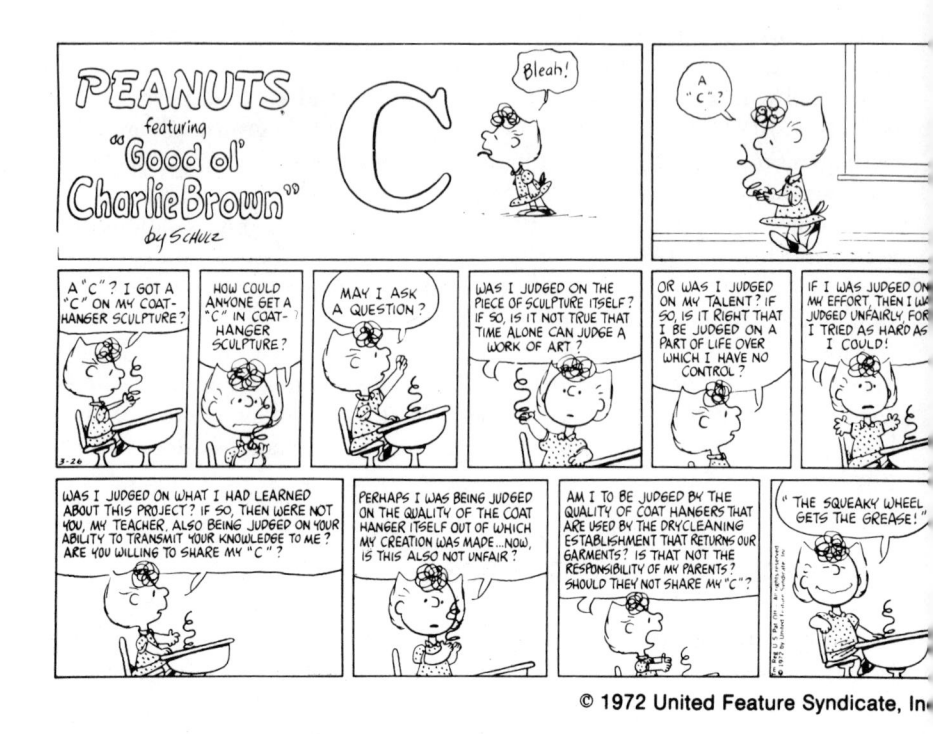

In fact, there may even be a basic tension between increasing esthetic conceptual sophistication, on the one hand, and encouraging emotive sensitivity, on the other. By making the students more intellectual in their approach to esthetic objects, we may detract from their ability to respond in a raw, emotional way. People, after all, can be too rational, too cerebral in their responses.

Though few of us make great or even mediocre art, the emotive, affective, feeling dimension of esthetics is vital to our lives. This is why the cognitive emphasis of the curriculum in so many schools, especially in esthetic areas like music and art, makes schooling less meaningful than it might be.

Strong evidence for the general importance of the nonrational in esthetics comes from the impact of music—the art form most readily available to the majority of people. The staying power of classical music over the centuries, and the mass appeal of "popular" music—be it rock, ballad, or country-western—suggest the importance of music. Music does evoke and express poignant, feeling-centered aspects of our lives, whether we are construction workers who like to listen to the juke box in a bar after a hard day's work or faithful symphony subscribers. And, each of us gives high esthetic marks to those art forms—music, literature, or the movies—that meet our emotional needs. This is worth keeping in mind as you interact with students.

Pop music is America's most pervasive art form. It wakes us up in the morning. It rides along in our cars. It accompanies us through the bars, supermarkets, and bedrooms of our lives.

—Maureen Orth. *Newsweek,* December 24, 1973.

Our argument, then, is that a variety of "art" forms serve legitimate affective functions; we are not saying that whatever evokes emotion is esthetic. Watching someone being strangled would arouse plenty of emotion, but anyone who found it a beautiful experience could correctly be described as psychopathic.

It follows that the rational and nonrational[1] aspects of human dignity are both relevant to decisions about esthetic curricula, because emotive expression *and* reasoned judgment are both important aspects of esthetics. But because the emotional force of music—and of movies, art, and literature—meets common, down-to-earth needs, each teacher of an esthetic curriculum must weigh the potential conflict between analysis and raw, emotive experience. To strive for conceptual refinement on the part of your students should be a conscious decision, one that takes into account the possible negative, as well as positive, impacts on enjoyment if "primitive" experiencing is tempered by cognitive sophistication.

By one set of statistics, the movie business—that volatile mix of money and esthetics—would seem to have it made. A book with 20,000 readers is a best seller. A hit play may be seen by a few hundred thousand theater-goers. By contrast, 900 million tickets will be sold at movie houses across the U.S. this year.

—Paul D. Zimmerman. *Newsweek,* December 24, 1973.

---

[1]Note that the words *nonrational* and *irrational* are not synonyms. Because something is *not rational* does not mean that it is opposed to rationality—that it is in any sense "contrary to reason; senseless; unreasonable; absurd," definitions of "irrational" found in *Webster's New World Dictionary* (Guralnik, 1972).

There are other implications for teaching. One has to do with the subtle shifts from the esthetic to the moral that we have already emphasized (see Chapter 2). Say, for example, that you yourself prefer refined esthetic judgments. If you do not hold this preference in proper perspective, you may set a "preachy" classroom tone that clearly implies a repudiation of your students' esthetic values. Mutual alienation is likely to be the result.

Moreover, if you exclude from the classroom the very art forms that the students enjoy, you may even be open to a legitimate charge of hypocrisy. After all, how can you claim to be concerned with developing your students' esthetic sensitivities when you don't, at least initially, use music, literature, or art from their daily lives as your subject matter?

Rock resurrected the blues, dealt a temporary death blow to jazz, taught country singers to plug in their gee-tars and buried Tin Pan Alley forever. To a generation turned off by war and turned on to drugs, rock was the catalyst of a whole new life style.

—Maureen Orth. *Newsweek,* December 24, 1973.

Helping students to identify and verbalize the standards that underlie their current esthetic tastes need not prevent you from moving on to esthetic forms that you consider to be of superior quality and lasting significance.[2] What is critical is whether you accept the students' music and other esthetic forms as serious and worthwhile in their own right, or whether you show interest in them only as a stratagem to get your students interested in "really good" art.

. . . [W]hat's often forgotten is that all art is experimental at bottom. It's our tendency to equate the past with security that makes us think otherwise.

—Jack Kroll. *Newsweek,* December 24, 1973.

---

[2]You should be careful that concern for "lasting significance" doesn't lead to the judgment that anything older is better. Adults often use this argument, for example, in disputes with young people over the relative merits of classical and popular music. It should be clear that the length of time an art work has been around does not necessarily have anything to do with an individual's reaction to it. Even though many people have reacted favorably to classical music over the years, an individual or a group of people may not find it particularly pleasurable. And how can the criterion of longevity be applied to music like that of the Beatles, which has been in existence only a few years? Beethoven was a new composer once.

To develop esthetically, students will need to consider a wide range of literature, music, and art. One group of authors (Tovatt, Miller, Rice, and De Vries, 1965) has suggested that students should be invited to bring "popular" reading material to class because "expert opinion seems to agree that analysis of the 'bad' as well as the 'good' is important in developing reader judgment and taste . . ." (p. 2). But which literature is "good" and which "bad"? What is the effect when teachers prejudge popular literature? What if you overlook the function of "popular" literature and music, and see your role as moving your students away from it (the "bad") toward the classics (the "good")? Aren't your students likely to see you as condescending, even disparaging, toward them?

In short, if you are narrow about esthetic judgments, if you insist that your judgments and your criteria are always "right," you are denying your students' dignity. The educational impact of this denial is likely to be negative. The freedom of students to arrive at their own conceptions of what is beautiful and pleasurable—after being exposed to other forms and considering other criteria—may not be a basic value in the American Creed, but it certainly is consistent with our general commitment to human worth and dignity.

Nonesthetic Courses

If you do not teach an esthetic subject such as art or music, this discussion may seem irrelevant. But the earlier discussion of the hidden curriculum should suggest that it has important implications for you. In your formal and informal contacts with students, you make many judgments and convey many impressions. Your reaction to the paperback book a student is reading, your facial expression when music blasts out of a transistor radio between class periods, your response when you overhear students discussing a movie they have enjoyed—each gives clear signals about your appraisal of your students' tastes.

How teachers of nonesthetic courses react to their students' esthetic judgments involves more than their abstract faith in the ideal of human worth and dignity. Whether you accept students' tastes in music and literature, whether you avoid imposing your own esthetic standards (and avoid making moral judgments based on esthetic reactions) can seriously affect your capacity to teach science or math or social studies. It will partly determine whether you can relate to your students in a way that minimizes antagonism, defensiveness, and distrust, and maximizes the opportunities for learning—by letting them know that you accept and respect their individuality.

Esthetics are related to "nonesthetic" courses in another important but quite different way. Mathematicians often refer to the esthetic concepts of simplicity and elegance as criteria for mathematical proofs. And beauty—

simplicity (parsimony) and elegance—are also important in developing and judging scientific theories (see May, 1975). Judson (1980) emphasized that point in his discussion of "doing science," which includes an intriguing portrayal of science as art. Can students adequately comprehend mathematics and science as scholarly fields unless their teachers devote attention to the role of esthetics in creative intellectual activity?

What do esthetics have to do with mathematics? "Making School Weird," page 100, raises the question of whether a math teacher *should* deal with beauty.

Value Conflict

We have been emphasizing interpersonal—teacher versus student—value conflict without labeling it as such. Of course, esthetic judgments may also involve intrapersonal conflict, as when a person with broad interests in music must decide between buying a new symphony or a new rock concert recording. One of the goals of an esthetic curriculum should be to make such dilemmas more likely by broadening students' interests. Paradoxically, another goal should be to help resolve these dilemmas by making the students more aware of their own esthetic priorities.

There is another aspect to esthetic value conflict, however, that bears directly on instructional decision making. Consider, for example, two people with different esthetic tastes—John likes hard rock, Laura likes quiet baroque—who live in adjoining apartments. When John plays hard rock at peak volume, his choice conflicts with Laura's. Suppose that Laura knocks on John's door and asks him to turn down the volume. He refuses and an argument ensues. Their controversy is not likely to hinge on the relative merits of hard rock and baroque, or on the relative pleasures of low versus high sound intensity. Instead, the issue is likely to center on Laura's right to peace and quiet, to privacy in the sense of enjoying whatever she wants in her own apartment, and on John's right to play whatever he wants in his own apartment. In short, the argument stemming from an esthetic conflict will turn very quickly into an ethical argument revolving around moral values.

This shift is typical—perhaps we should say inevitable. But people seldom recognize that it has taken place. As teachers, we need to be aware that when interpersonal esthetic conflict leads to disputes over proper behavior, people shift from esthetic to moral values to support their positions. We can help our students to recognize such shifts and deal explicitly with the moral values involved (see Chapter 6).

Throughout this chapter we have been concerned with the potential conflict between teacher and student over esthetic values. This conflict raises the ethical issue: Can you justify imposing your esthetic preferences on your students? Your answer may depend on whether you see freedom of esthetic choice as intrinsic to your students' worth and dignity. But freedom of esthetic choice for your students may also be an instrumental value—if you use it in order to enhance your classroom effectiveness. It is to the handling of instrumental values that we turn next.

INSTRUMENTAL VALUES IN THE CLASSROOM—THE NEED FOR DIALOGUE

One of the major tasks facing each teacher is setting up and enforcing classroom and study standards. The standards are typically justified on the grounds that they establish a classroom atmosphere and regulate student behavior so that learning will occur. They are clearly instrumental in nature. We shall refer to them in this section as *instrumental teaching values*.

These values may be nonmoral or moral. Of the nonmoral ones, most are performance values. That is, they are based on a conception of how a good student—one who learns—will function. Included will be values that speak to such matters as attendance (it should be punctual and regular), assignments (they should be on time, legible, thoughtful, complete), and participation in discussions (it should be frequent, thoughtful, not quarrelsome).

Some nonmoral instrumental teaching values are esthetic. For example, students may be required to keep bulletin boards attractive or the room neat and orderly, on the assumption that pleasant surroundings have a positive influence on learning. To encourage involvement that will hopefully lead to learning, beautifully done maps may be given extra points in social studies classes.

Finally, many instrumental teaching values are moral. They are standards for judging whether student behavior is ethically proper. You may insist that your students not interrupt one another during discussions or you may penalize students who cheat. Cheating and lack of courtesy may be viewed as intrinsic—as simply wrong in themselves. But it is equally likely that they will be viewed as instrumental: Interruptions during discussions create a chaotic atmosphere which detracts from learning; those who cheat get around the study necessary to learn. .

Being conscious of one's instrumental teaching values is important for several reasons. In the first place, they *are meant* to be instrumental and must always be scrutinized from that point of view: that is, do they facilitate learning? They may be ineffective or counterproductive. (Having to sit quietly may keep very young students from learning.) They may conflict with one another. (A teacher's belief that spontaneity is part of being a good student may not square with her strict adherence to a rule against interruptions during discussion.) Perhaps more importantly, instrumental teaching values may conflict with your teaching goals. (What, for example, of a teacher who would like to encourage student creativity, but insists on highly structured discussions and assignments?) Or they may alienate students when their validity is not obvious.

Can the reaction of teachers to standards set for *their* performance provide a fruitful entree for consideration of their demands of students? See "Inservice Workshop," page 102.

Careful attention to your instrumental teaching values will also help you avoid unwarranted judgments of students. As has been emphasized throughout this book, values tend to shift in meaning. Nonmoral values—including performance and esthetic instrumental teaching values—may take on moral overtones. For example, students who turn in papers late or make negative comments about the bulletin board are likely to be viewed as offensive. Also, instrumental values often become intrinsic. For example, having assignments in on time may become an end value to be enforced even when it interferes with learning. Avoiding the potential misuse that can result from shifts in the meaning of instrumental teaching values is a matter of fairness to students.

Another reason for analyzing instrumental teaching values is that they may run counter to the basic commitments of a democratic society. Is an emphasis on quietness so stringent as to deny dignity to students? Does a rule that students may not challenge their grades run counter to due process? Are grading standards that call for verbal skills that minority students lack a denial of equality of opportunity? Questions such as these lead to another reason for concern with instrumental values in the classroom.

What students learn from the environment of the classroom, established largely by the teacher's instrumental teaching values, is at the heart of the hidden curriculum. Are students learning that people who do not fit the teacher's concept of a "good student" are also regarded as less morally good? Might they be learning that following instructions and conforming to rules are the most important outcomes sought by schools? Are they learning that basic values and rationality are not important? These questions will be taken up again in Chapter 6 where we focus on moral values in the school and classroom.

TEACHING IN A DEMOCRATIC CONTEXT: ESTHETIC & INSTRUMENTAL VALUES 97

> ... [W]hat is wrong with elementary and secondary education—or for that matter higher education, journalism, television, social work, and so on—has less to do with incompetence or indifference or venality than with mindlessness.
>
> If this be so, the solution must lie in infusing the schools and the other educating institutions with purpose—more important, with thought about purpose, about the ways in which techniques, content, and organization fulfill or alter purpose.
>
> —Charles E. Silberman. *Crisis in the Classroom,* 1970.

Clearly, then, your instrumental teaching values merit attention—but not only by you. School is a major part of students' lives. The concept of dignity suggests that they should be helped to understand the reasons for the rules that govern such a large chunk of their being; it also suggests that they should have some say in determining whether the rules are reasonable. Moreover, because the classroom is the students' "real life," it provides excellent opportunities for helping students to reason soundly about values.

Competition—a good means to an end? See "Means and Ends," page 104.

Potential Outcomes

Identifying and scrutinizing your instrumental teaching values can have several valuable outcomes. Whether done alone or in dialogue with fellow teachers, this self-examination is likely to make you more introspective and observant about the way you treat students. You may find yourself removing or relaxing unnecessary behavioral controls that arouse antagonism or impede learning. Such self-examination, then, can lead to a more reasoning and reasonable classroom, one more consistent with the notion that the ideal of dignity also applies to students.

Once you are clear in your own mind about your instrumental classroom management values and their justification, you will be in a position to show basic respect for your students by discussing those values with them. You can emphasize their functionality as the reason for abiding by them, rather than simply insisting that students conform. The fact that you can justify these values in a way that makes sense to your students does not mean, of course, that students will never challenge them. But it does mean that such challenges can lead to rational means-ends discussions, rather than to shouted invectives or the quiet but seething confrontations so common in schools.

If you want to explain, justify, and discuss your instrumental values, and then use them rationally in managing the learning environment, you will have to confide your goals and objectives to your students. This may seem obvious, but it is likely to be a threatening proposal to some. Moreover, you may find it necessary to involve your students in decisions about the goals that ought to be desired for *their* education. If students are to take part in assessing your instrumental values, they must also consider the reasonableness of the learning outcomes that are sought. This, too, is a logical extension of a commitment to dignity.

Some teachers might overdo the examination of teaching purposes and instrumental values and neglect other important activities. But this is not likely, given the content orientation of most American schools. William Glasser (1969) suggests in *Schools Without Failure* that regular classroom meetings be held to work out management and other problems. Certainly a few minutes spent this way once or twice a week would not be excessive. As a minimum, a period or two should be taken at the beginning of the term to explore the goals and classroom procedures for each of your classes. Then, if regular times are not scheduled, you should at least be obviously open at any time, in or out of the classroom, to students' queries about instructional goals and instrumental values.

Although greater adherence to classroom procedures is likely to result from this approach to instrumental values, the potential for positive impact on students' feelings of self-worth is even more valuable. If you show your students that their opinions count by involving them in decisions about the goals for their own schooling and by having them help set the standards for the conduct of daily classroom business, their self-images are certain to be enhanced.

You must be particularly careful, though, not to use the process of rationalizing instrumental values simply to dupe students into conforming. Many young people are rightly wary after years of being put down by the system. They can readily sense—and even imagine—insincerity, and they will take it as evidence that you do not respect them. You must give serious consideration to your students' opinions, without being condescending and without making explicit or implicit threats of retribution toward students who speak their minds.

If you open the ends and means of the classroom to discussion, treating students as humans capable of thought, you must be ready to have your own assumptions and conclusions challenged. This will be uncomfortable, perhaps impossible to handle, if you need to rely on an authoritarian relationship to maintain a "superior" position over your students. But the values underlying such a relationship can also be examined and their effects altered.

Are you clear on the instructional implications of instrumental values? To check your comprehension, turn to Value Exploration 6, page 106. It will help focus your thinking on some basic questions.

RECAP

Showing respect for students' esthetic judgments and involving students in establishing instrumental values are both consistent with a commitment to human dignity. Both are also likely to make the school a more meaningful and less inimical place for the young. As the student's perception of the school changes and student-teacher relationships are transformed, the job of teaching could become much more pleasant than it often is now.

The basic question raised here has to do with how *you* view the young. Do you really see students as capable, functioning humans, deserving of your respect? Or do you see them as juveniles upon whom the judgments of mature adults must be imposed? Does your in- and out-of-classroom behavior truly reflect respect for students? Perhaps no questions are more critical than these to the development of the rationale from which you will make your value-related decisions as a teacher.

Making School Weird

Problem. *Is Mr. Graham teaching mathematics when he discusses esthetic values with his seventh-grade class of inner city students?*

"Hey, far out! What's he got now?"
"I don't know, man. Looks *weird!*"
Butch Morgan and Tino Muella were drifting into the strangely ordered world of Mr. Graham's seventh-grade math class, a place that always seemed to quiet the chaos of city streets outside. This was the class they both looked forward to each morning, though they had been hard pressed to explain why when Mr. Graham asked them to fill out a semester course evaluation.

It wasn't that the class was easy. Emphatically *no* on that one. It wasn't even that Mr. Graham was black and relaxed, though that counted for something. It was simply the "weirdness" of the class, as Tino liked to put it. You never knew what crazy thing he'd have you doing; and then, afterwards, he'd have you figuring out stuff you didn't know you could do on your own. Somehow, it was different from the other classes that put you mentally—and sometimes physically—to sleep.

"Hi, guys." Mr. Graham's glance flicked up, then back to his work. "How you making it?"

"Cool." Tino shrugged and jammed both hands into his hip pockets in a gesture of studied nonchalance. "What's happenin'?"

"Monday morning," Mr. Graham said.

"So what's that thing?"

"Nothing special. Called a geodesic dome."

Tino poked his tongue in his cheek and shifted his weight. Butch grinned at him.

"Get your homework done?" Mr. Graham asked, still concentrating on his work.

"Yeah."

"Good."

In a few minutes, twenty-four kids were jammed around the work table, and Tino was showing them how to clip the polygons together. A huge dome was taking shape. Meanwhile, Mr. Graham was taking roll and filling out the absentee form. A Monday morning with no kids absent. He took pleasure in this and smiled to himself as he moved into the crowd.

"What's it for?" Juanita was asking.

"Well, it could be the building of the future," Mr. Graham said. "Both on earth and out in space. Do you see why?"

"Easy to put up," Miguel said.

"And light," Gary interrupted. "Man, you could put jillions of these little sticks on a rocket ship! Give them astronauts something to do at night."

"Right on," Mr. Graham said. "Of course, this is just a model. Real buildings like this one are enormous. But you've got the idea. It's lightweight and incredibly strong for the weight of its separate pieces. And, to me, its simple lines are really kind of beautiful—you know? Tougher looking than the boxes we live in. And, of course, it's simple to put together, too—even you guys can do it, huh?"

"Hey, listen to that," Tino grinned. "We do *his* work, and he starts badmouthin' us."

Mr. Graham snickered in a friendly way and handed a triangle to Marsha so she could add it to the dome. "C'mon, now. Quit admiring the thing. You guys really think you can figure out why it's so strong for its weight?"

"Yeah," Butch grinned. "We'll figure it out. We ain't dummies, you know."

"True enough," Mr. Graham nodded. "Looks like you're *domeys* today!"

Follow-up. *Part of Mr. Graham's lesson plan involves having students try to crush a raw egg by squeezing it. In this way, they will learn something about how the fragile beauty of the eggshell distributes pressure. He hopes that such experiences will pique the students' curiosity and cause them to seek mathematical explanations. Is he teaching esthetic values if he has students compare the beauty as well as the strength and "usable life space" of a geodesic dome with other geometric forms such as cubes and pyramids? Should he do so?*

The "esthetic response" often occurs when you understand something in a new way—when the strange is made familiar, or the familiar strange. Try to remember an occasion in your schooling when a teacher helped you "see" the subject matter from an exciting or profound perspective. Or try to recall a time when you "put things together" on your own—the feeling when you really understood for the first time the basics of something you were studying. Discuss the personal value of such an esthetic experience with your friends. What does it do for you when it happens?

Inservice Workshop

Problem. *Do performance standards perform an important function when teachers are students?*

Glancing at his watch, Mr. Crockett put on a practiced sneer. One more minute and the consultant would be late.

"*Moral education,*" he grunted to a colleague. "Another better idea from the District Office."

His cynicism was undisguised. He wore it as a badge of professional identity.

"Well, it's good for a lane change," someone whined, mimicking the superintendent's nasal intonation.

Mr. Crockett smiled thinly. "A swift kick in the fanny—that's the only moral education these students understand."

"Mine don't even understand that," Coach Perkins grinned.

"Too lazy," Mrs. Norton murmured. "Or stupid. Or *both,* of course."

Mr. Crockett was warming up to the topic. "Take my last term paper assignment. Slipshod research, patched-together writing, out-and-out plagiarism, late papers—you name it. The students think that *anything goes*— if they can get away with it."

"Irresponsibility," Mrs. Norton agreed. "It's rampant. A decline of standards."

The consultant was in the open doorway, breathless, a briefcase in each hand. She moved quickly into the room, made her apologies, and began unpacking handouts for the workshop. Meanwhile, Mr. Crockett nodded knowingly to the others.

The workshop was quickly outlined: five sessions on moral education, two hours each; one graduate credit; fees to be split between teachers and the District Office.

Mr. Crockett raised a hand. "About the requirements," he inquired. "You have a syllabus, I presume?"

"Yes, of course," the consultant nodded, searching among her papers. "This is inservice, so it's been worked out with the District Office." She found the right stack and began distributing it. "This should explain everything."

Mr. Crockett scanned the sheet quickly and again raised his hand. "You say that this *has* been negotiated with the District Office?" A frown creased his brow.

"Why, yes. Is something wrong?"

Pausing, Mr. Crockett glanced at the others. "Well, no," he said. "Not exactly. It's just that—well, for an inservice workshop—the reading list, paper, and exam look a *bit* heavy."

"We normally just sort of kick things around in inservice," Coach Perkins added. "Share ideas and teaching methods. Nothing too formal. Nothing too theoretical."

Mrs. Norton's comment was precisely calculated. "After all, we are *professional* teachers. Perhaps we could, uh, *modify* the list a bit?"

The consultant clicked the twin latches on one of her briefcases. Her eyes scanned the group.

"I see," she said. "You're saying that standards should not be set for an inservice workshop. I assume you set standards for your students."

Mr. Crockett did not raise his hand this time. "The circumstances are hardly comparable. We're *not* tenth-grade students. We're adults."

"That's true," the consultant said. "But you're adults involved in a professional inservice activity."

"As professionals, we can judge what's good for us," Mr. Crockett rejoined. "And we have a lot of other demands on our time."

"Really? But don't *your* students say they're busy, and don't they say they know what's good for them? How do you react when they try to get out of *your* requirements?"

Mr. Crockett was struggling not to show his anger. "This is really ridiculous," he complained, holding up the syllabus. "Our time is valuable. I can take another inservice course and do *one-third the work* for the *same* credit."

The consultant stood her ground. "You're saying that a course with required reading, a paper, and an exam is ridiculous, but a course where anything goes because there are almost no requirements or standards is okay?"

"There is such a thing as *unreasonable* expectations," Mrs. Norton replied.

"Of course I want to be a *reasonable* instructor," the consultant said. "Just as you are *reasonable* teachers yourselves. Is it unreasonable to expect you to do some thoughtful research and some original writing and to get this work in on time? That's all I'm asking."

Coach Perkins was now scowling. "But you have us over a barrel. We need this workshop for a lane change."

"Well," the consultant nodded. "If you want the credit, you do the work. You certainly expect that of your students."

"Except that they don't *do* the work," Mr. Crockett grumbled. "They spend most of their time trying to get *out* of requirements."

"Hmmm," the consultant smiled. "I wonder where they learn such values?"

Coach Perkins raised his hand. "A couple of us will need to leave a bit early each time," he said.

Follow-up. *Should the inservice instructor change her syllabus? Is the teachers' implicit request for a relaxation of standards legitimate? Do performance standards serve a different instrumental function with adults than with younger students? Or does the teachers' position suggest hypocrisy? On the other hand, has the consultant allowed her performance standards to become intrinsic values?*

What should the consultant say next?

Means and Ends

Problem. *How can failure to think clearly about* means *affect the* ends *a teacher wishes to achieve?*

"T.G.I.F." Marty Donahue grins. "And *saluté!*"

There's great enthusiasm for Marty's impromptu toast around the table. Three other teachers hoist their beer mugs, echoing his gesture.

"Two days of freedom!" Gil Hunt says.

Judy Washburn, the girls' P.E. teacher, smiles and shakes her head. "Freedom? What a sick, sexist joke! Andrea and I have got a week's housecleaning to do, you muttonheads!"

"Ms. Washburn, that's *good* for your physical fitness." says Marty. "Keeps you in shape!"

"I ought to clobber you," says Judy.

"No, no," Gil frowns, "that would be out of order during our serious discussion of the week's problems."

Judy sips her beer and tries to keep from laughing. "Okay," she says. "I guess I'm really having a problem in my P.E. program right now. You see, my chart isn't working."

"Tell us more," says Gil. "Marty and I will help you sort things out."

Judy takes a deep breath and starts to outline the problem. How she thought that a huge locker-room chart which showed the relative skills of each girl would increase motivation and help spark her program, but how things have been going from bad to worse ever since she implemented the idea.

"To compete or not to compete," says Marty. "A real value dilemma—wouldn't you say, Gil?"

Andrea Thomas, who has been hanging back until now, comes into the discussion. "That's *exactly* what it is, you clowns. The way I see it, Judy's working through a problem in instrumental values."

Marty and Gil exchange stunned, silent looks.

"We're not following you," Gil says.

"Okay." Andrea nods. "Judy's told us that she thought competition, created by a master chart, would motivate the girls. In other words, she's used competition as an instrumental value—a way to help the girls achieve the things she wants them to in P.E."

"Right," Judy says. "And it isn't working."

"Could be because the girls with really low skills are discouraged by this kind of competition," says Andrea. "Nothing makes a kid feel crummier than a public record of low achievement."

"So competition is a bad thing?" Marty asks.

Andrea shrugs. "I guess it depends. If you've got a chance of winning you probably feel challenged by competition. But if it looks hopeless, you're probably going to feel pretty discouraged and threatened."

A smile begins to edge across Judy's face. "Maybe I could get them to compete against their own *past* performance," she says.

"Might be worth a try," says Andrea. "After all, it's not competition against each other that you're really concerned about, is it? The competition's just a means to help you achieve your goals."

"Wait a minute," Gil says. "Hold everything, I'm confused. I thought competition was the basis of Western Civilization! I thought we were trying to prepare students for *life!* Isn't competition a part of life?"

Judy is wearing the patient expression she reserves for slow learners. "Mr. Hunt, competition is indeed a part of life. But it probably isn't a *moral* value that's good in and of itself. That's just a phony bill of goods!"

"Women's Lib," Gil grunts. "Whoever heard such screwy ideas before, huh? I think we need another beer!"

Follow-up. *Can competition be both an instrumental and an intrinsic moral value? What do your friends who are reading this book think?*

Were you surprised when Andrea Thomas said, "Judy's working through a problem in instrumental values"? How do you think teachers who hadn't read this book would react if you said something like that during a bull session? What would you say if the reaction was "Horsefeathers!" or "What's this nonsense about instrumental values"?

Value Exploration 6

Turn back to "Instrumental Values, Kids, and Potted Plants" on page 43. Reread it with the following questions in mind:

- Is there any evidence that Mrs. Ashcroft has periodically reexamined her instrumental values of neatness, predictability, and order?
- Could it be that these values have become end (moral) values in her mind?
- Are her instrumental values likely to be counterproductive for some kinds of learning? What kinds?
- Do you think Mrs. Ashcroft could handle (tolerate) the suggestions made in this chapter for involving students in setting up and scrutinizing instrumental values?
- If you were the principal of her school, would Mrs. Ashcroft's approach bother you? If so, how might you go about trying to change her outlook and behavior? If change were not possible, would you consider dismissing her?

Discuss your responses to these questions with others who have read "Instrumental Values, Kids, and Potted Plants." In particular, try to express divergent views so that the assumptions underlying the above questions will be explored. For example, despite her approach, which may seem restrictive to some, Mrs. Ashcroft may be a very loving teacher who respects and has the respect of her students, and teaches them some significant attitudes toward rules.

Chapter 6

TEACHING IN A DEMOCRATIC CONTEXT: MORAL VALUES

In the last chapter, we focused on esthetic values and a small subset of instrumental values that are of great significance to teachers and students: those set up for the purposes of classroom management and instruction. Now we turn to moral values—our standards for judging whether aims or actions are good or right—as goals of instruction.

Moral values are an essential basis, implicit or explicit, for our ethical decisions. And, of particular importance to schools, they are central to the nature of our society. For these reasons, concern with moral values should be a priority for teachers in every field, not just in social studies where the emphasis on citizenship education makes moral values particularly relevant.[1]

Some time you may have the chance to help develop a sequential program for moral values education. More likely, however, you will find yourself dealing with moral values in bits and pieces—in short units or incidentally in the formal and informal curriculum. In any case, a rationale for dealing with moral values needs to consider the components of intelligent valuing and some of their implications for teaching. The purpose here is not to propose a

---

[1]Interestingly, practicing teachers seem to agree with this point. A summary of three recent National Science Foundation–sponsored studies of status in precollegiate mathematics, science, and social studies concluded that teachers in all three fields are concerned with socialization of students for citizenship, including "the advocacy of 'American' values and a commitment to inculcate them" (Shaver, Davis, & Helburn, 1979, p. 151). We hope that this book, and this chapter in particular, will make clear that more than advocacy and inculcation is needed.

program for values education. We do, however, want to relate some notions about democracy and the nature of values to teaching about moral values.

COGNITIVE ASPECTS OF MORAL VALUES EDUCATION

Our discussion of the nature of values in Chapter 2 emphasized their cognitive and affective aspects. By the same token, in our consideration of democracy, we have stressed the intellectual relevance of values (rationality as an underlying component of our commitment to human dignity and the need to untangle our value commitments in order to make sound decisions) and their emotional relevance (value commitments as the context for meaningful disputation and as the "cement" for a vast, multicultural society).

In the following discussion, we deal first with cognitive aspects of valuing: identifying and clarifying our values; the importance of value labels; dealing with the consequences of acting on our values which includes handling value conflict; relating moral values to decisions. Then we discuss value inculcation. Here we will deal with a fundamental question raised by the affective side of values.

Identification and Clarification of Values

Our democratic commitment to rationality does not assume a purely intellectual approach to life. Our behaviors are, and should be, influenced by our emotions. But it is desirable to be aware of the forces that move us. That is, remembering that values are both cognitive and emotive, one step in the direction of rationality is to try to state what our values are. What are our standards? How strongly do we feel about them? Answering such questions we call *value identification*.

Statements of identified values often lack clear cognitive or emotive meaning. Emotions are hard to put into words. And trying to be aware of and convey to others the cognitive meaning of a value can be difficult because one tends to confuse feeling with intellectual meaning. In addition, values are not static—either in the society or in any one individual—so a statement that is accurate at one time may not be so at another. For all these reasons, it is important to help your students go beyond a surface identification of principles and related feelings. The point is to help them be as certain *as is possible* at any time about the parameters of their commitments. So moral education must involve not just value identification, but *value clarification*[2] as well.

---

[2]"Value clarification" is used here in its generic sense to refer to any process for becoming more clear about one's value commitments. It is not intended to refer to the particular approach to values education which has been labeled "values clarification," about which we have serious reservations (see Chapter 7).

TEACHING IN A DEMOCRATIC CONTEXT: MORAL VALUES 109

> IN THE SCHOOL I USED TO GO TO I GOT A'S IN ALL MY TESTS.
>
> AND ALL THE KIDS WOULD ASK ME, "HOW DID YOU DO IT, JOEY?"
>
> AND I TOLD THEM, "I STUDIED."
>
> SO THEY WOULDN'T PLAY WITH ME ANYMORE. "THE BRAIN!" THEY CALLED ME. "THE PROFESSOR!"
>
> EVEN MY FATHER! "I WANT YOU TO BE A NORMAL AMERICAN BOY!" HE YELLED AT ME.
>
> SO WE MOVED AWAY IN DISGRACE.
>
> NOW IN THE NEW SCHOOL I GO TO I STILL GET A'S IN ALL MY TESTS.
>
> AND ALL THE KIDS STILL ASK ME, "HOW DO YOU DO IT, JOEY?"
>
> BUT NOW I TELL THEM, "I CHEATED."
>
> IT'S GREAT TO BE THOUGHT OF AS REGULAR.

Reprinted by permission of Jules Feiffer

As we have suggested, value clarification is not easy. Witness the difficulties faced by the Supreme Court in defining the basic values underlying most of its decisions. What is meant by "due process of law," for example? Has it been denied to a defendant who did not have an attorney when he was tried? What does "equal protection of the law" mean? Can it be considered to exist when laws require that students be segregated by race? How about when the segregation is *de facto* (existing in fact) rather than *de jure* (by law)? The Court has answered differently at different times—on these and other issues—as citizens have challenged current definitions or applications of values. If you are interested in obvious transitions in value meaning, study any of the series of cases that report the Court's attempts over the years to define various basic values.

AMERICA—Love It or Leave It. A bumper sticker is used to provide an opportunity to clarify the meaning of "good citizen." But are basic values adequately identified and clarified? See "Civil Disobedience," p. 126.

Value Labels

Thinking about values, like thinking about anything, depends on language. We need to pay special attention to *value labels*, especially labels for the central moral values that we call basic values. Value identification and clarification are partly a question of defining value labels clearly. But there is more, too. Moral education in a democratic society should teach students to use value terms that relate their unsophisticated value concepts to the more basic, more general values of the society. This we call *label generalization*.

The terms that adults as well as children use in applying their values to concrete situations often are not the same as those used in political-ethical debate, even though the conceptual meaning is similar. Take, for example, the notion of "fairness" which children and youth develop and apply in play as well as in the classroom. "It's not fair" may be said of a playground game in which, via some biased process, all of the best student athletes arrange to be on the same team. Or, "It's not fair" may be used to protest a referee who favors one team over the other. In the first instance, the idea of "fairness" is akin to the political-legal concept of equality of opportunity. In the second, it is akin to the political-legal concept of equal treatment before the law. And a youngster who protests, "I've got a right to say what I want," when an adult shushes him during an argument, is calling on a value that might appropriately be termed freedom of speech.

Helping students to begin to use labels with basic value meanings serves several related functions: (1) It provides a basis for value identification and clarification.[3] (2) It gives students a more powerful conceptual scheme as they relate their own untutored commitments to the basic values of the society. (3) It gives students a more powerful value language for analysis, discussion, and persuasion. And (4) it helps to insure a nationwide values vocabulary at the basic value level among people who, unlike news commentators, politicians, and lawyers, frequently would not otherwise use such terms in their thinking and disputes. In short, the process of label generalization is important because it relates the student's own developing value vocabulary and conceptual schema to the broader and more powerful basic values of a democratic society.

— — — — — — — — — — — — — — — —

A news item sparks a heated discussion.

"Well, I don't think it's *fair!*" a white ninth grader blurts out.

"*Fair?*" comes the incredulous challenge from a black student.

Turn to "Current Events," page 128, and consider the value clarification and identification problems involved.

— — — — — — — — — — — — — — — —

Consequences and Value Conflict

Another basic element in rational valuing is the *examination of consequences*. This simply means asking: "What will happen if people do (or do not)

---

[3] Two questions are pertinent here: Is the value that is being applied to a personal situation similar to the value referred to by the broader value term? Is it appropriate to apply the broader value to this particular situation? The latter question is not the same as asking whether the value is being applied correctly. The distinction is between "Is John's freedom of speech really at issue here?" and "Should Mrs. Jones have denied John his freedom of speech by telling him to shush?"

act in accord with, or support, a particular principle?" We are not likely to be clear about the dimensions of our value commitments until we examine what may happen if we act upon (or ignore) them.

When students examine consequences, they will probably discover that acting on the basis of one moral value commonly leads the person to violate another one. Such value conflicts involve personal values, middle-level values, and the basic values that are used to justify decisions about personal and societal questions of proper aims and conduct.

Value conflict recognition ought to be treated as more than an incidental outcome of examining consequences. Our values are inherently inconsistent and their relative importance changes over time. Because the potential of value conflict is so pervasive, students ought to learn to recognize and deal with value dilemmas openly and rationally.

Disputes that make value conflicts obvious may not occur in classes that are homogeneous. People with similar frames of reference are less likely to conflict on basic ethical issues, or to stimulate one another to self-examination. To bring out different points of view, you may have to take a devil's advocate position, or use student role-playing, films, or outside reading. The devices you use should awaken your students to the existence of, and reasons for, conflicting opinions in the society (see, e.g., Fraenkel, 1980, pp. 244–251).

Once value conflicts are recognized, they should be confronted and handled. This stage of valuing we call *value conflict resolution*. As Coombs and Meux (1971, pp. 54–61) have pointed out, it may involve any or all of the following: (1) examining similar situations to see if you would be willing to accept the consequences of acting on one or another value in each case; (2) changing places (usually in a simulation of some sort) with a person who will be affected by the application of the value, in order to consider whether you could accept the principle if you were in that person's shoes; (3) asking if you could accept the consequences if everyone acted on the principle in question. The examination of consequences, then, is obviously important both as a means of making value conflicts salient and as a means of arriving at an acceptable resolution.

Handling value conflict is especially important when we apply basic values to the justification of political-ethical decisions (decisions about public issues). The search for human dignity demands that we weigh conflicting basic values (such as equality and freedom), and deliberations about public issues should proceed from that perspective. In fact, it is important to teach students to search out the basic values that support the position of their opponent—or, if they are not directly involved in a dispute but are trying to make a disinterested decision, to look for the basic values that are on each side of the issue.

We must be willing to keep our value choices open to reexamination. We have used the phrase *value conflict resolution* for want of a better term. As we noted in Chapter 2, however, our value weightings shift, and the same value conflicts occur in settings sufficiently different that our value choices change. Value conflicts can, therefore, be resolved once and for all only by individuals who are cognitively inflexible.

Although it is seldom possible to resolve value conflicts permanently, it is important to use some consistency in applying one's values. No one wants to be in a constant state of quandary. Moreover, other people are entitled to have some reasonable expectations as to your behavior. We want to avoid the implication that shifting value emphases is "good" in itself—any more than it would be intrinsically "good" to maintain a consistent value position in the face of changing circumstances. We should use our rationality to weigh our value priorities, remembering that "stability" and "adaptability" are both values to be taken into account.

Summary. You will assist your students along the road to rational decision making if you can do two things: (1) Make them aware that value conflict is inevitable, so that they do not see having to confront value dilemmas as a sign of abnormality or malfunctioning. (2) Help them learn to weigh values—for example, in terms of the consequences of following conflicting commitments—and come to tentative conclusions, accepting that value dilemmas are usually not resolvable in any final sense. These are not impractical goals. If you succeed in achieving them, perhaps you will help to reduce deception on the part of government officials, the questionable business practices so common today, and the unconscionable treatment of blacks and other minorities in this country. In short, you may help people to do better at matching what they say to what they do.

Valuing and Decisions

A decision is the desired result of the ethical reasoning process. In particular, we should help students arrive at *qualified decisions*. A qualified decision is one that takes into account the possible negative consequences of a policy or action to be supported, and the circumstances under which you might change your mind and support a different value. A qualified decision might also take into account the extent to which it depends on particular definitions of key terms, including value labels.[4]

Cheating on a quiz—time for a lecture or an opportunity for some value analysis? See "Story Within a Story," page 129.

---

[4]For a discussion of qualified decisions, see Shaver and Larkins (1973a, Ch. 9).

Judging decisions.   The democratic society's commitment to human worth and, consequently, to rationality suggests that all sides of an issue should be given consideration in decision making. This does *not* mean, however, that differing positions must automatically be given equal weight. Teachers can judge the complexity and soundness, and therefore the acceptability, of their students' position statements (see e.g., Newmann and Oliver, 1970, pp. 278–284; Oliver and Shaver, 1974). And they can help young people learn to apply criteria of adequacy to their own and other persons' position statements.

For example, one can question whether the consequences of acting on a given value have been adequately examined and taken into account. This may involve asking whether the person considered conflicting commitments before he arrived at a position.

Value conflict and relativism.   A few educators have expressed concern that our value conflict rationale might lead students to believe that because value conflicts cannot be finally resolved, decisions cannot, or need not, be made. That is, students might use their awareness of value conflict as an excuse for copping out and not confronting a decision on the relativistic grounds that anyone's position is as good as anyone else's.[5]

We have already noted that positions can be judged by the adequacy of the reasoning behind them. Moreover, it should be clear that decisions do have to be made. Neither personal lives nor world affairs stand still merely because value conflicts are difficult to grapple with and resolve. This is where the qualified decision comes in. Since decisions must be made, the rational person takes into account the qualifying circumstances that condition his or her stand. In your classroom, therefore, you should emphasize that decision making is inevitable, that action is necessary, and that even inaction implies a decision—the decision not to act.

This brings us back to a question we discussed in Chapter 4. In dealing with issues that involve value conflict, should a teacher ever take a stand during classroom discussions? We suggested in the earlier discussion that your willingness to be identified with a position may go a long way toward convincing students that you are not a phony or an uncommitted person. Now we want to add a second point: If you refuse to let students know where you stand on issues, your refusal may be interpreted as relativistic. Such a stance certainly does not provide a model of involvement in decision making appropriate to a democratic society.

Letting your students know what you believe is not likely to cause much

---

[5]If the relativistic argument interests you, you may wish to read an argument by Oliver and Shaver (1974, p. 50) that relativism is an inappropriate and nonfunctional basis for curriculum development and teaching in a democratic society.

consternation when you are dealing with historical issues. For example, no one is likely to be too upset if you express moral revulsion at the Nazis' "final solution" to the "Jewish problem," toward the institution of slavery, or toward the treatment of Indians in the nineteenth century.

But what about issues of current, even local, concern? Is it realistic to ask you to take a stand on matters that may frighten or enrage parents (and, consequently, administrators)—especially when to do so may cost you your job?

Here the value conflict model is again relevant, because it provides you with the means of taking a stand. Once the model has been taught as a rational framework for dealing with issues, you have available a basis for stating your position. Using the qualified decision, you can take a stand which does not attack those who disagree with you, but rather takes into account their deep concerns. Note, however, that stating qualified decisions is likely to avoid emotional responses by your students only to the extent that they understand value conflict and are accustomed to taking contradictory values into account in their own decision making.

In other words, when students have been helped to develop an adequate frame for analyzing controversial issues (see, e.g., Shaver & Larkins, 1973a), your statement of opinion in the classroom is potentially less "dangerous." Students are less likely to take it as an attempt to impose your views on them or as a pronouncement to be accepted unthinkingly.

We make the following statement from experience: When you and your students share an analytic frame, and when, in addition, you conduct discussions in a context of dignity, clearly based on the assumption that your students are intelligent, worthwhile beings whose thoughts and comments are to be respected, your position simply becomes one among others to be considered. You can let students know that you stand for something—and do so in a rational setting that makes clear that you do not intend to indoctrinate them.

Your students ask you to take a stand. How might you respond? Value Exploration 7, page 131, asks you to deal with that question.

The mention of indoctrination leads us to our next important point.

AFFECTIVE ASPECTS OF MORAL VALUES EDUCATION: INCULCATION AND DIGNITY

There are important affective considerations beyond the emotions that might be raised by discussions of value-related issues. These become apparent when we raise the basic question: Should teachers in a democracy indoctrinate values? Or, put another way, should your role as a teacher include value inculcation, especially when this involves instilling deep emotional commitments to certain values?

We have already made our position clear in regard to esthetic values and instrumental teaching values. In the area of esthetics, the teacher should not indoctrinate. Rather, he or she should try to help students develop their own sets of criteria for beauty. In fact, attempts to implant values in areas such as music and English often misfire. Pious comments about the students' failure to appreciate the "right" kinds of music or literature often only confirm the image that many young people have of teachers as, at worst, inconsiderate and disrespectful, and at best, well-intentioned, but rather bumbling souls out of contact with reality.

By the same token, the teacher should not inculcate the instrumental values of the classroom or school. If you respect your students, you must explicate and examine with them your justifications for management and instructional instrumental values—that is, how you expect these values to help obtain the end results you want. And you must alter or discard those values when they appear to be nonfunctional or dysfunctional. And, of course, instrumental values which lead to violations of dignity ought to be abandoned, regardless of the other ends they achieve. Inhumane methods are not to be justified on the basis of valued ends.

Moral values beyond classroom standards call for a different initial approach, but the end result in terms of teaching behavior is similar. To begin with, recall the earlier discussion (Chapter 3) about the fundamental function of the American Creed. Not only do the values in it provide a linguistic and emotive frame for political debate among the diverse groups in our pluralistic society, but as a corollary they provide the cohesive force (the "cement") that holds divergent groups together as a political entity.

Teachers, as professionals in a democratic society, therefore have special obligations in regard to these values—as distinct from personal and even middle-level values. Teachers have no business attempting to impose personal values, and must approach middle-level values with a great deal of caution. But they are obligated to encourage emotive commitment to the basic values of society, as well as growth in the cognitive processes of value identification, value clarification, and value conflict resolution.

In colonial America, freedom of the press could not be taken for granted. John Peter Zenger, a German immigrant and editor of the *New York Weekly Journal*, was imprisoned for criticizing the governor of New York. In 1735, after ten months in jail, he came to trial on libel charges. To the British court, the only question was whether Zenger had published critical articles. His attorney, Alexander Hamilton, argued that he should be convicted only if what he said was untrue. The jury agreed with Hamilton and the foundation was laid for freedom of the press in this country.

Emotive commitments tend to be formed at an early age—studies of political attitudes (Massialas, 1969) suggest before and during elementary school. Literature and other materials (such as dramatization of the John Peter Zenger free press episode) can be used to build commitment to basic values by exemplifying their importance and the dedication to them in our society. Such experiences should especially be an important part of elementary school teaching (see, e.g., Oliver, 1960), but they should not be ignored at higher grade levels. As Diane Ravitch (1980) has pointed out:

> Children can learn to love the rights and freedoms we hold dear, such as freedom of the press, freedom of religion, freedom of speech, and universal suffrage, only by learning how difficult it has been to secure them over the centuries, and how few are the societies where such rights and freedoms have been enjoyed, either now or in the past. (p. 2)

But for teachers at all levels the teaching role is more likely to be the *reinforcement* of often unverbalized value commitments, rather than the instilling of new values. That is, you may be able to make existing commitments stronger, but the commitments themselves will usually have been established in the powerful environment of family and peer groups, and via television.

In a very important sense, then, the issue of value inculcation or indoctrination by teachers is a red herring, because forces other than the school are relatively more powerful. Unfortunately, this issue is still so emotionally loaded that it often prevents us from exploring the teaching behaviors that are legitimate in a democratic educational context.

Value inculcation is a red herring in another sense—if one agrees with our discussion of values, especially the emphasis on the affective and cognitive aspects and functions of values, in Chapters 2 and 3. It should be obvious that *the legitimate inculcation* (or more realistically, the reinforcement or strengthening) *of commitment to basic democratic values does not entail indoctrination of any particular cognitive definition of the values or any particular political position*. How the values are to be defined and which opposing values are to be given preference must be left for students to decide themselves. If you as a teacher emphasize, for example, values having to do with freedom— and neglect the opposing values of equality and security (or vice versa)—you are violating your students' human dignity. Here the distinction between values and value judgments (see Chapter 2) is crucial. *It is justifiable to build emotive commitment to the values basic to a democratic society. It is not justifiable to indoctrinate specific judgments based on those values.* You would be out of line, for example, in trying to convince your students that welfare was bad policy[6] because it deprived people of their independence—or, on the other hand, that it was good policy because it made people more equal.

Finally, it is important to stress that our own position rests on a strong faith in the self-evident validity of the American Creed. As students consider the conflicts between our basic values and confront the difficulty of choosing between them, the result will be durable commitment. As Ravitch (1980) has put it: "The ideals and principles of a free society . . . may be taught by debate, by challenge, and by a critical 'problems of democracy' approach . . . because of our belief that these values are so compelling that they can survive critical analysis and prevail in the free market of ideas."

A sitdown strike: What are the implications for value inculcation? This question is posed by "Pep Assembly," page 131.

How About Parents?

You may be asking yourself, But what about my students' parents? Won't they be upset by my attempts to indoctrinate or consolidate emotive commitments to *any* values? These questions recall the discussion of the teacher as professional in Chapter 4. They should remind you that it is important to have a carefully thought-out rationale for making teaching decisions and for discussing these decisions with fellow teachers, administrators, and parents.

Parents may find it harder to tolerate rational valuing than inculcation. They are likely to think that teaching is subversive when it leads youngsters to challenge the unexamined value assumptions of the home. That is another reason why you should be circumspect about translating value commitments into value judgments.

Parents are particularly likely to tolerate inculcation of certain middle-level moral values, such as honesty, punctuality, and dependability, because they

---

[6]Note that we have used the word *policy* instead of *value judgment*. Policy is a broader word. A value judgment is an assertion based on a value: a policy is a plan or course of action. A typical policy may be thought of as a complex judgment based on a value (or values), but also on factual assumptions that may themselves be very complex.

want youngsters to exhibit these daily in their interactions. They may not, for example, be particularly happy if, rather than insisting that "Honesty is good," you ask such questions as:

"What is meant by honesty?"
"What may be some consequences of not being honest?"
"Under what circumstances (that is, when confronted with the violation of what other values) could one justifiably choose not to be honest?"

Such a pattern of questioning is essential, however, if you are to help students build rational bases for their value stands.

As a professional educator in a democratic society, shouldn't you be prepared to argue not only that parents should tolerate such inquiry, but that they should encourage it as a legitimate and needed educational function of the school? Certainly, this task is not likely to be carried out systematically elsewhere. One seldom overhears this kind of dialogue at parties or in more intimate discussions among friends. The home itself, where so much education takes place, is a difficult environment for critical inquiry into values. The relationships there are too complex, too fraught with emotive power. Moreover, it is too difficult for parents, in their intense relationships with their children, to stand outside their own frames of reference, to be analytic, and to ask questions in ways that are not overt or subtle reminders (deliberate or not) of what the child *ought* to believe, rather than invitations to contemplation.

Moreover, the concept of human dignity, emphasizing individual choice and rooted in the notion of pluralism, demands that, important as the home may be, a broader context for value development is necessary—for the good of the maturing individual as well as in the interests of the society. Kahlil Gibran (1923) has expressed, as only a poet could, what human dignity means in child rearing. With slight modifications, his words are also a poignant reminder to teachers who would impose their own value interpretations and choices on their students:

> Your children are not your children.
> They are the sons and daughters of life's longing for itself.
> They come through you but not from you,
> And though they are with you yet they belong not to you.
> You may give them your love but not your thoughts,
> For they have their own thoughts.
> You may house their bodies but not their souls,
> For their souls dwell in the house of tomorrow, which you cannot visit, not even in your dreams.
> You may strive to be like them, but seek not to make them like you.
> For life goes not backward nor tarries with yesterday.
> You are the bows from which your children as living arrows are sent forth.
> . . .
> Let your bending in the archer's hand be for gladness. . . .

You may want to explore with some of your fellow teachers the implications of Gibran's words for your interrelations with parents and with students. How many parents or teachers can accept such an expression of dignity for youngsters? Do we unjustifiably deny the worth of the young by trying to mold them in our own images rather than "shooting forth the arrow"? Does Gibran's statement have any relevance to the frequent alienation between parent and child, or between school and student?

About teaching itself, Gibran says:

If he [the teacher] is indeed wise he does not bid you enter the house of his wisdom, but leads you to the threshold of your own mind.

TEACHER AND SCHOOL

We began this book with the caution that it is impossible to avoid teaching about values. You will teach values implicitly, even if you avoid formal instruction about them, through your choices of content and instructional methods as well as through your various interactions with students in and out of your classroom. And, of course, the same is true of the total school. The manner in which the school is organized and run, along with the students' contacts with various school personnel—whether the principal, the school secretary, custodians, or school lunch workers—will have value implications. In fact, it is now the vogue in education to argue that more value instruction takes place informally through the "hidden curriculum" than is, or could be, done through the formal curriculum.

Concern for the lessons taught outside of the classroom is not new. In 1909, John Dewey admonished educators that "the school is fundamentally an institution erected by society . . . to [perform] a . . . function in maintaining the life and advancing the welfare of the society." And, if the school is to execute properly its responsibility for moral training, "there cannot be two sets of ethical principles, one for life in the school, and the other for life outside of the school" (p. 7).

Unfortunately, school people have frequently not structured schools by the basic values of our society. This lapse has been the subject of many lawsuits involving student rights, and the courts have ruled that the society's basic values are germane to the school. For example, in cases involving equality of opportunity, courts have said that in San Francisco the school district must provide special language programs for non-English-speaking Chinese students (*Lau v. Nichols,* 1974); that school districts must make special efforts to obtain certification for Spanish-speaking teachers to teach Spanish-speaking students (*Serna v. Portales Municipal Schools*, 1972); that achievement or "intelligence" tests with strong Anglo middle-class biases may not be used to classify black or bilingual Hispanic students as mentally retarded and that tracking systems may not be based on cultural-ethnic differences (McClung, 1973); that handicapped children have a right to appropriate free public education (*Mills v. D.C. Board of Education*, 1972); and, perhaps most basic of all, that schools segregated by race are a denial of equal educational opportunity (*Brown v. Board of Education*, 1954).

Some cases have dealt directly with the application of constitutional values to the manner in which students are treated in school. In *Goss v. Lopez* (1975), the Supreme Court held that students have the right to at least "minimum" due process—a notice and opportunity for a hearing—before being suspended from school for disciplinary reasons. And in *Tinker v. Des Moines* (1969), the Court ruled that students should not have been suspended from school for exercising their freedom of expression by wearing black armbands to school to protest the Vietnamese War. One comment by the Court in the *Tinker* case is of particular interest to teachers concerned with the applicability of basic societal values to the school:

> It can hardly be argued that either students or teachers shed their constitutional rights to freedom of speech or expression at the schoolhouse gate.
>
> Students in school as well as out of school are "persons" under our Constitution. They are possessed of fundamental rights which the State must respect, just as they themselves must respect their obligations to the State.

The Supreme Court has even spoken directly to the powerful influence of the hidden curriculum. In 1943, the Court decided the case of *West Virginia State Board of Education v. Barnette*. A young member of the Jehovah's Witnesses had been expelled from school for refusing to salute the American flag during opening exercises because to do so was interpreted as bowing to a graven image, contrary to religious faith. The Court ruled that such an expulsion was a denial of religious freedom. And, in an interesting bit of dictum, the Court also said:

> [Boards of Education] have, of course, important, delicate, and highly discretionary functions, but none that they may not perform within the limits of the Bill of Rights. That they are educating the young for citizenship is reason for scrupulous protection of Constitutional freedoms of the individual, if we are not to strangle the free mind at its source and *teach youth to discount important principles of our government as mere platitudes*. (Italics added.)

The statements by Dewey and the courts reinforce the notion of the hidden curriculum and its importance. As you think about your role as a teacher in regard to basic moral values you need to consider what you do in your classroom in the context of what goes on in the total school. In particular, it will be important for you to confront a difficult ethical question that each teacher should face: To what extent should I try to influence the environment of the school in which I teach?

Once you decide to be concerned with what happens outside of your classroom a number of other questions arise: On what sorts of occasions will I be willing to speak out to try to influence what happens to students? Will I try to influence other teachers—for example, during faculty room discussions or by reacting to the specific treatment of students which I observe? Will I try to influence the political structure of the school through suggestions to the principal and through the positions I take in faculty meetings on such matters as disciplinary procedures and student involvement in school decisions?

A carefully thought-out rationale based on a conception of the school's role in a democratic society will help you to make up your mind on these important questions. Moreover, it will provide a sound basis for being persuasive with other school personnel. To serve those functions well, your rationale should, in particular, speak to a question that we have not yet addressed directly—"What is a democratic school?"

Democratic Schools

It will not come as a surprise that, in our view, a democratic school is one which reflects the basic values of the society. More specifically, in such a school those values are embodied in classroom and school procedures and exemplified in the decisions and behavior of school personnel.

Defining precisely what such a school might be like is difficult, however—for at least two reasons. First, there is disagreement over how to define and weigh our basic values in applying them to specific settings (as we emphasized in Chapters 2 and 3). Second, basic values cannot necessarily be applied directly to the school as they have been defined for other settings. For example, the Supreme Court stated in *Goss v. Lopez* (1975) that due process is a constitutional concept that is applicable to schools. But the Court also stressed that the application needs to be appropriate to the situation, and that the due process accorded a student charged with a disciplinary violation need not involve the same complex standards and procedures as for a person charged with a crime.

Also, the nature of a democratic school may vary with the age level and maturity of the students. For example, taking part in decisions that affect one's own well-being is an important aspect of human dignity. The involvement of students in decisions about the curriculum as well as in setting and enforcing standards for classroom and school behavior would, in itself, be consistent with democratic commitments. It would also provide splendid opportunities to fulfill the democratic mandate to prepare youth to be intelligently involved citizens. But the extent of participation of students on school curriculum committees or in course development in individual classrooms, their attendance at faculty meetings, even the type of decisions turned over to student governance bodies (e.g., student councils and courts) ought not be the same for first graders as for seniors, nor for the first graders or seniors in every classroom or school. The common ingredient should be real involvement in personally important decisions. And although serious questions need to be raised about the types of insignificant decisions usually delegated even to high school student councils, along with the typically ever-present specter of administrative veto, it also is evident that there are no pat answers to questions about the extent to which students should be involved in school decision making.

FUNKY WINKERBEAN By Tom Ba

Courtesy Field Newspaper Syndic

Although commitment to basic societal values does not provide precise guidelines for democratic schools, it is clear that such schools would *not* be permissive places in which students do pretty much as they wish. The curriculum must be based on professional judgments about goals and the instructional activities to reach them. Student interests are important considerations, but they ought not be the only ones. John Dewey was clear on that point, although his position has often been misconstrued. He stressed that student interest and spontaneity should be taken into account in making instructional decisions. But he did not believe that students should be left free to set their own objectives, because among the results would be shallow aims and projects and activities lacking the continuity necessary for productive thinking and growth. Teachers are responsible for structuring the learning environment. At the same time, they should heed Dewey's caution that they ought not act arbitrarily as "magistrates" and impose objectives and activities alien to their students (Dewey, 1964a, pp. 153–155; 1964c, pp. 9–10).

Democracy does not call for permissiveness in standards of behavior either. Classrooms and schools need rules, as the broader society needs laws, for stability. (Of course, the rules need not be imposed and enforced arbitrarily, and will not be in schools based on democratic principles.) Permissive schools would not only be unrealistic, but nondemocratic—because they would not give students essential experience in learning about and acting with regard for their responsibilities to other people and to society.

Responsibility is an important value in our society against which students' rights must be balanced in democratic schools. The Supreme Court reminded us of that in *Tinker v. Des Moines* (1969). The case was decided in favor of freedom of expression by students. At the same time, the justices were mindful of "the need for affirming the comprehensive authority of the states and of school officials, consistent with fundamental safeguards, to prescribe and control conduct in the schools." "Appropriate discipline" must be maintained to avoid disruptions that "would substantially interfere with the work of the school or impinge upon the rights of other students."

In short, school governance, like the governance of the society, must proceed from a value conflict model such as that laid out in this book. This means that democratic schools will not be ideal mini-societies in which everyone is treated as he or she wishes. The basic values of the society do conflict when applied to specific situations, and no solution is likely to be viewed as perfect by all the parties involved. For this reason, dissension is as inevitable in school as in the broader society. Unfortunately, it is too often suppressed arbitrarily rather than dealt with, even through the explanation of decisions, in terms of the need to weigh conflicting values including responsibility.[7]

Aside from value conflicts, life itself is not perfect. One of the naive applications of the notion of the hidden curriculum is the conclusion that anything negative that happens to students in school is "bad," in the sense that it results in mislearning. Yet the students involved in *Tinker v. Des Moines*, for example, probably learned a great deal both about coping with bureaucratic inflexibility and about the role of the judiciary in a democratic society.

Even with the best of intentions, teachers and administrators will make errors of judgment that result in unjustifiable denials of students' rights. But if

---

[7]For an excellent treatment of the value issues involved in students' rights, see Richard Knight, *Students' Rights: Issues in Constitutional Freedoms* (1974). This booklet will be especially helpful to teachers who wish to explore such issues with students.

you help students to understand the school as a political-social institution and encourage them to analyze occurrences there as a basis for comprehending and dealing rationally with political-social settings generally, even seemingly negative experiences can be the basis for valuable learning.

> Other students are also part of the "less-than-ideal" mini-society of the school. Should the teasing of a handicapped student be used as a take-off for values education? See "After School," page 132.

Respect for the dignity and worth of the individual does not, then, dictate permissiveness or an ideal mini-society in classroom or school. It does, however, call for the rational understanding and application of the basic values of the society by school people. The result will be what we call "democratic schools," schools that reflect democratic commitments and dilemmas. Again, we urge that you consider what your role should be in encouraging the school in which you teach to be such an institution.

> How should teachers respond to racism and anti-Semitism when it touches their school? Value Exploration 8, page 134, asks you to consider that question again.

RECAP—AND BEYOND

Each of the various components of valuing—values identification and clarification, label generalization, examination of consequences, value conflict and resolution, and commitment—needs to be considered in making teaching decisions. The components are not valued ends themselves. They take on importance in light of the democratic commitment to human dignity, and therefore to intelligent decision making. Each of these components of valuing is significant to the extent that it helps individuals to make sound decisions in the ethical domain by increasing the probability that these decisions will be consciously related to their commitments.

The cognitive aspects of moral values education discussed in this chapter are not intended as an exclusive definition of rational moral valuing. We think that these components are significant; but we present them here as suggestive and heuristic, not as definitive, final answers. Consider them as you contemplate what to do about values. But remember, they can be refined and expanded.

Note, too, that the discussion in this chapter is focused on operations for clarifying and dealing with values. We have almost totally ignored other aspects of intelligent decision making. For example, we only touched on the problem of handling factual questions in making decisions—by suggesting that people should examine potential consequences when making value choices. Another important area, language clarification, is hinted at in the discussion of label generalization. Many other concepts and skills are needed to handle factual and language problems in making warranted, sound decisions. But to discuss them all is beyond the scope of this book.[8]

Another caveat: The order in which we have discussed the aspects of a values education program is not necessarily the order in which you ought to teach them. That is, in teaching about values, you will not necessarily proceed through a set sequence from values identification to the making of qualified decisions. In real life the categories tend to overlap. As students identify their commitments, they are likely to raise questions about the consequences of acting on them. Examining the consequences of acting upon values may lead them to better insights about their commitments. In fact, a good way to involve students in value identification and clarification is to force them to confront the conflicts between values in their own frames of reference. Another good tactic is to make them face the consequences of acting generally upon values that are implicit in their classroom or playground behavior.

In short, a *logical* sequence for examining the components of moral values education moves from the identification of value commitments, through awareness of value conflict, to the confrontation of full-blown ethical problems. However, the greatest *psychological* effect may come from following a different sequence—one which first engages students in the consideration of ethical problems with which they can identify, so that they become immersed emotionally. Then they can be helped to become aware of the difficulties in arriving at rationally defensible answers. The feelings of disequilibrium and the interest generated by this approach can motivate students to consider values and valuing systematically.

It is also important to remember that values have a strong emotive (affective) component. Their emotive force helps to hold society together. But for you as a teacher, emotions can also be a source of contention. Administrators and parents may object when you try to teach students to handle loaded issues rationally. It is here that having a strong rationale, set in the context of a commitment to human dignity, can be a good survival strategy. Remember, too, that when students have been helped to develop the vocabulary and conceptual tools for value analysis, it is less likely that you will be accused of indoctrination—even when you do take stands on moral issues.

Finally, in considering what to do about moral values as a teacher, it is

---

[8]A discussion of concepts for handling ethical decisions involving public issues can be found in Shaver and Larkins (1973a), *Decision-Making in a Democracy*.

essential to keep in mind the school in which you teach. Whether it reflects basic societal values, including rationality in decision making, will have an impact on your efforts to help students be committed to and apply basic moral values. For that reason alone, there is a serious question as to whether one can justify playing a passive role in school affairs outside one's own classroom.

Civil Disobedience

Problem. *Does Miss Watson have a firm grasp of democratic values?*

Miss Watson stated that the bumper sticker she held before her twelfth-grade class had been popular among certain conservative groups during the 1960s and early 1970s: *AMERICA—Love It or Leave It*. She explained to the students that while this particular message might be dated, the issue of protest in a democratic society was still very much alive. She also pointed out that negative reactions to protest were by no means a recent phenomenon—that this had been a tough problem for Americans of many eras, including Colonial supporters of American independence, opponents of slavery, pioneers of the women's suffrage movement, civil rights activists, and supporters of hundreds of other causes.

The class was soon itemizing issues that had evoked protest in more recent years—rights for the handicapped, nuclear energy, the ERA, draft registration. Miss Watson set up a discussion by emphasizing a personal belief: that responsible democratic citizenship required careful thought about protest.

"This bumper sticker—if you think carefully about its intent—is really an anti-protest protest," she said to her students. "Do you see why?"

The class looked puzzled. A hand or two tested the air.

"Well, it's saying that people either should like the way things are or they should have to leave the country," Vicki commented.

"That's what I mean by an anti-protest protest," Miss Watson said. "It's protesting people who didn't fully support America's policies at the time."

Joel had a grin on his face. "So it's okay for a bumper sticker to make *its* protest, but it's un-American for other people to make theirs?"

Miss Watson nodded in Joel's direction. "That's the irony of this bumper sticker. On the surface, it seems to be a super-patriotic, very American sort of message. But as you think more deeply, the message seems very *un-*American."

Mark raised his hand, "Why un-American? I mean, it sounds okay to me. People who are against the country shouldn't be wrecking it for others."

Miss Watson sensed the need to go more slowly—to explain some of the "leaps" in reasoning that Vicki and Joel had easily made.

"Let's talk logic," she said. "Think for a moment about the underlying value judgment in the bumper sticker. *You either love America or you don't.* That perhaps *sounds* reasonable, but is it? *Either-or* statements are very tricky. Think of colors," Miss Watson said. "There are lots of shades between the extremes of black and white. The same logic applies in other situations. Is it true, for example, that you either love or hate everyone you know?"

"Well, no," Mark said.

Maria spoke up. "But I agree with Mark. People shouldn't have the right to just tear down the country. Some people are just negative. They complain about what's *wrong* with America. Why don't they ever talk about what's *right* with the country—I mean, build it up?"

Miss Watson spoke in a clear, reassuring way. "I sometimes feel as you do," she said. "After all, it's hard to listen to criticisms and to realize that reality may not match our aspirations. Listening to all sides of an issue, weighing facts and opinions, making decisions rationally—these are tough things to do. But they're the very *foundation* of our way of life. We're fortunate that our society *respects* the right of individuals to think for themselves."

Two or three more hands were up.

"Back to the bumper sticker," Chuck said. "I don't understand what you meant before—about it being un-American and all."

"Let me explain," Miss Watson said. "The bumper sticker implies that if you *love* America, you support all policies unhesitatingly. In other words, you believe *everything* you're told. You go along with whatever authority is currently in power, regardless of your own beliefs. Above all, you don't try to change the way things are—to try to make things better. Those to me are un-American ideas."

"Well, if you put it *that* way," Chuck mumbled, "I guess you have a point."

"Peaceful protest is a basic right of citizenship," Miss Watson continued. "It helps keep our system of government reasonable and balanced. It's the avenue for *improvements* in the system."

Tonya was frowning. "But what about protestors who break the law? I mean, that isn't good, is it? You can't be a good citizen if you're breaking the law. That doesn't make sense."

Miss Watson turned to the chalkboard and put Tonya's question before the class:

Can you break the law while being a "good citizen"?

"Your question is a very important one, Tonya," she went on. "Some people, such as Henry David Thoreau and Martin Luther King, Jr., have said that breaking *bad* laws—and *accepting the consequences* for one's actions—actually expresses the highest respect for the law. In other words, under some circumstances, breaking the law might actually be a patriotic act."

The class thoughtfully considered what Miss Watson had said as she took a moment to contemplate what to say next.

Follow-up. *Can you identify the values implicit in the discussion? Can you identify points in the discussion where it might have been more helpful to the students had Miss Watson been more explicit about her values? What should Miss Watson do next to help the students identify and clarify their values as they relate to being a "good citizen"? Find out if others who are reading this book agree with your identifications of values and with your suggestions for the way in which the discussion might have been conducted and continued.*

Current Events

Problem. *Focus on the value of "fairness" as you read this section.*

A news item I read to my ninth-grade homeroom said that a white college student had been denied admission to law school because the institution had a "quota" system—a system that gave preferential admissions to minority students. The white student was suing the school because his qualifying entrance scores were higher than those of blacks who had gained admission.

"What's your reaction?" I asked.

Dick Simmons was grinning from ear to ear. "That white dude, he knows what it's like now! About time, too!"

"What do you mean?"

"Oh, you know, man! Step to the back of the bus and all that jive? So let him sweat it out."

"Well, I don't think it's *fair*," Joanie blurted out. "I mean . . ."

"*Fair!*" Dick interrupted in a half-shout. He swung round in his desk. "You gonna talk about *fair* to me? Huh? You think Whitey was talking *fairness* and all that honky crap when they sent the slave ships over? You think working blacks on the plantations was *fair*? Or breaking up the families? Or white masters screwing the black women? You think being denied the right to vote was *fair*? Or segregated housing and restaurants and schools?" Dick let the questions hang and then drove in his point. "Hey—you *owe* us—and you better get used to payin' up!"

Joe Sheridan didn't even bother to raise his hand. "Dick, you're full of it. Joanie don't owe you *nothing*. And neither do I. Nobody owes nobody—that's what I think."

Dick's sneer was cool and stylized. "Four hundred years, dig? That's what you owing blacks in this country!"

The challenge was unmistakable in Dick's voice.

"Whites can't turn back the clock and neither can blacks," I said. "That's the terrible thing about history. But it's also great, too, because it shows us how far we've really come in the past few years."

"Blacks ain't been nowhere 'cept down the river," Dick said.

"I don't know," I shrugged. "I mean, look at this news clipping we've been discussing. Why, fifteen or twenty years ago we couldn't have had this kind of talk."

Dick fell silent.

"Let's talk over this value of fairness," I added. "Maybe this kind of discussion can help us work things out for ourselves in the future."

Follow-up. *Dick and the other students who entered into the discussion seem to have different meanings for the value of "fairness." Can you identify the various definitions—such as justice, equality of opportunity, retribution—and whom they fit? Which are basic democratic values?*

How would you work with this class to help them identify and clarify their commitments and relate them to basic value labels?

Story Within a Story

Problem. *Notice how a classroom difficulty can provide the basis for value analysis.*

I looked over the scores on a science quiz I'd given my fifth graders and felt a twinge of anger. Once again there was that same strange pattern—a cluster of nearly identical scores from the back corner of the room.

"The honor system!" I thought to myself. We'd spent time at the beginning of the year talking it over, and the kids had agreed that they were "grown up" enough to handle the responsibility of taking tests without my constant supervision. Now some of them were apparently taking advantage of me.

I glanced at the classroom clock and wondered what to do. Throw out the test scores? Give the test over? Vent my anger in front of the class? Accuse the kids whose scores were suspicious? Announce that the honor system was going to be replaced by teacher monitoring?

I meditated on the alternatives for maybe a minute and then reached into my desk drawer for a ditto master. A narrative "springboard" for discussion was quickly scribbled out in longhand:

> *What Should Sue Do?*
>
> "C'mon, Sue," came the whisper. "Number four--please?"
> Sue looked down at her paper. Her mouth felt dry and tight. She could feel the stare of her best friend, who wanted help on the test.
> It isn't right, she thought to herself. It's cheating.
> "Sue--c'mon! Number four."
> Maybe just this once, Sue thought. For my best friend.
> Sue hesitated and bit her lip.

By the time my kids were in from lunch I had run off enough copies to start the discussion.

"What do you think?" I asked. "What *should* Sue do?"

Almost immediately a hand went up. "Is it an honor system?" Scott wanted to know. "I mean, is the teacher around?"

"It's an honor system," I shrugged with a smile.

"Hmmmmmm," Connie murmured. "That's a hard one. It's really her *best* friend?"

"Her best friend," I answered.

"Maybe it would be okay just once," Mark volunteered.

"But it's *cheating*," countered Simone.

"Yeah, but just once—"

"If you do it once, they'll just keep asking you," Karen blurted out.

There was a lull as the kids mulled over what Karen had said. I decided not to pursue the cause-effect question she had raised, but instead to focus on the values—honesty and friendship—at stake here.

"On the one hand, Sue wants to be honest," I said. "But she wants to have friends, too. Let's hear from some other people. Don, what do you think Sue should do?"

Don's voice was little more than a whisper. "Uhmm, I don't know." He glanced up at me, then back to his ditto sheet.

"Well, this is a pretty hard problem," I said. "And it's one we all have to work out for ourselves sooner or later. You know, I wonder if it might help if we talked for a moment about these two terms, 'honesty' and 'friendship.'"

I went to the board and wrote down the terms for the value conflict. "Okay," I nodded. "Now, how can we figure out what Sue should do—and what *we* should do if we ever find ourselves in this situation?"

Hands started going up.

Follow-up. *With somebody playing the teacher and several playing students, role-play the discussion that might follow. The "teacher" should attempt to get the "students" to define value terms, to examine the possible consequences of acting on one value or the other, and finally to state qualified decisions. After a few minutes of discussion, switch roles.*

Value Exploration 7

Reread "Inner Office Conference" on page 84. Imagine that Miss Dunning has returned to class. One of her students says, "After all the work we've done, you still haven't told us where *you* stand on this water pollution thing."

"Yeah," another chimes in. "Don't you think it's about time for a strong water pollution law?"

The students wait for an answer.

Assume that Miss Dunning has acquainted her students with the terminology and processes of value analysis that we have discussed in this chapter. She decides that it *is* time to take a stand. Explore with others the kind of *qualified statement* she might make to avoid imposing her opinion on students. In doing this, assume first that she is in favor of water pollution legislation—then that she opposes it.

Pep Assembly

Problem. *What values does Allison Hunt appear to be using to judge her pep assembly experience?*

Allison Hunt—a young, white teacher, only one month on the job—sidestepped her way to her official sentry position high on the right side of the new Wolverine grandstands. The sky was electric blue, the field an unreal green, carefully manicured for the afternoon's football contest.

Trumpets and blaring trombones crescendoed into the chorus of the school rally song as a small pack of sullen-looking youths straggled through the north gate, herded down the track by a beefy assistant principal. A squadron of paper airplanes sailed down from somewhere beneath the Dads' Club Press Box, looping gracefully over the heads of the Pep Club. Allison turned and tried to impale one whole section of Hispanic students with her iciest teacher stare. This was met with uncomprehending grins and eyebrows arched in mock innocence.

Tightening her mouth, she turned back to the Rally Squad, which was going through a zippy new dance routine. She heard snickers and giggles behind her. Three black students were making a small show of bravado in their swaggering ascent of the concrete steps.

The problem with minorities, she thought with a sigh, was their disrespect—pure and simple. It was something you could feel—just in their attitude.

The grandstand exploded in an enormous bellowing cheer, and the rally girls down on the field went wild, their lithe bodies dancing and jerking like marionettes, orange-and-blue pompons spangling the autumn air with color. The noise came in waves.

Then the crowd quieted as the student body president smoothed his school sweater, leaned forward, and blew a quick test into the microphone at the fifty-yard line, where the players and coaches were lined up. It was time for the Pledge of Allegiance. Allison stiffened her small slim back and put her hand above her left breast as she had been taught to do.

It was then she noticed that a whole section of black students in the rows below her had remained seated. The first words of the Pledge began to echo through the grandstands. The students were still sitting, erect, tight-lipped.

So now it's *this,* she thought. *Refusing* to participate—and denying their American heritage in the process. The surly attitude. Any excuse to draw attention to themselves and their "cause." So what did they want? A society without *any* kind of order and stability?

The pledge was finished, and the crowd sat down. Allison had an unmistakable bitterness in her mouth. As a teacher, she couldn't ignore what had happened today.

> **Follow-up.** Do you think Allison Hunt's concerns are legitimate? List the value judgments that Allison seemed to be making during the pep assembly. Then list the value or values underlying each. Check your lists against those of others who have read the vignette.
>
> Then consider each value. Would Allison be justified in trying to inculcate that value in her students? How about the value judgments? Would she be justified in trying to impose any of them on her students?
>
> In light of the position on values presented in Chapter 6, how might she proceed to handle the problem in class or in a faculty meeting?

After School

> **Problem.** Identify the two separate—but related—value issues in the following story based on a real incident.

Mr. Morris had just gathered up a stack of his third graders' work to correct at home when a tall, chunky man dressed in work overalls entered his classroom. His daughter, Theresa, was in tow, her eyes filled with tears.

"Theresa," Mr. Morris said. "You've been absent. I've been worried about you. I hope you're feeling better."

"That's what we come to talk about," Mr. Steel said heavily. "You sit down, Theresa."

Mr. Morris closed his briefcase. "What seems to be the problem?"

Mr. Steel cleared his throat and sat down, knitting his brows into deep furrows. "It's them kids in your class. You need to discipline 'em better." His speech was thick and labored.

"You'd better start at the beginning," Mr. Morris said. "Does this have something to do with Theresa's absence this week?"

"She don't want to come to school," Mr. Steel said. "Them kids has been teasing her again—making life real miserable. If I had my way, I'd whip some sense into the lot of them." His anger was visible.

Mr. Morris turned to Theresa. "What happened?"

The little girl simply shook her head.

"Them kids is real mean," Mr. Steel said. "Making fun of Theresa, calling her a retard and all."

"I see," Mr. Morris said. "I'm sorry to hear that, Theresa."

Theresa looked up, her eyes red and watery.

"Theresa maybe ain't the brightest girl," Mr. Steel went on. "But this discussion you had—that's what set it off."

Mr. Morris quickly thought back to an exercise he had handed out three days earlier—the last day Theresa had been in class. The activity, called "Goal Setting," had called for students to say what they saw themselves doing twenty years in the future. How had this created a problem for Theresa? he wondered.

Mr. Morris turned to Theresa. "You'll have to remind me what you put down on your value exercise," he said.

Theresa swallowed. "Just that I want to have a big family like my mom and clean the church like she does."

Mr. Morris now remembered the snickers as Theresa had volunteered her goal statement.

"Did the other kids tease you?" Mr. Morris asked.

"At recess," Theresa said, biting down on her lip.

Mr. Morris guessed right away who the ringleaders in all of this had been.

"Theresa helps her mom clean the church," Mr. Steel said. "They do a real good job."

"I'm sure they do," Mr. Morris said, turning to Theresa.

"Let me tell you," Mr. Steel added, "Theresa is a real good worker. It ain't fair for them kids to make fun of her. She can't help the way she is—handicapped, like you school folks call it."

Mr. Morris turned to Theresa. "Your value statement is very worthwhile," he said. "Your mom and dad are lucky to have a girl like you."

"That's why I come down," Mr. Steel said. "I don't want them kids to tease her no more."

"I'll take care of it," Mr. Morris said firmly. "Of course, I can't guarantee that Theresa won't be teased sometime in the future, but I can *assure* you I'll deal with *this* matter. I appreciate your coming to see me."

Mr. Steel cleared his throat again. "I just hope you make them kids behave. That ain't the proper way to act."

"Don't worry," Mr. Morris said. "I'll take care of it."

Follow-up. *What might Mr. Morris do tomorrow to deal with the problem raised by Mr. Steel's visit? How could he help all of the students in his class, as well as those he suspects of teasing Theresa and Theresa herself, to be more sensitive to the moral issues?*

What long-range steps might Mr. Morris take to help avoid such problems in the future? Should he abandon his "Goal Setting" activity and others like it?

Is Mr. Morris's responsibility to "take care of" the matter any greater because his class activity apparently precipitated the teasing? What if he simply observed the teasing on the playground?

Value Exploration 8

Turn back to "Faculty Meeting," on page 85, and reread it in light of the discussion of democratic schools in this chapter. Would you still give the same advice to the principal, Miss Wilson, about what to do about the students wearing swastika armbands? How could the treatment of those students by the principal be made a valuable lesson in democracy for the entire school?

Chapter 7

TWO OTHER APPROACHES TO MORAL VALUES

"Values clarification" and "cognitive moral development" have become familiar terms to many educators and parents in recent years. Each is the label for an approach to values that has gained widespread attention. You are likely to encounter both in preservice and inservice education activities, and ideas from both have been incorporated in many instructional materials.

In this chapter, we review the two approaches briefly and critique them from the point of view of the rationale sketched out in earlier chapters. Our intent is not to suggest that either the values clarification or the cognitive moral development approach should be rejected out of hand. Rather, we want to illustrate the kinds of questions a rationale such as the one proposed in this book may lead you to ask in making curricular and instructional decisions.

VALUES CLARIFICATION

You will recall that in Chapter 6 we emphasized the clarification of one's values as an important component of intelligent valuing. The names of Louis Raths and Sidney Simon have become associated with an approach to values which is focused on helping students to clarify their values. The "values clarification approach" was first detailed in the book *Values and Teaching*

(Raths, Harmin, & Simon, 1966). A revised edition, containing the essence of the first edition plus some additional material, was published in 1978.

Although the values clarification approach is applicable to moral values, its use is not restricted to them (see Harmin, Kirschenbaum, & Simon, 1973; Hawley, Simon, & Britton, 1973). In fact, the popularity of the approach in a variety of curriculum areas is probably due in part to its applicability to esthetic values, as well as to its emphasis on the personal concerns of students.

We believe that each person has to wrest his own values from the available array. ... [V]alues that actually penetrate living in intelligent and consistent ways are not likely to come any other way. Thus it is the process of making such decisions that concerns us. "Instead of giving young people the impression that their task is to stand a dreary watch over the ancient values," says John Gardner (1964), "we should be telling them the grim but bracing truth that it is their task to recreate those values continuously in their own time."

—Louis Raths, Merrill Harmin, Sidney Simon. *Values and Teaching*, 1966

The values clarification approach centers on the valuing process. It is concerned with techniques for stimulating students to think about and clarify their own values. Fundamentally, the strategy involves responding briefly to what the student says, usually on an individual basis, always without moralizing, and in such a way as to make the student reflect on his or her statement. The purpose is to set up situations that will encourage individuals to arrive at "values" themselves by considering their own decisions and becoming involved in "choosing, prizing, behaving" (Raths et al., 1966, Ch. 1 and 3).

The approach can be applied to all aspects of the teacher's interactions with students—casual discussions, classroom dialogue, reactions to written assignments. A central "strategy" is the "clarifying response": the teacher's reaction, orally or on written work, aimed at encouraging a student to think. Raths, Harmin, and Simon (1966, pp. 56–62; 1978, pp. 58–66) list and discuss thirty clarifying responses and present sixty-five in graphic form. Included are responses such as, "Are you glad about that?" and "How did you feel when that happened?" Ten criteria are provided for "effective" clarifying responses (Raths et al., 1966, pp. 53–54; 1978, 55–56). The first criterion stresses that it is important to avoid "moralizing, criticizing, giving values, or evaluating" and also to avoid hinting at "'good' or 'right' or 'acceptability,' or their opposites."

As well as providing guidance for interchanges with students, the values clarification approach suggests activities that teachers can use to help students clarify their values. Three chapters (Ch. 6, 7, and 8) are devoted to "additional techniques that teachers can use to get students involved in value-related discussions, thinking, and activities" (p. 82). In addition, a book by Simon, Howe, and Kirschenbaum (1972) details seventy-nine more activities, or "strategies," for initiating discussion about values.

It is difficult to review such an array of activities, but their general nature can be illustrated. One suggested activity is called "rank orders." For example, students might be asked to indicate in class whether they would rather be "wealthy, wise, or good-looking"; or to indicate, by ranking, whether they would prefer to be told directly, receive a note, or not be told that they "had bad breath." They might similarly be asked to indicate, by ranking, their preference for being "a black American, a black African, or a black Mexican" (Raths et al., 1978, pp. 150–51). Other values clarification activities include having students complete open-ended sentences, such as "My bluest days are . . .," "Secretly I wish . . .," "My advice to the world would be . . ." (pp. 162–63); having the class respond by show of hands to such items as whether "you feel lonely often, sometimes, or seldom," "How many feel strongly about some religion or religious beliefs?", "How many of you have no fathers living in your home?" (pp. 178–79).

One of the more popular and dramatic techniques is the "public interview" (Raths et al., 1978, pp. 168–175). In this activity a student volunteers to be interviewed, usually by the teacher but sometimes by his or her classmates, in front of the class. The student can choose the topic or let the interviewer do so. The student is told that he or she may refuse to answer any question by saying, "I pass," or terminate the interview at any time by saying, "Thank you for the questions." A list of questions suggested for use when the student being interviewed opts for the teacher to select the topic includes: "Are there things you would not tell even best friends? What kinds of things and why?" "Would you bring your children up differently from the way you are being brought up? How and why?" "Did you ever steal something? Recently? How come?" Teachers are admonished again to "not moralize or take issue with the student being interviewed."

The "value sheet" (Raths et al., 1978, 86–120) is another central technique. A sheet of paper with a provocative statement and a series of questions duplicated on it is given to the students. Each student completes his own value sheet in response to the questions. The responses can be used as the basis for class discussion. The suggested topics for value sheets range from personal matters, such as what is friendship, whether to try to pass a highway toll booth without paying, and how to use leisure time, to content area concerns, such as reactions to George Eliot's *Silas Marner*, quotes from Shakespeare, statements on civil rights, or statistics on international trade in military arms. Again, among the "do's and don'ts" is the avoidance of moralizing.

> There is an assumption in the value theory and the teaching strategies that grow from it that humans *can* arrive at values by an intelligent process of choosing, prizing, and behaving.
>
> —Louis Raths, Merrill Harmin, Sidney Simon. *Values and Teaching,* 1966.

There has been some research to determine the effects of the values clarification approach on students. According to Raths, Simon, and their associates, "the small amount of empirical research that has been done . . . and the large amount of practical experience . . . by thousands of teachers" (Simon, Howe, & Kirschenbaum, 1972, p. 20) indicate such positive results as students who are "less apathetic, less flighty, less conforming . . . less over-dissenting, . . . more zestful and energetic, more critical in their thinking, and . . . more likely to follow through on decisions." They also say that the approach has helped underachievers become more successful in school (Simon, Howe, & Kirschenbaum, 1972, pp. 20–21; also Raths et al., 1966, pp. 47–48, 205–229, 1978, pp. 248–49). Nevertheless, Hersh and his associates (Hersh, Miller, & Fielding, 1980) concluded, in regard to nineteen studies that had been taken to support values clarification, that "most . . . are at best vague in their results and lack the sophistication and statistically significant results required by most researchers" (p. 92). According to Lockwood (1978), studies of the values clarification approach conducted in the early 1960s "produced inconclusive results" (p. 330). He reviewed thirteen studies conducted since then and found that although they were "superior in design" to the earlier studies (p. 330), they still provided very little basis for warranted claims about the effects of values clarification (p. 344).

Some Reservations

When it comes to adopting new teaching techniques, teachers usually find the opinions of other teachers more persuasive than research evidence. And there is no question but that the values clarification approach has had a frequently enthusiastic reception by teachers. At the same time, critics (e.g., Steward, 1975, Lockwood, 1975, 1977) have raised serious questions about the approach, and you would be well advised to read what they have to say before adopting values clarification as a teaching approach.

Our intent here is not to critique the values clarification approach or to review the available critiques, although we will touch on most of the points made by the major critics. Rather, we want to consider the types of questions that ought be raised about such an approach from the perspective of a rationale such as is presented in this book. The purpose is to suggest implications for the development and use of a rationale.

In the comments that follow, we consider the approach basically as it is laid out in the book *Values and Teaching*, both the 1966 and 1978 editions which are in most respects similar. There have been efforts, especially by Howard Kirschenbaum (1977; Kirschenbaum, Harmin, Howe, & Simon, 1975), to modify and defend the values position of *Values and Teaching*. But as Hersh and his associates (1980, p. 92) have noted, the basic tenets of the approach remain intact. At the same time, it is important to recognize that different advocates take varying positions; and in actual practice, there will be diversity in use of the approach from teacher to teacher.

Defining "value." One serious reservation concerns the way in which Raths, Harmin, and Simon use the term "value," in contrast with our own definition given in Chapter 2. Indeed, it is difficult to tell what a value is to Raths and his colleagues. As we have already mentioned, Raths, Harmin, and Simon (1966) stress the *process* of valuing. So they define "value" in a special way:

> . . . [I]t would be well to reserve the term "value" for those individual beliefs, attitudes, activities, or feelings that satisfy the criteria of (1) having been freely chosen, (2) having been chosen from among alternatives, (3) having been chosen after due reflection, (4) having been prized and cherished, (5) having been publicly affirmed, (6) having been incorporated into actual behavior, and (7) having been repeated in one's life (p. 46).

At the same time, they also discuss beliefs, attitudes, and activities as "value indicators" which "approach" being values (1966, pp. 30–32; 1978, pp. 29–30).

Their definition, with its behavioral emphasis, is discrepant from the definition of "value," and the consideration of the nature of values, that we have proposed as a productive basis for building a teaching rationale. You will recall that we defined a "value" as a standard or principle by which one judges worth.[1] We stressed that values are an inevitable and integral part of one's frame of reference, developing from and shaped by each person's experiences.[2] And we noted that values are cognitive and affective (they involve concepts about which one has feelings). Finally, we pointed out that our attitudes are based partly on our values, and we also emphasized the distinction between the value judgments we make and the values that underlie those judgments.

---

[1] See Chapter 2, p. 17.
[2] Raths and his colleagues also assert that values come from experience. But from that start, they seem to conclude that values are only personal preferences, "an area that is not a matter of proof or consensus, but a matter of experience" (1978, p. 34).

From our point of view, if teachers adopt the Raths-Simon definition, there may be some unfortunate consequences. Their definition confounds values, beliefs, attitudes, activities, and feelings. It thereby obscures important distinctions with implications for teaching decisions. Moreover, the values clarification definition also obscures the distinction between emotive and cognitive meanings, and so ignores the differing functions of each. The definition also fails to distinguish between value judgments and the principles underlying them. This distinction, we have suggested, is important to making and analyzing decisions.

Moreover, the definition does not square with what is known about how our standards and principles develop. Often they are not "freely chosen" from among alternatives, after reflection, but are the unconscious result of our experience. By the same token, saying that values must be publicly affirmed is misleading. Everyone *must* have standards by which to make judgments—even though they may not have been publicly affirmed. To imply that some people lack values or may not develop them (Raths, Harmin, & Simon, 1966, e.g., pp. 42, 47, 194), which is a logical extension of the definition, is to deny this obvious fact. We could not function without values (as we have defined them), for consciously or unconsciously we are continuously applying standards and principles of worth as we make judgments. That individuals are not likely to have *explicated* their values is a legitimate matter for educational concern, as we indicated in Chapter 5. But it should not lead us to the erroneous conclusion that such persons lack values.

Values, then, may or may not have been "publicly confirmed" or "incorporated into actual behavior." Whether they are is often contingent upon opportunity. If a person has never had a given value tested, and so has never had a chance to act on it, we could not say that he or she lacked that value. We could only say that we lacked evidence as to whether the person had the value, and if so, how he or she would apply it given the opportunity.

Then, too, public confirmation of one value may run counter to one or more other values. Suppose, for example, that a high school student leader remains silent when American Indian students are denied the floor to protest during a Student Council meeting. We might question whether she really has a commitment to freedom of speech (i.e., whether it is a value in her frame of reference). However, we could not conclude that she lacked the value—even if, to our knowledge, she had never acted on it publicly. Although our doubts about her commitment would gain strength if she consistently failed to support the value publicly, we should still be cautious about concluding that she lacked it. Even though she believes in freedom of speech, she may not see its relevance in the present case. Or she may be consciously choosing to support another value.

To summarize: Given a rationale which accepts value conflict as inevitable, it is not automatically a cause for consternation when a person fails to act in accord with his or her stated values. Nor does any particular action, or lack of action, deny the presence of unstated values. At the same time, as our discussion in Chapter 6 suggests, if a student consistently acts contrary to a stated value, especially one of the basic democratic values, the teacher not only can, but should, try to help him to clarify his reasons for doing so.

To always act in accordance with all of one's values is impossible. To assume one can do so is to adopt a shallow and dangerous perspective from which to teach or to make other value-related decisions. A teacher with such a perspective will find it difficult to handle value conflicts realistically. Even worse, that teacher is likely to impose on students a value (consistency) and a value judgment (that one should always be consistent) that are unrealistic, and thus open the way for unwitting violations of values.

Which values? In our rationale, not all values and value questions are not taken to be the proper business of the school. In *Values and Teaching*, however, all values are treated as equal. No distinctions are made between moral and nonmoral values or between instrumental and intrinsic values. Indeed, the question of which values a teacher should feel free to probe appears not to be of concern. Consideration of types of values is not included as part of the process of making value-related teaching decisions. The focus instead is on topics (1966, pp. 194–96) or issues (1978, pp. 244–45) that might be the focus of clarification efforts. Equally important, suggested guidelines for selecting topics or issues do not address the matter of distinguishing between personal decisions not within the prerogative of the school and decisions about matters of societal concern. It is not that teachers are told never to deal with societal issues, but that the impression given is that such issues are not more important or no more within the school's proper domain than personal matters. So the suggested topics include such matters as rejection by friends; bad breath (1978, p. 151); whether one would rather live without parents, friends, or brothers and sisters; whether one would rather have a loving, cheerful, or famous father (p. 152); and secret wishes (p. 163).

Predictably, parents have objected (see, e.g., McGough, 1976, 1977; Bennett & Delattre, 1978) when teachers have used values clarification in their classrooms. From our view, many of the complaints are legitimate. To initiate discussion of personal decisions can frequently not be justified in terms of the school's societal role; involved are personal and middle-level moral values that many parents properly consider to be privileged matters for the home. Decisions to discuss such values in the classroom must be based on careful justfication—certainly not an easy task if the concerns of all parties are to be met adequately. Consider the continuing controversy over sex and parenting education classes, even when based on the reasoning that premarital pregnancies and early marriages are causal factors in *societal* problems (such as high divorce rates and child abuse), and thus are fit topics for schools.

But our reservations about treating such issues in the classroom involve more than the objections of parents. Also involved is a basic moral value—privacy—which can be violated too easily by values clarification activities involving personal matters. Despite the continued insistence by values clarification advocates that students are always free to "pass" during activities, we are concerned that the pressures to go along with the group and to please the teacher make it difficult for students to withhold participation. Even conscientious teachers will often be unaware of the consternation faced by reluctant students. In fact, one must ask why, on many such issues, students should be put in a position where they have to decline to participate. The personal cost can be high, and there is the potential implication that they have something to hide. Moreover, public comments made in such settings can reveal more about the individual or about others than the student will, in retrospect, wish he or she had revealed. One of the "reports from the field" by teachers using values clarification (Raths et al., 1978, Ch. 15) includes an account of a girl encouraged in a literature class to tell about being busted for smoking pot and her parents' reactions. We question the suitability of such discussions.

Interviewer: "Why do you say in the Introduction in the Handbook that in an area like relations between the sexes it's particularly unwise to encourage pupils to talk about personal experiences?"

Editor: "Because if you're in a group, the climate of a group which works together is very supportive in general. It's so supportive that people can be encouraged by this to talk about their personal lives in a way that they wouldn't like revealed to other people, and you can't guarantee confidentiality in the group. . . . When people talk in a group they can, unless they've been alerted to it, go farther then they would have wished when they reflect on it afterwards. Therefore they wish they hadn't said as much as they have said. It's quite clear also that there are cases where one person could be in a group and the other people who were involved in an experience or an incident, parents, . . ., somebody's girlfriend or boyfriend, is not in the group, and their private lives could be disclosed in a way they objected to. I think it's a matter of confidentiality really."

—Donald Hamingson (Ed.). *Towards Judgement,* 1973.

Alan Lockwood (1975) has argued that the values clarification approach with its concern for the student's emotional state and its techniques to encourage the expression of personal thoughts and feelings has much in common with psychological therapy, especially of the client-centered, Rogerian variety. We share his belief. The potential for invasion of privacy and harm to the student and to others is great when therapy-like techniques are used by nontherapist teachers in a public setting, despite the numerous admonitions in *Values and Teaching* not to embarrass students or push them to participate. And the issue of privacy is compounded by the fact that school attendance is compulsory.

"I want to be interviewed about drugs. . . . You know—like narcotics and that."

To examine potential tensions between value clarification and personal privacy, see "Jeremy and the Public Interview," page 155.

Relativism. There is an issue other than privacy involved in our criticism that the values clarification approach does not deal with the question as to which values are properly the business of teachers. In our rationale, the schools have no business supporting particular esthetic values or even personal moral values. Support of middle-level values may often be warranted, but in a context of rational justification that includes making students aware of value conflicts. Basic societal values are so fundamental to the reason for the existence of public schools that they are not only to be supported but even inculcated, with increasing attention to their rational bases as students gain in intellectual ability (see Chapter 6). And, of course, in the context of value conflict, pluralism, and respect for human dignity (see Chapter 3), teachers must accept and respect the differing decisions that students come to—as long as they are based on careful consideration of the basic values of the society. As Lockwood (1975) noted, our approach is one which rejects *both* relativism and authoritarianism.

The values clarification approach, on the other hand, has been criticized, and rightly so, for being relativistic. In answer to the criticisms, the values underlying the approach have been elucidated and their relevance to basic American values pointed out (e.g., 1978, pp. 290, 299; Kirschenbaum, 1977; Kirschenbaum et al., 1975). However, the values clarification definition of values continues to focus on the *process* of arriving at values, suggesting that if one uses the process whatever values one arrives at are all right. The definition emphasizes that values can only be arrived at personally. The suggested strategies, too, appear to promote a relativistic view—i.e., that anyone's values are as good as anyone else's as long as they are arrived at freely, prized, and acted upon. Although teachers can express their own personal values (e.g., 1978, pp. 241–42), the general tone is one of acceptance of whatever students say. As noted earlier, teachers are not to "moralize" or give advice, show distaste or support, nor act as if some values are better than others or ask the "why questions" that would force students to consider whether their positions are defensible (see, e.g., 1978, pp. 26, 34, 176, 241, 242).

Again, the failure to distinguish between types of values and levels of moral values has potential for teaching decisions which are, from the point of view of our rationale, unjustifiable. By default, all values seem to be equal in validity. How, from that perspective, can students be helped to see that some behavior is morally justifiable or reprehensible on grounds more than personal preference? How can students address questions such as one suggested by Lockwood (1977): How are the views and actions of people such as Adolf Hitler or Charles Manson, as contrasted with those of such people as Martin Luther King, Jr., or Albert Schweitzer, to be judged when all clearly fulfill the values clarification criteria for determining whether one "has a value" (see the definition on page 139)? Our rationale, we believe, speaks clearly to such judgments in the context of the society's basic values with their roots in human worth and dignity as the ultimate intrinsic value.

Raths, Harmin, and Simon do propose classroom activities that are easy to use and often of interest to students. Indeed, if selected with care, some of their activities could be used in the value identification and clarification component of moral values education discussed in Chapter 6. Your decisions about how, when, and to what extent to use the values clarification approach, however, should be based on an explicit rationale. Not just incidentally, a carefully worked out rationale will also enhance your capacity to explain and justify what you are doing to other teachers, to administrators, and, perhaps most important, to parents.

COGNITIVE DEVELOPMENT: MORAL STAGES

The "moral stages" approach of Lawrence Kohlberg is first of all a psychological theory. Implications for schooling have been drawn from the theory and from research based on the theory. The theory itself is based on Jean Piaget's seminal studies in cognitive development (see, e.g., Flavell, 1963) and on Kohlberg's own research. Kohlberg has also argued that his cognitive moral development model is not only grounded in research evidence but is philosophically sound.

Unlike the values clarification approach discussed above, Kohlberg's cognitive development approach has been the subject of innumerable papers, articles, and books. Most of the criticisms are in the technical research and philosophical literature and present difficult reading for persons without appropriate backgrounds. Kohlberg himself has written prolifically about his approach. Most of his writings are very readable, but some are quite technical. Moreover there is considerable redundancy among them, and there have been subtle changes in his position over the years.

One of the best and most recent interpretations of Kohlberg's work is that of Hersh, Paolitto, and Reimer (1979). Fortunately, their book was written with teachers in mind. Moreover, Kohlberg gave the book a high compliment: "It is the best introduction to the cognitive-developmental approach to moral education of Piaget or myself currently available" (Hersh et al., 1979, p. ix). Hersh, Miller, and Fielding (1980) also have an excellent chapter on Kohlberg's approach in their book *Models of Moral Education*. What follows on the next pages is a brief summary based on Kohlberg's writings and those of Hersh and his associates. It is meant to serve as a basis for contrasting Kohlberg's approach with our rationale.

Piaget and Cognitive Development

To understand Kohlberg's work, one must begin with the thought of Jean Piaget (see Hersh et al., 1979, Ch. 2). Piaget was trained not as a psychologist but as a naturalist and biologist (he published over twenty scientific papers on mollusks before he was twenty-one). As a biologist, he knew that organisms develop according to genetically determined patterns. Yet he found that when mollusks were moved from large lakes to small ponds, structural changes took place over several generations that could be explained only by the reduced wave action of the smaller bodies of water. From experiences such as these, Piaget concluded that development—both physical and mental—is the result of genetic maturation *and* adaptation to the environment (Wadsworth, 1979).

From Piaget's point of view, then, cognitive development takes place—frequently spontaneously and unintentionally—as the maturing mind carries out its intrinsic function of coping with the environment. The environment may be manipulated so that children will learn, but the development of thinking capacities is not due primarily to such manipulations.[3]

The significance of this view becomes particularly evident when it is contrasted with the long-standing emphasis on behaviorism in American educational psychology and the current stress on behavioral objectives and competency-based instruction. These movements identify the teacher's task as defining what students should learn and then devising the means to teach them. From Piaget's developmental view, however, the teacher's basic task is

---

[3]Note that in this sense Piaget's view corresponds to the one we expressed in the discussion of education and schooling in Chapter 4. He too sees learning as a constant, inevitable life process, not something that happens only in school or when one is "taught"; and development is inevitable unless it is thwarted in some dramatic way (Elkind, 1970, pp. 7–10).

to set up circumstances to *facilitate* the cognitive development which is more or less inevitable.

Piaget did not believe, however, that mental growth goes on helter-skelter, depending solely on the experiences that each individual happens to encounter. Mental development, he maintains, is also very much a product of the genetic structure of the brain. And because humans have similar organic structures, we can expect considerable uniformity in the mental development of different persons. In fact, Piaget proposes that predictable stages of cognitive development take place during certain periods of children's lives. (See Table 1.)

It should be noted that the limits of the age ranges in Table 1 are not rigid. Although most children will tend to move through the stages at about the ages indicated, some will move sooner and some later. Also, a person may be at more than one stage of development at one time; so a youngster may vary in level of cognitive functioning from task to task and even from time to time.

Development is accumulative according to Piaget. That is, cognitive development proceeds in the order of the periods and stages of Table 1, and the child does not skip stages. Each period is the foundation for the one that follows; and moving from one to another involves important changes in the quality of thinking. So it is not just that older children *know more;* they *think differently*.

Another important point: It is to be expected that all "normal" children will achieve the concrete operations period, although perhaps not by age seven. However, some people never attain the formal operations level of reasoning. Some data (Hersh et al., 1979, p. 37) suggest that this may be true of as much as 50 percent of the adults in our society.

Piaget's theory of cognitive development has many implications for teaching about values. Value Exploration 9, page 157, raises some questions to help you explore Piaget's relevance to values and teaching.

Kohlberg's Moral Stages

Building on Piaget's work, especially in moral development (Piaget, 1932) and on the findings from his own research, Kohlberg defined three levels of moral development—the preconventional, conventional, and postconventional levels. Each level had two stages. The three levels and six stages are presented in Table 2 (based on Kohlberg, 1968, and Kohlberg and Gilligan, 1971).

Table 1 Piaget's Periods of Cognitive Development

Sensorimotor Period* (0–2 Years)

Stage 1 (0–1 months):	Reflex actions only.
Stage 2 (1–4 months):	Hand-mouth coordination.
Stage 3 (4–8 months):	Hand-eye coordination.
Stage 4 (8–12 months):	Means-ends behavior begins. Absent objects take on permanence (child will search for articles taken out of sight).
Stage 5 (12–18 months):	Child tries out different means (experiments) to get what it wants.
Stage 6 (18–24 months):	External objects are represented in the mind; symbols are used. Child thinks out different means to get what it wants.

Preoperational Period (2–7 Years)

Problems are solved through thinking about them.

Rapid language (2–4 years) and conceptual development takes place.

Thought and language are egocentric (they reflect the child's point of view, not the views of others).

Orientation is perceptual (judgments are made in terms of how things look to the child).

Imagined or apparent and real events are confused ("magical" thinking).

Attention tends to center on one thing at a time.

Concrete Operational Period (7–11 Years)

Reversability is attained (child understands, e.g., that the volume of liquid is the same even if the shape of the container is changed).

Logical operations develop and are applied to concrete problems.

Complex verbal problems cannot be solved yet.

---

*Sometimes the word "era" is used instead of "period."

(Continued overleaf)

Table 1 continued

Formal Operations Period (11–15 Years)

All types of logical problems, including deductive hypothesis-testing, and complex verbal and hypothetical problems, can be solved.

Analysis of the validity of ways of reasoning becomes possible.

Formal thought is still egocentric in the sense that there is difficulty in squaring ideals with reality.

Source: Table adapted from Wadsworth (1979, pp. 126–127) and Kohlberg and Gilligan (1971, p. 1063).

Table 2 Kohlberg's Stages of Moral Development

Preconventional Level

Stage 1: Punishment and obedience orientation (physical consequences determine what is good or bad)

Stage 2: Instrumental relativist orientation (what satisfies one's own needs is good)

Conventional Level

Stage 3: Interpersonal concordance or "good boy-nice girl" orientation (what pleases or helps others is good)

Stage 4: "Law and order" orientation (maintaining the social order, doing one's duty is good)

Postconventional Level

Stage 5: Social contract-legalistic orientation (values agreed upon by society, including individual rights and rules for consensus, determine what is right)

Stage 6:* Universal ethical-principle orientation (what is right is a matter of conscience in accord with universal principles)

*Kohlberg has recently decided that Stage 6 may be incorporated in Stage 5. See page 150.

Insight into the meanings of the stages can be obtained from Kohlberg's own summary (1972, pp. 297–298) of the reasons people give for moral decisions. Note the differences in justification at the six different stages.

1. Obey rules to *avoid punishment*.
2. Conform to *obtain rewards*, have favors returned, and so on.
3. Conform to *avoid disapproval*, dislike by others.
4. Conform to *avoid censure* by legitimate authorities and *resultant guilt*.
5. Conform to *maintain the respect of the impartial spectator* judging *in terms of community welfare*.
6. Conform to *avoid self-condemnation* (italics ours).

Kohlberg's developmental schema clearly reflects Piaget's. As with Piaget's cognitive periods, Kohlberg assumes that movement through the moral stages always occurs in sequence and that stages are not skipped. Also, as with Piaget's formal operations period, there is no guarantee that all persons will reach the highest stage of moral reasoning. In fact, it appears likely that a majority of people may not move beyond Stage 4.

There is also a correspondence between Piaget's periods of cognitive development and Kohlberg's stages of moral development. Reaching certain intellectual levels is necessary before the moral stages can be attained. The major considerations are that the concrete operational period is a prerequisite to Stage 2, and the formal operational period must be reached before the child can move into Stage 3 moral reasoning (Hersh et al., 1979, pp. 64–65). However, reaching a logical period does not insure that moral development through the corresponding moral stages will occur. A person at the formal operations stage might still be at Stage 1 or Stage 2 morally. As with cognitive development from Piaget's point of view, moral development in Kohlberg's view depends not just on genetic maturation, but also on appropriate interaction between the individual's cognitive structure and the environment. And just as a large proportion of people appear not to reach the formal operations stage, so a large proportion probably never reach the postconvention level of moral reasoning (Hersh et al., 1979, pp. 64, 77, 102).

Kohlberg and Piaget agree, moreover, that teachers need to be aware of their students' stages of cognitive or moral development. Youngsters cannot handle problems that require thought at higher stages than they have attained. Problems more than one stage above their own level will be both incomprehensible and frustrating. However, teachers can encourage growth by presenting problems that require students to think at the stage immediately above their present one.

Kohlberg has advocated this as a teaching strategy. Students are to be presented with moral dilemma situations to discuss, and the teacher must see to it that two things happen. Each student should listen to and be involved in arguments about the situations with other students who are at the next stage of reasoning. And the teacher should support the use of higher level arguments. Experimental evidence with small numbers of children suggests (Hersh et al., 1979, pp. 107–108) that movement through the stages can be accelerated in this way.

Unlike Raths and Simon, whose approach emphasizes value neutrality, if not ethical relativity, Kohlberg clearly states that his moral stages involve "higher" moral reasoning. Reasoning becomes more complex as one moves through the stages, and more consistent as well. The Stage 6 level of conscience-based decision making assumes a conception of justice based on Kant's categorical imperative (act as you would want everyone to act in the same situation) as a "basic and universal principle" (Kohlberg, 1970a).

Kohlberg's conception of Stage 6 has been criticized as based too narrowly on justice (e.g., Peters, 1971, 1975) and as reflecting a limited view of justice which leads to an over-emphasis on the rights and interests of individuals to the exclusion of other possible universal values (see, e.g., Hall & Davis, 1975, pp. 104–106; Bennett & Delattre, 1978). Moreover, Kohlberg has been able to identify Stage 6 reasoning only in the writings of persons with philosophical training, not in his longitudinal samples. As a result, Stage 6 has been dropped from the most recent manual for scoring interviews and is currently seen as an advanced substage of Stage 5 reasoning (Kohlberg, 1978, p. 86; Muson, 1979, p. 57).

His own cross-cultural research in Malaysia, Taiwan, Mexico, and Turkey, as well as in the United States, has convinced Kohlberg (1968) that his stages (except for Stage 6) are adequate world-wide descriptions of moral development. Variations in development are, he believes, due to differences in social context that push the members of some societies toward higher levels of reasoning than others.

To Kohlberg, then, the stages are universal in two senses. They describe moral development in all societies; and movement through them represents higher, morally more adequate reasoning (see Hersh et al., pp. 83–94) in all cultures.

Can you apply Kohlberg's moral stages to the reasons that students might give for their decisions? Value Exploration 10, page 159, gives you a chance to find out.

Research based on Kohlberg's theory of moral development has not been particularly decisive. Simpson (1974) raised serious questions about the cross-cultural research evidence that Kohlberg's moral stages are universal (see

Hersh et al., 1979, Ch. 4). And Lockwood (1978, pp. 347, 358) concluded, after his review of twelve selected studies, that the discussion of moral dilemmas does appear to produce stage development, but the changes are small, not consistent for all students, and only in the Stage 2 to Stage 3 range.

Similarities

As with the values clarification approach, moral dilemma discussions are being promoted (e.g., Galbraith & Jones, 1976; Beyer, 1976) and teachers are using them, despite questions about the underlying research. However, in contrast with the values clarification approach, Kohlberg's approach has a great deal in common with the position on values which we have been developing in earlier chapters. And the similarities grow as experience in schools leads the cognitive moral development advocates to temper the theory.

Like us, Kohlberg believes that it is important to think about schooling in the context of the values of a democratic society. Initially, this led Kohlberg to argue that any attempt to instill values was inherently undemocratic, as well as philosophically and psychologically unsound. He has in recent years modified that stand (Kohlberg, 1978, pp. 84–85; Muson, 1979, p. 51), recognizing that concern with the cognitive structure of moral reasoning is not enough. Commitment to the values that underlie democratic processes and provide community stability is also vital, if the society is to survive.

Kohlberg also stresses the importance of going beyond inculcation. Like us, he and his colleagues emphasize that it is important for students to face value conflicts and to be confronted with the "why" questions that force justification of their stances on moral issues (see Hersh et al., 1979, pp. 153–54).

As noted earlier, Kohlberg no longer views Stage 6 as a separate stage of reasoning but believes that the concern for universal values may be an elaboration of Stage 5 reasoning (Kohlberg, 1978, p. 86). That change has also increased the similarity of our approaches because the conception of basic democratic values rooted in a commitment to human worth and dignity (which we have presented in Chapters 2, 3, and 6) meshes well with such an elaborated Stage 5 (see Table 2). In other words, the positions share the belief that schooling decisions ought to be made in terms of the commitments vital to a democratic society and agree that emotive commitment accompanied by the rational examination of value positions is indispensable. They also share a similar view of the appropriate frame of values that students should be helped to apply to moral societal issues.

A shift also seems to be occurring in the prime teaching suggestion emanating from the cognitive moral development approach—the dilemma discussions. The theory and research indicated that the teacher should challenge students with arguments one stage above that which they evidence in discussions of moral issues. This recommendation has been challenged on the grounds that (1) it would be difficult for teachers to assess their students' level of moral reasoning; (2) impromptu reactions at different levels would be difficult; and, (3) if the theory is correct, some students would be confused and frustrated by the higher level arguments in discussions involving groups of students at more than one stage.[4]

The emphasis on one-stage-higher teacher responses appears to be disappearing. Beyer (1976), for example, in his article on "conducting moral discussions" barely mentions it and Hersh and his associates (1979, 1980) certainly do not emphasize it. Without the requirement of one-stage-higher challenges, moral dilemma discussions seem akin to the recommendations of other educators that children confront value conflicts in discussing public issues (e.g., Oliver & Shaver, 1974). Clearly, such discussions are consistent with our recommendations for teaching moral values in the classroom.

Our position and Kohlberg's are also alike in recognizing that the school cannot properly discharge its obligations in moral education by having teachers teach an occasional lesson on values. Concern for moral issues must be integrated throughout the curriculum (see Hersh et al., 1979, ch. 6). Formal programs of instruction are needed, but they are not sufficient. Concern for democratic values must permeate the school or the "hidden curriculum" will contradict the lessons of the formal curriculum.

Recognizing the importance of the total atmosphere of the school, Kohlberg has attempted to establish "just community" schools, which have at their core the intimate involvement of students in democratic governance (see Hersh et al., 1979, ch. 7). One result of this effort has been a shift in emphasis (Kohlberg, 1978, p. 85) from personal development to the importance of group norms and expectations. So far, the just community concept has been tried only in a small number of alternative schools operating within a larger school. The concept has proven difficult to put into practice, and the results have been mixed (Muson, 1979).

Our rationale is not inconsistent with the just community approach to schooling. But our emphasis on rationale-building suggests a focus on individuals rather than institutions, even though the end sought is institutional change. It is our hope that every teacher and principal will carefully consider the basic values of a democratic society and try to guide their own behavior by those standards, recognizing that to do so will entail the continual weighing of

---

[4]For a more extensive critique of the problems involved in applying Kohlberg's developmental theory to the classroom, see Rest (1974) and Fraenkel (1976).

conflicting values (for example, the balancing of due process and the welfare of other students in dealing with students who violate school rules).

The principal told his high school students that they could not have a radical speaker because the speaker was against the government and the school was an agency of the government. If he had understood our constitutional system at the Stage 5 level, he would have recognized that the school as an agent of the government has a responsibility for communicating conceptions of individual rights which the government was created to maintain and serve. I am not arguing that the principal had a Stage 6 moral obligation to heroically defy an angry community of parents to see that a given radical speaker was heard. He was failing as a moral educator, however, if all he could transmit was Stage 4 moral messages to students, many of whom were quite likely already at a Stage 5 level.

—Lawrence Kohlberg. "The Moral Atmosphere of the School," 1970.

Kohlberg's experience confirms again how difficult institutional change is. Yet most adults can recall one or two teachers who markedly influenced them. You can significantly touch your students' lives if you teach from a rationale that consciously builds on the commitments of a democratic society. And by example, as well as by reasoned discussion, you also can influence your fellow teachers, even your principal. It seems to us that the necessary changes are more likely to occur from within, through careful reflection by teachers and administrators, than from without, through efforts to restructure the school.

Differences

Despite the similarities between our rationale and the cognitive moral development approach, there are differences. They illustrate, we believe, a contrast between using a psychological theory as the basis for schooling prescriptions and starting from a rationale that addresses the school's role in a democratic society. That contrast is illustrated in the following paragraphs.

Kohlberg's early work, which continues to influence recommendations for schooling, focused on the cognitive structure within which decisions about ethical issues are made. From our approach, the emphasis on structure casts too narrow a perspective. Kohlberg (1978) has recognized this, too, with his admonition that "the abstract concept 'moral state' [including the stimulation of moral reasoning stages through discussion] is not a sufficient basis for moral education" (p. 84).

The emphasis on cognitive moral development has, for example, tended to exclude concern with the analytic concepts which—consistent with the democratic commitment to rationality—will help students make better warranted decisions, whatever their stage of moral reasoning. As we noted in Chapter 6, having students confront value conflicts and then challenging their responses is not sufficient instruction from the point of view of a rationale in which rational decision making is valued. The students must be helped to develop strategies and skills for assessing factual claims, for dealing with the effects of language, and for weighing conflicting values. Using the moral discussion model, the teacher probes at such matters (see Hersh et al., 1979, Ch. 5) but does not provide the explicit instruction in decision making that we believe is crucial to an adequate treatment of moral values in the school.

Another difference in position has to do with the selection of topics for classroom discussion. We agree with Kohlberg that it is important to have students deal with problems that are real to them so that they can conceptualize, interpret, and become morally involved in the issues presented. But in our view, developmental psychology (or even Kohlberg's more recent sociological bent) does not speak adequately to the question of which are fit topics for classroom discussions.

From the developmental point of view, it appears that topics are acceptable if they are meaningful and of interest to the students and if they raise issues appropriate to the students' stage of reasoning. Kohlberg's approach does, in contrast with the values clarification approach, distinguish between moral and nonmoral issues, and it has no place for the discussion of the latter. But levels of moral values (see Chapter 2) seem not to be considered. The result is that the dilemmas suggested to teachers frequently center on values toward the personal end of the curriculum—for example, personal choices in regard to sexual activity—as opposed to dilemmas centered on basic societal values. As with the values clarification approach, we believe that many of the resulting discussions might be validly viewed by parents as unwarranted intrusions on their prerogative to shape their children's values and as having, as well, potential for infringement on the privacy of students. Such doubts are heightened by the contention of some parents (see, e.g., McGough, 1979) that some of the moral discussions suggested for the use of teachers—such as the survival game in which children are asked to decide who to banish from an overloaded life raft or the discussion of whether the wife of a paralyzed man should seek sex elsewhere—imply objectionable values by the very dilemmas they pose. For example, the survival game, it is argued, assumes that one has the right to make life-and-death decisions about other people.

There is no simple formula that provides unequivocal guidelines for selecting topics for classroom discussion. However, teachers ought to be aware of the ramifications of the issues they choose to treat as dilemmas, and they should be able to defend their choices in terms of the values of a democratic society. Although theories of human development should be taken into account in making teaching decisions, they alone are not an adequate basis for those decisions. Theories that attempt to describe what happens or what could happen do not provide justification for what *should* happen. Decisions about what you should do as a teacher require the careful explication and examination of values, for they provide the moral justification which facts cannot.

"You're trying to indoctrinate my son with values I don't approve of—such as dishonesty. And I'll not have it!"

An angry parent lets a teacher know that she thinks her efforts at values education have overstepped the bounds of propriety. What do you think? See "The Dilemma," p. 161.

RECAP

This chapter has presented overviews of two widely advocated and used approaches to values education, along with commentary on them. The descriptions of both approaches were only detailed enough to allow us to suggest how they might coincide with and differ from a rationale such as proposed in the prior chapters of this book. The intent was not only to suggest the types of questions that might be asked of advocates of the approaches, but to indicate the role that a rationale such as we have proposed might play in your consideration of instructional and curricular recommendations.

Clearly, the cognitive moral development approach, especially as it has evolved in recent years, is much more compatible with our rationale than is the values clarification approach. Yet, we have concerns about both. In particular, it seems important to emphasize that in contemplating any approach to value-related teaching decisions, you should not only ask whether such an approach will evoke interest in your students—although student interest is an important value for teachers—but also inquire whether, given your conception of the school's role and the nature of values in a democratic society, the approach is morally justifiable.

Jeremy and the Public Interview

Problem. Which is more important: Clarifying values or protecting the privacy of an individual student?

"One more, one more!" the kids were chanting. "C'mon, just one! Please?"

"I don't know," I said. "I don't think so."

The clamor intensified. Any second now I expected my cooperating teacher in the next pod to come bursting in to bring the class back to order.

"Okay, okay," I finally relented in a cowed whisper. "Just hold it down, huh?"

The tenth graders quieted, and I realized that I'd been holding my breath. Just like a runaway stagecoach, I thought to myself. Give the horses their head and they'll take you all over the countryside.

"Who'll do the 'public interview' next?" I asked.

"Jeremy's turn!" Liz shouted.

"Yeah, let Jeremy do it!" came another voice.

Jeremy bounded up front and took a round of applause from his audience. I reviewed the rules of the strategy for him: He could either choose the topic or have me suggest one; after we got started he could "pass" on any question he didn't want to answer; and he could terminate the interview whenever he wanted. My job, as teacher, would be to ask questions and make clarifying responses.

"I want to be interviewed about drugs," Jeremy said in a cool, worldly way. "You know—like narcotics and that."

The class began hooting and giggling. "Okay," I nodded. "Would you like to tell us what you think about drugs?"

"Yeah. Like there's a lot of it going down at this school." He grinned at a buddy.

"You think it's a problem, then?"

"Yeah, you could say that. I mean, you start fooling around with some of that junk and it scrambles the circuitry upstairs."

"Well, how many kids do you think are using drugs regularly as opposed to experimentally?"

"Some of both." Jeremy winked. "But mostly just messing around. I guess. Like, you know, grass and pills—stuff like that."

"What's behind this experimentation?"

Jeremy hesitated and his mood seemed to grow a shade quieter. "I don't know," he said slowly. "Something to do, I guess—just being in with the guys. Or maybe just to see what's it like. Or to get back at your old man and old lady. There could be a hundred different reasons."

"That makes sense."

"I mean, maybe you're at this party and somebody starts a joint moving around. It's pretty hard to pass it up when everybody's watching."

"So it starts innocently enough," I said. "But—"

"But then they expect you to smoke after that," Jeremy said. "Whether you want to or not."

My throat was dry and tense. "That could be a pretty tough problem," I said.

"Yeah."

"I'm not entirely sure of your attitude toward drugs," I said. "On the one hand, you seem to take a kind of cavalier attitude. But you also seem to regard the drug scene as a really serious problem—"

"Well, some of that stuff can really screw up your head," Jeremy interrupted. "I mean, so you can't think straight, you know?" The classroom was utterly quiet.

"We're running short of time," I said. "Maybe we'd better wind this up."

"I remember this one time that me and Andy Elliott and some other guys—Cleaver and Butch—"

"Jeremy, I'd like to conclude this interview."

"Cleaver was really flipped out. I mean, like it was *really* a bad trip. Anyhow, the awful part was—"

Dave Cleaver lunged out of his desk and through the open classroom door. The sound of his running echoed down the hall.

Follow-up. *Certainly not all value clarification episodes end in this traumatic way. We have selected an extreme example to raise questions in your mind such as the following: (1) What topics, when used in value clarification exercises, are particularly likely to lead to violations of personal privacy? (2) Can you identify any criteria based on your rationale that would assist you in selecting appropriate topics for value clarification? (3) What sorts of basic understanding should there be between teacher and class before engaging in value clarification work?*

Considering the specifics of this case: How would you have responded when Jeremy said he wanted to be interviewed about drugs? Is there any point in the story where you would have directed the discussion in a different way? If you were the teacher conducting the class, what would you do now about Dave Cleaver?

Value Exploration 9

In Chapter 6, we discussed several aspects of moral values education. Now we want to raise some questions about how your students' cognitive development might affect the ways you teach the various aspects of valuing. Table 1, page 147, should provide you with helpful guidelines in considering your answers.

Preoperational Children

If you are in early childhood education or elementary, which of the valuing aspects do you think can be dealt with at the two-to-seven-year age level? For example:

> Are children in this age range likely to be using "fairness" as an implicit standard for judging behavior?
> Could incidents on the playground and/or in the classroom be used to develop a concept of "fairness"?
> Could children be helped to use labels such as "equality of opportunity" at this age level?
> Can the term "value," as defined in this book, be meaningfully introduced to children at this age? Can it be illustrated by reference to the standards they use implicitly or explicitly in their play and work?

Concrete Operational Students

Using your own experiences with children in the seven-to-eleven age spread, and through discussions with others who may have had more experience, what can be done with values during this period? Can you identify problems of esthetics, instrumental values, and ethics that students at this age level deal with in their own lives (maybe by interviewing some students)?[5]

What do you think of the suggestion that the child's life is to a large extent a microcosm of the larger society, and that the value choices that occur "out there"—in regard to such matters as respecting the rights of others, relating to authority, allocating scarce resources, to name a few—occur in simplified form in the child's encounters in the home, at school, and on the street? If so, does that suggest that these situations could be used as the basis for preparing the student to deal with values in broader, more abstract situations as he or she moves into the formal operations period?

Formal Operational Students

Remember that current findings suggest that perhaps as much as 40 percent of the population never reach the formal operations stage. Consider such questions as the following:

---

[5]You may want to examine materials prepared to engage students at this age level in the consideration of value conflicts through role-playing. See, for example, the book by F. R. Shaftel and G. Shaftel (1967), as well as their film strips (1970) and films (n.d.). You may also want to examine value conflict materials prepared by Kohlberg and Selman (1972–73) and by Fenton and Kohlberg (1979).

TWO OTHER APPROACHES TO MORAL VALUES   159

How much can you expect to accomplish in teaching rational valuing at this developmental level?

What do the differences between the concrete and formal operations stages suggest about why students vary in their enthusiasm for dealing with problems, such as social issues, on a nonpersonal level?

How can you use the student's own daily life experiences to help him relate to broader problems? For example, can students fruitfully examine the ways in which their encounters with the school principal are similar to adult encounters with government in regard to such values as due process of law, freedom of speech, the right to personal privacy? (See, for example, Knight, 1974.)

The multitude of considerations raised above might best be approached as a brainstorming effort shared by you with other readers of this book. In addition, you might find it helpful to have on hand a very readable discussion of Piaget's theory, such as Wadsworth (1979), *Piaget's Theory of Cognitive Development*, or Hersh et al. (1979), *Promoting Moral Growth—From Piaget to Kohlberg*.

Value Exploration 10

Reread "Story Within a Story," page 129. Set forth in the following table are some reasons that children might give for their decisions about what Sue should do. Indicate what stage of moral development you think each statement illustrates and the age at which such reasoning could first occur (according to Piaget's periods of cognitive development).

Response (Sue should . . .)	Reason	Moral Stage	Age of Possible First Occurrence
1. help	. . . because her classmate will take it out on her somehow (hit her, keep her out of friendship groups) if she doesn't.	1	2
2. not help	. . . because the rules of the school must be followed or who knows what will happen.		
3. help	. . . because her classmate will do something for her in return.		

(Continued overleaf)

Response (Sue should . . .)	Reason	Moral Stage	Age of Possible First Occurrence
4. not help	. . . because people agree that cheating is not good, and she feels an obligation to do what most people judge is right—partly to gain their respect.		
5. help	. . . because the person asking for help comes from a poor family, must work, doesn't have enough time to study; and she'd surely lose the respect of other people if she didn't help such a person.		
6. not help	. . . because her friends (or more likely, teachers or parents) would think she was being bad.		
7. not help	. . . because the teacher will punish her if she gets caught.		
8. help	. . . because her friends won't think she's a good kid if she doesn't.		
9. not help	. . . because she can't see how doing so will help herself at all.		
10. help	. . . because following the rules of her "gang" is very important, and giving help to anyone in trouble at school is one of those rules.		

After you've made your choices, look at "Our Decisions," on the next page, to see how we think the reasons should be categorized. Any differences between your decisions and ours, or between your decisions and those of other people who do this value exploration, would be a good basis for a discussion to clarify your thinking about Kohlberg's and Piaget's theories.

Our Decisions

Example Number	Moral Stage	Age of Possible First Occurrence
1	1	2
2	4	11
3	2	7
4	5	11
5	5	11
6	3	11
7	1	2
8	3	11
9	2	7
10	4	11

Using the situations in other vignettes (for example, the decisions facing Miss Dunning in the "Inner Office Conference," page 84, and in Value Exploration 7, page 131), can you construct the reasoning for "pro" and "con" decisions that might be used at different moral stages?

Also, reread "Civil Disobedience," page 126, and try to discern the levels of moral reasoning used by the different students.

The Dilemma

Problem. *Is this teacher violating a parent's right to shape her child's values?*

Shirley Bowes drove through the deepening dusk, thinking again about her phone call from Mrs. Roth. How insistent she had been that Mrs. Bowes was indoctrinating her seventh-grade son, Glen, with values that went against his home training.

Shirley jumped at the sound of a car horn. "My heavens," she thought. "I ran a stop light. I'd better forget my school problems for now."

But her thoughts wandered back to Mrs. Roth. *She was angry!*—over a simple discussion of a dilemma Mrs. Bowes had posed for her seventh-grade class. It involved a high school English teacher who had caught a student cheating on a test. Ordinarily, that meant an F—and for this student, the result would be an F in the course. But this wasn't just *any* student. It was the star center on the basketball team—due to go to the state tournament next week, but without the star if he failed his English course. The coach and the principal had informed the teacher of that in the principal's office later in the day.

"What," Mrs. Bowes had asked her students, "should the teacher do? Fail the star center or overlook the cheating so that he would get a passing, even if low, grade?"

She had explained to Mrs. Roth that these sorts of dilemmas come up in life, and it's important that students learn to reason about them.

But Mrs. Roth had been adamant. "That situation does *not* present a dilemma! Cheating is *wrong.*" In fact, she had punished Glen for cheating while playing a card game with his sister just last week. Now, she had fumed, Mrs. Bowes was teaching that cheating may be okay.

"But, Mrs. Roth," Mrs. Bowes had pleaded, "people do have to make such decisions."

"Certainly," Mrs. Roth replied, "and sometimes they'll do the *wrong* thing and reward dishonesty. But when you tell my son that there really is a choice involved, and imply that it might be morally all right not to fail a cheater because he's a star basketball player . . .," her voice had risen, "well, that simply teaches him a value that I don't want him to learn!"

A touch of the brakes, a quick turn of the wheel, and Shirley was in her driveway. She shut off the key and sat quietly. "How can I convince Mrs. Roth that children must be helped to deal with such dilemmas—that they can handle value conflicts, if they are helped to do so?"

Follow-up. *Would you be more likely to side with Mrs. Roth or Mrs. Bowes? If you agree with Mrs. Roth that the discussion of the English teacher's "dilemma" was inappropriate, pretend that you are a teacher in the same school to whom Shirley Bowes has come with her problem. If you agree with Mrs. Bowes, pretend that you are in her place and must call Mrs. Roth the next day to try to resolve her complaint. In each case, use the ideas about values and democracy discussed in this book to decide what to say, and then try it out on another reader of the book.*

What if the dilemma situation to which Mrs. Roth objected involved a young woman (unmarried or married) trying to decide whether to have an abortion? What if it involved an eighteen-year-old deciding whether to register for the draft? What values might be objectionable to Mrs. Roth, or some other parent? Would your position be the same as on the "English teacher" dilemma?

Chapter 8

EPILOGUE: THE TEACHER AS PHILOSOPHER

Clearly, our "model teacher" is inclined to reflect on the assumptions—in particular, the value assumptions—that underlie his or her decisions about students, whether in or out of the classroom. In other words, we would like rationale-building—the explication and examination of reasons, including their interrelations and their implications—to be a persistent concern of each teacher.

Hersh and his associates (1980) reviewed our rationale-building approach as one of the six "main approaches to moral education currently in operation in the American public schools" (p. 8). They commented, aptly, that the "fundamental purpose [of *Facing Value Decisions*] is to sharpen teachers' understanding of the moral basis of teaching" (p. 26). In that sense, they noted, our approach "speaks to the core concerns of all models of moral education." It "seeks to help teachers understand the way values in general and moral values in particular affect [teaching] decisions . . . [and] is especially sensitive to the pressures and risks that teachers face in confronting moral questions in the classroom" (p. 8). And, finally, Hersh and his coauthors observed that our "primary concern is with the realm of judging . . ., [with] teachers' moral decision making" (p. 8), with "the *teacher as philosopher*" (p. 26, italics ours).

The exploration of values which we advocate in this book *is* very much akin to philosphy. In fact, we would like teachers to think of themselves as philosophers—persons given to the careful analysis and statement of reasons. We have, however, hesitated to use that terminology earlier in the book for fear that it might create the false impression that our goal was academic sophistication, rather than simply more thoughtful value-related teaching decisions.

Is it presumptuous to speak of teachers as philosophers? Some may say so, and even contend that our use of the term to describe the rationale-building efforts of teachers engaged in the hectic demands of the classroom and school is an unfortunate distention of the meaning of "philosopher." We do not agree, nor did one well-known philosopher, John Dewey.

Dewey refused to view educational philosophy as a "poor relation" of general philosophy. Instead, he saw it as "ultimately the most significant phase of philosophy" (Dewey 1964d, p. 16). Dewey was neither negative nor condescending toward the philosophical efforts of teachers or administrators who might lack the time, resources, or even the intellectual acumen to match his own depth of thought. Indeed, he rejected the idea of "any inherent sacredness in what is called philosophy," and argued that "any effort to clarify the ends to be attained is, as far as it goes, philosophical." Efforts at clarification were crucial to Dewey, because education not based on a "well-thought-out philosophy," he argued, is likely to be "conducted blindly, under the control of customs and traditions that have not been examined or in response to immediate social pressures" (1964d, p. 17). (Or, as Beard, 1934, put it, teaching based on an unexamined frame of reference will likely be guided by "small, provincial, local, class, group, or personal prejudices," p. 182.)

Dewey emphasized that philosophy—rationale-building—is not an exercise to be completed prior to teaching. In fact, he called on teachers and administrators to "test and develop [ideas] in their actual work so that through union of theory and practice, the philosophy of education will be a living, growing thing" (1964d, p. 18). This emphasis on intertwining work and thought is consistent with Dewey's general view of how thinking and, consequently, learning occur.

Reflective thinking arises out of one's own direct experiences (Dewey, 1933, p. 99), and it is through experience-based thought that we learn. Dewey believed that (1916):

> No thought, no idea, can possibly be conveyed as an idea from one person to another. When it is told, it is, to the one to whom it is told, another given fact, not an idea. The communication may stimulate the other person to realize the questions for himself and to think out a like idea, or it may smother his intellectual interest and suppress his dawning effort at thought. (p. 159)

To Dewey, then, each person must wrestle with self-recognized problems, and seek and find their own solutions, to think and learn (p. 160).

The implications are clear, and consistent with the intent of this book. No one can *give you* a rationale for teaching. You must develop your own, if you are to have one. That is, you must be your own philosopher. Although others can stimulate your thinking (as we hope to have done with this book), your own rationale can only develop validly as a result of the thinking stimulated by your own teaching experiences, as an outcome of your own efforts to make sense of life. And, of course, your efforts at rationale-building are anything but trivial, for they will influence what happens to the many students whom you encounter daily.

A LIFELONG COMMITMENT

It should be clear from the above discussion that the goal is not a tightly structured, unchallengeable philosophical position, but continuing reflection and, as necessary, adaptation. As Dewey (1964d) noted, it is important that your "philosophy of education be a living, growing thing" (p. 18). Your rationale will hopefully become more comprehensive, better substantiated, its parts more clearly formulated and the logical relationships among them more clearly perceived, and its implications for teaching better understood. But you ought never to consider your rationale as complete and final, for that would mean that you had stopped responding to and learning from experience. Most of us would likely agree with Dewey (1964c) that "a truly healthy person is not something fixed and completed" (p. 4). And the same is true of a rationale. If ossified, it will become dysfunctional.

In a real sense, rationale-building can be likened to education, an analogy that should be attractive to teachers. You may recall that in Chapter 4, we referred to education as life, "a continuous process of reacting and adapting to experience—that is, learning" (p. 72). We agree with Dewey (1964c) that what is important about education is not a product, but the "process of development, of growth" (p. 4). Education is the "continuing reconstruction of experience" (Dewey, 1964b, p. 434). So is rationale-building. In a real sense, then, rationale-building is a conscious continuation of your education, vital to your personal and professional growth.

PHILOSOPHY AS ACTION

Personal and professional growth are for many teachers ends in themselves, terminal values. But when growth is sought *only* for its own sake, the result can be counterproductive—as, for example, when teachers take university courses to learn more and more about their content areas, but pay little attention to whether the increased knowledge helps them to produce greater interest or learning in the classroom.

Absorption in "doing philosophy" can also be dysfunctional. A person can become overly engrossed in the development of reasons, with primary satisfaction coming from the process of reasoning rather than from its influence on his or her teaching. Our interest is not in intellectualization as a terminal value, but in the effects on teachers' day-to-day behavior of diligent, thorough thought about reasons.

Dewey spoke of joining theory and practice through the "on-the-job" development and testing of ideas. Certainly, your classroom experiences will be one vital basis for developing and testing your value assumptions. If, for example, you note unrest and lack of interest among your students, that should provide an impetus to re-examine the premises from which you teach. Equally important, that inquiry should bear some relationship to your teaching behavior, whether it leads to a decision to change or a reaffirmation of what you have been doing. After reflection, you might conclude, as an English or social studies teacher, that learning to organize and express thoughts on complex matters through the exactness called for in written expression is so important that you will continue to assign lengthy essays, despite student protests that they are too time-consuming. On the other hand, what if you recognize that your tendency to call on boys more than girls in your mathematics classes and to devalue girls' responses more frequently than boys' (as research shows teachers frequently do) clashes with your commitment to equal opportunity? This awareness could result in significant changes in your classroom behavior. It is in this sense that we refer to philosophy as action: Thought about values should influence your behavior, just as your experiences should stimulate your thinking about values.

WHY FOCUS ON VALUES, NOT ATTITUDES?

We have emphasized in earlier chapters that values are the essential ingredient in defining a democratic society. In particular, the core values of the society are recognized as basic in debating and judging public policy and in making judgments about the morality of intents and actions toward one's fellow citizens. It can be argued that certain attitudes—for example, discriminating attitudes toward minority groups—are nondemocratic because they are opposed to basic values. But note that attitudes are judged against values, not vice versa. And a rationale that is to be securely founded on an adequate conception of a democratic society must start from fundamental commitments, from values, not from attitudes.

In a personal sense, too, values are more primary than attitudes. As noted in Chapter 2, Rokeach (1973) has pointed out that we have literally thousands of attitudes but only several dozen values. We have, of course, an even fewer number of moral values, and a small number of basic moral values. As a teacher, you will have attitudes toward a great variety of things—school, subject matter, approaches to discipline, teaching methods, types of homework assignments, lunchroom and other extra-classroom duties, boys, girls, ethnic groups, athletes, cheerleaders, specific boys and girls, and on and on. But you will have a much more limited number of relevant values. So, if you focus on values rather than attitudes in rationale-building, the task of articulation and analysis is much simpler, at least quantitatively.

But a more fundamental reason for centering on values is that they are major determinants of our attitudes, not vice versa, and so merit prior attention. In fact, there is evidence that getting people to reflect on their values can influence not only their attitudes but their behavior.

Rokeach (1973, Ch. 8) has theorized that when individuals are dissatisfied with their values, they will change those values and, as a result, their attitudes and behavior. He has developed an experimental method for inducing self-dissatisfaction (Ch. 9). People are asked to rank two sets of values (typically, the eighteen "instrumental" and eighteen "terminal" values[1] on a Value Survey). Then, the experimenter provides information on how others have ranked the values and interprets the rankings.

For example, in research with students at Michigan State University, the experimenter pointed out that previously gathered data indicated that freedom was ranked before equality by Michigan State students. That finding was interpreted to mean that "MSU students in general are much more interested in their own freedom than they are in freedom for other people" (p. 237). The students were then asked to take a stand on civil rights demonstrations (whether they were sympathetic participants, sympathetic nonparticipants, or unsympathetic), and additional data were presented on MSU students' civil rights stands. The data were interpreted as raising a question as to whether "those who are *against* civil rights are really saying that they care a great deal about *their* own freedom but are indifferent to other people's freedom" (p. 238, italics in original).

Rokeach found (1973, Chs. 10 and 11) that students who were exposed to his self-dissatisfaction treatment later ranked both equality and freedom higher than previously. The increases were greater than those for a "control group" of students who had not received the treatment. Moreover, the experimental students also tended to shift toward more favorable attitudes

---

[1] You may recall that in Chapter 2 (p. 28), we took issue with Rokeach's definitions of instrumental and terminal values. It should also be noted that in listing values, he does not distinguish between moral and nonmoral values or between levels of moral values. Consequently, we do not see his conceptualization as adequate for use in the analytic activities of rationale-building, although it is suitable as a basis for research investigating value change and its relations to attitudes and behavior.

toward blacks (interestingly, there was a "sleeper" effect—changes didn't show up until three to five months later). The experimental students also showed a greater tendency to respond to membership solicitations by the NAACP and to register in ethnic relations core courses.

Several studies have indicated that self-dissatisfaction can lead not only to changes in values but to long-term changes in behavior in a variety of areas. The research most pertinent to this book was done by Greenstein (1976). Building on Rokeach's earlier findings, he attempted to create self-dissatisfaction (which he called "self-confrontation") in teacher education students. During the first week of their student teaching, he had the experimental students compare their rankings of values with the rankings of "good" and "mediocre" teachers (those who scored in the highest and lowest 10 percent on a "behavioral measure of teaching ability"). In particular, the students' attention was drawn to the fact that the good teachers ranked the value "mature love" above "a sense of accomplishment," while the mediocre teachers ranked the two values in reverse order. Thirteen weeks after this self-dissatisfaction treatment, the experimental students ranked the value "mature love" higher than did control students, although there had not been a difference on the pretest. (There was no difference on either test for "sense of accomplishment.") A more important finding came from the student teaching evaluations completed routinely by the students' supervisors, who were unaware of the research project. On the average, the experimental students were judged to be better teachers.

Rokeach's and Greenstein's studies, then, help to answer the question, Why focus on values? Potentially, the payoff is great. The conscious articulation, consideration, and testing of values as they apply to the classroom and school setting can help to insure that your teaching behavior is consistent with basic democratic values.

THE CULTIVATION OF SELF-CONFRONTATION

In the research based on Rokeach's ideas, self-dissatisfaction has been induced via experimental treatment. However, self-dissatisfaction does not have to be brought about by someone else—which is why we like Greenstein's use of the term "self-confrontation." Dewey (1933, pp. 13–15) emphasized that reflective thinking arises when a person's experiences leave her or him perplexed, confused, in doubt. And those states are likely to occur when one is open-minded—not in the sense of "empty-headed," but willing to recognize problems, including the possibility of one's own error, and to actively seek out and consider alternatives. If you are conscious of your frame of reference, of the influence of values on your behavior, and of the pervasiveness of value-related teaching decisions, you are more likely to engage in self-confrontation about your values.

Many daily teaching occurrences can be sloughed off as unimportant incidents, examples of lack of student self-discipline, or simply inevitable student complaints about school. After all, students frequently complain that subject matter is uninteresting, assignments too difficult, and rules for conduct too severe. But these complaints and incidents can be signals for self-confrontation, for reexamination of assumptions, for continued growth, personally and professionally. For some, the results may be as radical as they were for Eliot Wigginton (1972).

With an A.B. in English and an M.A. in Teaching from Cornell, Wigginton began teaching ninth- and tenth-grade English and geography in a small, rural Georgia school. After six weeks of teaching he sat back to "survey the wreckage." His lectern had been scorched by a student's cigarette lighter during class. The desks were covered with graffiti. His chalk and "the thumbtacks that held up the chart of the Globe Theatre" were gone—along with the nine water pistols he had confiscated that same day. His thoughts at that point demonstrate that values are at the pith of teaching decisions and that self-confrontation can have powerful effects:

> It was with a deep sigh that, as I launched one of several paper airplanes within easy reach, I began to ponder greener pastures. Either that or start all over.
>
> The answer was obvious. If I were to finish out the year honorably, it would be necessary to reassert my authority. No teenagers were going to push me around. Besides, my course was too important. First offense would be an "X" in the grade book. Second, a paddling. Third, to the principal. Fourth, out of class for two weeks.
>
> It frightens me to think how close I came to making another stupid mistake. First, I had bored them unmercifully. Now I was about to impose a welcome punishment. Two weeks out of that class would have been more pleasure than pain.
>
> Those who cannot remember the past not only relive it; they tend to impose it, mistakes and all, on others. My own high school—monumentally boring texts and lectures, all forgotten; punishments and regulations and slights that only filled a reservoir of bitterness; and three blessed teachers who let me make things, helped me make them, and praised the results.
>
> Luckily, it took only a few rewards to keep me going. How many students were denied even those few scraps of self-esteem from anyone other than their peers? And how many was I now denying?
>
> I am not sure what the magic formula is or whether I have it pegged yet, but it involves a chemistry that allows us to believe we may have worth after all. Someone says, "You've done well," and we hunger to make that happen again and again. Too often we, as teachers, slip, and that first flush of success our students get comes after they've survived a night of drinking Colt 45, stuck up the local gas station, or taken two tabs of acid and made it out the other side alive.

We could catch some of those if we would.

The next day I walked into class and said, "How would you like to throw away the text and start a magazine?" And that's how *Foxfire* began. (Wigginton, 1972, p. 10)

From that point on, the central activity in Wigginton's classes—with the idea of involving everyone—was the production of *Foxfire* magazine, devoted to local folklore.

What values were involved in Wigginton's self-confrontation? As we "listen to him speak," we discern at least three—all prevalent among teachers. There was authority—which he was going to reassert; self-pride—no teenagers were going to push him around; subject matter—his course was what was important. And, then, there was reflection—remembering the past and using that knowledge to shape the present; and there was self-esteem—which had been so elemental to his own development. Re-evaluation of the relative importance of these values provided the catalyst for change.

Most of us will not be able to make such dramatic changes in our teaching. Clearly, Wigginton had special talents that made the *Foxfire* magazine project viable. And he had strong support from his school and community, as he recognizes in the Acknowledgments to *The Foxfire Book*. But we should not allow awareness of those perhaps exceptional factors to obscure the gist of his message. Most, probably all, teachers face a similar sense of frustration, even failure, at some time. If the signals of student distress can be received and used as the basis for personal value analysis, rather than ignored or discounted, even subtle teaching changes can have rather striking effects on your students' lives and on yours.

Reflection Without Crisis

The perplexity that can lead to self-confrontation does not have to be the result of crisis, such as a disintegrating classroom. Being reflective can be a standard part of your *modus operandi*, if you are conscious of your values and the ways in which what you do may contradict them. For example, reflectiveness and rationality are values that apply to what and how you teach students as well as to your reactions to what happens in the classroom. Self-confrontation might start by asking if you are committed to those values and, if so, what are the implications for teaching. Do you (or will you), for example, include conscious instruction in decision-making concepts and skills in your courses?

Every course is loaded with opportunities to help students develop more adequate thinking—whether logic in English, the analysis of public issues in social studies, scientific inquiry in science and social science, or personal decision making in health courses. And, as we suggested in Chapter 5, classroom and school rules and their enforcement can, and should, be focal points for modeling and encouraging reasoning. Based on personal public school teaching experience, we can say that students are both surprised and pleased when they are taught thinking skills and involved in decision making—even if it is no more than the sharing of reasons for decisions that the teacher must make.

What of other values? If equality of opportunity is important to you, what are the implications for your interactions with students who are likely to be ignored—those from lower socio-economic families, those who demonstrate less of the type of "intelligence" needed to do well on abstract school tasks, those from ethnic minority groups? Interestingly, Anyon (1980) has gathered evidence that supports the claim that the work students are asked to do differs markedly according to their predominant socio-economic status. Assignments for working class students seemed to be aimed at following directions with little decision making or choice; in a middle-class school, the work appeared to be aimed at getting the right answers, with figuring and choosing somewhat important; for a school in an affluent professional area, creative activity carried out independently was the dominant mode of student work; and in a school where the students were largely the children of elite executives, developing analytic intellectual powers—reasoning and understanding—was at the center of school work. Anyon's findings are tentative but certainly provocative for rationale-building. Do your interactions with students reflect different career expectations based on your knowledge of their families' current socio-economic status? If so, is equality of opportunity being served?

We could go on laying out examples of value exploration. But, as we have emphasized in our references to Dewey in this chapter, we cannot *give* you a rationale. Each of us must reason out our own. The results can exert a powerful influence on your teaching—and on the learning of your students. Clearly, facing value decisions is not idle speculation, but thought that affects action.

References

Anyon, J. Social class and the hidden curriculum of work. *Journal of Education*, 1980, *162*, 67–92.

Beard, C. A. *The nature of the social sciences*. New York: Charles Scribner's Sons, 1934.

Bennett, W. J., & Delattre, E. J. Moral education in the schools. *The Public Interest*, 1978, *50*, 81–98.

Beyers, B. K. Conducting moral discussions in the classroom. *Social Education*, 1976, *40*, 194–202.

Bloom, B. A. (Ed.). *Taxonomy of educational objectives: Cognitive domain*. New York: Longmans, Green and Company, 1956.

Bowe, F. *Rehabilitating America: Toward independence for disabled and elderly people*. New York: Harper & Row, 1980.

Bronowski, J. *The identity of man*. Garden City, NY: The Natural History Press, 1965.

Broudy, H. S. *Enlightened cherishing: An essay on aesthetic education*. Urbana, IL: University of Illinois Press, 1972.

Brown v. Board of Education of Topeka. 347 U.S. 483 (1954).

Butts, R. F. *Public education in the United States: From revolution to reform*. New York: Holt, Rinehart and Winston, 1978.

Butts, R. F. *The revival of civic learning*. Bloomington, IN: Phi Delta Kappa Educational Foundation, 1980.

Clement, D. C., & Johnson, P. A. The cultural deprivation perspective. In G. P. Nimnicht & J. A. Johnson, Jr. (Eds.), *Beyond "compensatory education": A new approach to educating children*. San Francisco: Far West Laboratory for Educational Research and Development, 1973.

Combs, A. W. Educational accountability from a humanistic perspective. *Educational Researcher*, 1973, 2(9), 19–21.

Coombs, J. R., & Meux, M. O. Teaching strategies for value analysis. In L. E. Metcalf (Ed.), *Values education: Rationale, strategies, and procedures*, 41st Yearbook, National Council for the Social Studies. Washington, D.C.: National Council for the Social Studies, 1971.

Dahl, R. A. Decision making in a democracy: The role of the Supreme Court as a national policy-maker. *Journal of Public Law*, 1958, 6, 279–95.

Dewey, J. *Moral principles in education*. Carbondale, IL: Southern Illinois University Press, 1909.

Dewey, J. *Democracy and education: An introduction to the philosophy of education*. New York: Macmillan, 1916 (paperback, 1961).

Dewey, J. *How we think*. Boston: D.C. Heath, 1933.

Dewey, J. Individuality and experience. In R. D. Archambault (Ed.), *John Dewey on education: Selected writings*. New York: Random House, 1964. (a)

Dewey, J. My pedagogic creed. In R. D. Archambault (Ed.), *John Dewey on education: Selected writings*. New York: Random House, 1964. (b)

Dewey, J. Need for a philosophy of education. In R. D. Archambault (Ed.), *John Dewey on education: Selected writings*. New York: Random House, 1964. (c)

Dewey J. The relation of science and philosophy as a basis for education. In R. D. Archambault (Ed.), *John Dewey on education: Selected writings*. New York: Random House, 1964. (d)

Edel, M., & Edel, A. *Anthropology and ethics* (2nd ed.). Cleveland: Case Western University Press, 1968.

Elkind, D. *Children and adolescents: Interpretive essays on Jean Piaget*. New York: Oxford University Press, 1970.

Engel v. Vitale. 370 U.S. 421 (1962).

Fenton, E., & Kohlberg, L. *Values in a democracy*. Sound filmstrip series. Pleasantville, NY: Guidance Associates, 1979.

Fields, C. M. Supreme Court hears arguments in minority-admissions case. *The Chronicle of Higher Education*, 1974, 8(22), 1, 8.

Flavell, J. H. *The developmental psychology of Jean Piaget*. Princeton, NJ: D. Van Nostrand Company, 1963.

Fraenkel, J. R. The Kohlberg bandwagon: Some reservations. *Social Education*, 1976, 40, 216–22.

Fraenkel, J. R. *Helping students to think and value: Strategies for teaching social studies* (2nd ed.). Englewood Cliffs, NJ: Prentice-Hall, 1980.

Frankena, W. K. *Ethics* (2nd ed.). Englewood Cliffs, NJ: Prentice-Hall, 1973.

REFERENCES

Galbraith, R. E., & Jones, M. *Moral reasoning: A teaching handbook for adapting Kohlberg to the classroom*. Minneapolis: Greenhaven Press, 1976.

Gallup, G. H. The 12th annual Gallup poll of the public's attitudes toward the public schools. *Phi Delta Kappan*, September 1980, 33–46.

Gibran, K. *The prophet*. New York: Alfred A. Knopf, 1923.

Gillespie, J. A., & Patrick, J. J. *Comparing political experiences*. Washington, D.C.: The American Political Science Association, 1974.

Glasser, W. *Schools without failure*. New York: Harper & Row, 1969.

Goss v. Lopez, 42 L.Ed. (2d.) 725 (1975).

Greenstein, T. Behavior change through value self-confrontation: A field experiment. *Journal of Personality and Social Psychology*, 1976, *34*, 254–262.

Guralnik, D. B. (Ed.). *Webster's new world dictionary* (2nd ed.). New York: World, 1972.

Hall, R. I., & Davis, J. U. *Moral education in theory and practice*. Buffalo, NY: Prometheus Books, 1975.

Hamingson, D. (Ed.). *Towards judgement*. University of East Anglia, England: Centre for Applied Research in Education, 1973.

Harmin, M.; Kirschenbaum, H.; & Simon, S. B. *Clarifying values through subject matter: Applications for the classroom*. Minneapolis: Winston Press, 1973.

Hawley, R. C.; Simon, S. B.; & Britton, D. D. *Composition for personal growth: Values clarification through writing*. New York: Hart, 1973.

Hersh, R. H.; Miller, J. P.; & Fielding, J. D. *Models of moral education: An appraisal*. New York: Longmans, 1980.

Hersh, R. H.; Paolitto, D. P.; & Reimer, J. *Promoting moral growth—From Piaget to Kohlberg*. New York: Longmans, 1979.

Himes, C. *Black on black*. Garden City, NY: Doubleday, 1973.

Hogan, R., & Schroeder, D. The joy of sex for children and other modern fables. *Character*, 1980, *1*(8), 1–8.

Jensen, A. R. How much can we boost IQ and scholastic achievement? *Harvard Educational Review*, 1969, *39*, 1–123.

Jensen, A. R. The differences are real. *Psychology Today*, December 1973, 80–82, 84, 86.

Judson, H. F. The rage to know. *The Atlantic Monthly*, April 1980, 112–17.

King, M. L., Jr. *Stride toward freedom: The Montgomery story*. New York: Harper & Brothers, 1958 (paperback, 1964).

Kinsey, A. *Sexual behavior in the human male*. Philadelphia: Saunders, 1948.

Kinsey, A. *Sexual behavior in the human female*. Philadelphia: Saunders, 1953.

Kirschenbaum, H. In support of values clarification. *Social Education*, 1977, *41*, 401–2.

Kirschenbaum, H.; Harmin, M.; Howe, L.; & Simon, S. B. *In defense of values clarification: A position paper*. Saratoga Springs, NY: National Humanistic Center, 1975.

Kleinfield, S. *The hidden minority: A profile of handicapped Americans*. Boston: Little, Brown, 1979.

Knight, Richard S. *Students' rights: Issues in constitutional freedoms*. Boston: Houghton Mifflin, 1974.

Kohlberg, L. The child as a moral philosopher. *Psychology Today*, September 1968, 25–30.

Kohlberg, L. Education for justice: A modern statement of the platonic view. In N. F. & T. R. Sizer (Eds.), *Moral Education*. Cambridge, MA: Harvard University Press, 1970. (a)

Kohlberg, L. The moral atmosphere of the school. In N. Overley (Ed.), *The unstudied curriculum*. Washington, D.C.: The Association for Supervision and Curriculum Development, 1970. (b)

Kohlberg, L. Indoctrination versus relativity in value education. *Zygon*, 1972, 285–310.

Kohlberg, L. Revisions in the theory and practice of moral development. In W. Damon (Ed.), *New directions for child development: Moral development*. San Francisco: Jossey-Bass, 1978.

Kohlberg, L., & Gilligan, C. The adolescent as a philosopher: The discovery of the self in a postconventional world. *Daedalus*, 1971, *100*, 1051–85.

Kohlberg, L., & Selman, R. L. *First things: Values*. Pleasantville, NY: Guidance Associates, 1972–73.

Krathwohl, D. R.; Bloom, B. S.; & Masia, B. B. *Taxonomy of educational objectives: Affective domain*. New York: David McKay, 1964.

Kroll, J. The arts in America. *Newsweek*, December 24, 1973, 34–35.

Kurtines, W., & Greif, E. B. the development of moral thought: Review and evaluation of Kohlberg's approach. *Psychological Bulletin*, 1974, *81*, 453–70.

Lau v. Nichols. 42. U.S. Law Wk. 4165 (1974).

Lockwood, A. L. A critical view of values clarification. *Teachers College Record*, 1975, *77*, 35–50.

Lockwood, A. L. What's wrong with values clarification? *Social Education*, 1977, *41*, 399–401.

Lockwood, A. L. The effects of values clarification and moral development curricula on school-age subjects: A critical review of recent research. *Review of Educational Research*, 1978, *48*, 325–64.

Maslow, A. H. *Motivation and personality* (2nd ed.). New York: Harper & Row, 1970.

Massiales, B. G. Citizenship and political socialization. In R. L. Ebel (Ed.), *Encyclopedia of educational research* (4th ed.). London: Collier-Macmillan, 1969.

Masters, W. H., & Johnson, V. *Human sexual response*. Boston: Little, Brown, 1966.

Masters, W. H., & Johnson, V. *Human sexual inadequacy*. Boston: Little, Brown, 1970.

May, R. *The courage to create*. New York: Bantam Books, 1975.

McClung, M. School classification: Some legal approaches to labels. *Inequality in Education*, 1973, *14*, 17–37. Harvard University: Center for Law and Education.

McGough, K. One parent's gut reaction. *Social Education*, 1976, *40*, 607.

McGough, K. A parent's perspective—Values clarification: Your job or mine? *Social Education*, 1977, *41*, 404, 406.

McGough, K. A parent's perspective—Who's playing the organ? *Social Education*, 1979, *43*, 232–240.

Mills v. D. C. Board of Education. 348 F. Supp. 866 (D.D.C. 1972).

Muson, H. Moral thinking: Can it be taught? *Psychology Today*, February 1979, 46–68, 92.

Myrdal, G. *An American dilemma*. New York: Harper & Brothers, 1944.

National Assessment of Educational Progress. *Citizenship: National results* (Report No. 2). Washington, D. C.: U.S. Government Printing Office, 1970.

Newmann, F. M., & Oliver, D. W. *Clarifying public controversy: An approach to teaching social studies*. Boston: Little, Brown, 1970.

Nichols, R. C. Policy implications of the IQ controversy. In L. S. Shulman, *Review of research in education*, Vol. 6. Itasca, IL: F. E. Peacock, 1978.

Nimnicht, G. P.; Johnson, J. A., Jr.; & Johnson, P. A. A more productive approach to education. In G. P. Nimnicht & J. A. Johnson, Jr. (Eds.), *Beyond "compensatory education": A new approach to educating children*. San Francisco, Far West Laboratory for Educational Research and Development, 1973.

Oliver, D. W. Educating citizens for responsible individualism. In F. R. Patterson (Ed.), *Citizenship and a free society: Education for the future*, 30th Yearbook, National Council for the Social Studies. Washington, D. C.: National Council for the Social Studies, 1960.

Oliver, D. W., & Shaver, J. P. *Teaching public issues in the high school*. Logan, UT: Utah State University Press, 1974 (Originally published by Houghton Mifflin, 1966).

Orth, M. Pop: Messiah coming? *Newsweek*, December 24, 1973, 47.

Peters, R. S. Moral development: A plea for pluralism. In T. Mischel (Ed.), *Cognitive development and epistemology*. New York: Academic Press, 1971.

Peters, R. S. A reply to Kohlberg: Why doesn't Lawrence Kohlberg do his homework? *Phi Delta Kappan*, 1975, *56*, 678.

Piaget, J. *The moral judgment of the child*. London: Kegan Paul, Trench, Trubner & Company, 1932.

Postman, N., & Weingartner, C. A careful guide to the school squabble. *Psychology Today*, 1973, *7*(5), 76–86.

Raths, L. E.; Harmin, M.; & Simon, S. B. *Values and teaching: Working with values in the classroom*. Columbus, OH: Charles E. Merrill, 1966 (second edition, 1978).

Ravitch, D. Educational policies that frustrate character development. *Character*, 1980, *1*(7), 1–4.

Rescher, N. *Introduction to value theory*. Englewood Cliffs, NJ: Prentice-Hall, 1969.

Rest, J. Developmental psychology as a guide to value education: A review of "Kohlbergian" programs. *Review of Educational Research*, 1974, *44*, 241–59.

Rice, B. The high cost of thinking the unthinkable. *Psychology Today*, 1973, *7*(7), 89–93.

Robinson, P. A. The case for Dr. Kinsey. *Atlantic Monthly*, May 1972, 99–100, 102.

Rokeach, M. *The nature of human values*. New York: The Free Press, 1973.

Russell, G. K. Vivisection and the true aims of biological education. *American Biology teacher*, 1972, *34*, 254–57.

Schempp v. School District of Abbington Township. 374 U.S. 203 (1963).

Schmidt, J. A Christmas call to conscience: Do you hear the animals crying? *Family Weekly*, December 23, 1973, 5.

Scriven, M. *Primary philosophy*. New York: McGraw-Hill, 1966.

Scriven, M. The values of the academy (moral issues for American education and educational research arising from the Jensen case). *Review of Educational Research*, 1970, *40*, 541–49.

Serna v. Portales Municipal Schools. 351 F. Supp. 1279 (1972).

Shaftel, F. R., & Shaftel, G. Dimension Films. Los Angeles: Churchill Films, no date.

Shaftel, F. R., & Shaftel, G. *Role-playing for social values: Decision-making in the social studies*. Englewood Cliffs, NJ: Prentice-Hall, 1967.

Shaftel, F. R., & Shaftel, G. *Values in action* (filmstrips). New York: Holt, Rinehart, & Winston, 1970.

Shaver, J. P. Democracy, courts, and the schools. *Theory Into Practice*, 1978, *27*, 279–90.

Shaver, J. P., & Berlak, H. (Eds.). *Democracy, pluralism, and the social studies: Readings and commentary*. Boston: Houghton Mifflin, 1968.

Shaver, J. P.; Davis, O. L., Jr., & Helburn, S. W. The status of social studies

education: Impressions from three NSF studies. *Social Education*, 1979, *43*, 150–53.
Shaver, J. P., & Larkins, A. G. *Decision-making in a democracy*. Boston: Houghton Mifflin, 1973. (a)
Shaver, J. P., & Larkins, A. G. *Instructor's manual: The analysis of public issues program*. Boston: Houghton Mifflin, 1973. (b)
Silberman, C. E. *Crisis in the classroom*. New York: Random House, 1970.
Simon, S. B.; Howe, L. W.; & Kirschenbaum, H. *Values clarification: A handbook of practical strategies for teachers and students*. New York: Hart, 1972.
Simpson, E. G. Moral development research: A case study of scientific cultural bias. *Human Development*, 1974, *17*, 81–106.
Simpson, G. G. Notes on the nature of science by a biologist. In *Notes on the nature of science*. New York: Harcourt, Brace, & World, 1962.
Steiner, E., & Hitchcock, R. Teaching moral criticism in the sciences. *Viewpoints in Teaching and Learning*, 1980, 56(4), 63–73.
Stephens, J. M. *The process of schooling: A psychological examination*. New York: Holt, Rinehart and Winston, 1967.
Stewart, J. S. Clarifying values clarification: A critique. *Phi Delta Kappan*, 1975, *56*, 684–88.
Strong, W. J. *The development and exploratory field testing of situational materials for pre-service English education*. Unpublished doctoral dissertation, University of Illinois, 1973.
Sun, M. Briefing: Science teachers to ban testing harmful to animals. *Science*, 1980, *209*, 792.
Tinker v. Des Moines Independent Community School District. 393 U.S. 503 (1969).
Tovatt, A.; Miller, E.; Rice, D.; & De Vries, T. *Rationale for a sampler of practices in teaching junior and senior high school English*. Muncie, IN: Ball State University, 1965.
Wadsworth, B. J. *Piaget's theory of cognitive development: An introduction for students of psychology and education* (2nd ed.). New York: David McKay, 1979.
West Virginia State Board of Education v. Barnette. 319 U.S. 624 (1943).
Wigginton, E. (Ed.). *The foxfire book*. New York: Doubleday, 1972.
Zimmerman, P. D. Films: Creative chaos. *Newsweek*, December 24, 1973, 40.

SUBJECT INDEX

Abortion: vignette on, 41–42
Advocacy of political action, 80–81
American Creed, 34, 35, 49, 57, 58n, 78
  as context for debate, 57–58, 115
  and minorities, 60–62
  roots of, 59
  self-evident validity of, 117
  and societal cohesion, 57–58, 115
  and teaching of esthetics, 93
  universality of, 60
  in Value Exploration, 68–69
  and world community, 59–60, 68–69
Art: Peanuts cartoon on, 90
Art teaching: and esthetic values, 7, 24, 28, 89–93
Attitudes
  based on values, 139
  definition of, 19
Attitudes and values, 19–20
  relative importance of, in rationale-building, 166–68

Basic democratic values
  of domestic tranquility, 48, 50, 61
  of due process, 48, 49, 109, 121, 153, 159
  of equal opportunity, 22, 31, 34–35, 61, 69, 70, 158, 166
  of equal protection of the law, 22, 48, 50, 51, 109, 110
  of food and shelter, 24, 48
  of freedom from despotic government, 48
  of freedom of assembly, 49
  of freedom of association, 50
  of freedom of conscience, 49
  of freedom of press, 48, 49, 115–16
  of freedom of religion, 22, 48, 56, 57, 116
  of freedom of speech, 22, 23, 48, 49, 52, 61, 69, 85, 86, 116, 153, 159
  of justice, 78
  of liberty, 48, 61
  of life, 22, 23, 48, 78
  of local control, 57
  of majority rule, 47–48, 50, 57, 84
  of peaceful protest, 127
  of privacy, 142, 159
  of public interest, 51
  of the rational consent process, 52, 80, 81
  of respect for law, 128
  of respect for others, 81
  of responsibility, 48, 123
  of right to education, 24
  of universal suffrage, 116
Basic moral values, 21, 22–24, 30–31, 48–49
  dealing with violations, 82, 83

SUBJECT INDEX

Basic moral values *(continued)*
  democratic schools and, 121–24
  difficulty in defining, 109
  instrumental teaching values and, 96
  as instrumental values, 49–50
  the school and, 53, 83, 88–89, 119–24, 151–53, 158, 171
  Supreme Court and, 109, 119–21, 123
  taught by debate, 117
  and teacher's role in regard to the school, 121, 124, 152–53
  in vignettes, 63–64, 64–65, 69–70, 85–87, 87, 126–28, 131–32
  See also American Creed; Basic democratic values; Moral values
Basic values. *See* Basic moral values; Moral values
Beauty, 24, 28, 29
Bible reading in schools, 56, 57
Biology teaching: in vignette, 84–85

Campus Clatter cartoon, 97
Censorship of art, 25–26
Cheating, 95
  cartoons on, 97, 109
  vignettes on, 129–31, 161–62
Chemistry teaching: vignette on, 38–40
Civil disobedience, 61–62
  vignette on, 126–28
Classical music, 25, 90–91
Cleanliness, 23
Cognitive development, 144–46
  periods of, 146, 147–48
  Value Explorations on, 157–59
Cognitive dissonance, 33
Cognitive moral development
  criticism of stage six of, 148, 150, 151
  relationship of, to cognitive development, 149
  stages of, 146, 148–149, 150
  Value Explorations on, 157–60
  See also Cognitive moral development approach
Cognitive moral development approach, 144–45
  basic democratic values and, 151
  democratic schools and, 152-53

  and differences with rationale-building approach, 153–55
  and discussion of moral dilemmas, 149–50, 151–52
  narrowing effects of psychological theory in, 153–55
  parents' objections to, 154
  promoting stage movement in, 149–50
  research on, 150–51
  selection of discussion topics in, 154
  and similarities to rationale-building approach, 151–53
  teaching of decision-making skills in, 154
  and value inculcation, 151
  vignette on, 161–62
Compensatory education, 27–28
Competition: in vignette, 104–06
Consequences: examination of, 110–11, 113, 124
Constitutional rights: and diversity, 54
Cookery: and esthetic values, 24, 89
Culinary art: and esthetic values, 24, 89
Cultural deprivation, 27–28
Curriculum, hidden. *See* Hidden curriculum

Decision making, 53–54
  beyond values in, 124–25
Decisions
  judging, 113
  qualified, 112
Democracy
  and all teachers, 46, 76, 79–82, 107
  definition of, 47–50
  and republic, 47
  See also Pluralism
Democratic rights as basic moral values, 48
Democratic schools, 121–24
  age and maturity of students in, 121–22
  basic moral values and, 121–24
  dissension in, 123
  due process and, 121
  as ideal mini-societies, 123–24
  permissiveness and, 122–23
  responsibility as a value in, 123
  teacher's role in, 121, 124
  value conflict and, 123
  Value Exploration on, 134
Devil's advocate: vignette about, 64–65

SUBJECT INDEX

Dissension, 53-54, 123
  in vignette, 126-28
Diversity
  and schools, 54-55
  See also Pluralism
Dress standards, 28-29, 35
Drug use, 142
  vignette on, 155-57
Due process in schools, 121, 153, 159

Ecology: in vignette, 84-85
Education
  compared with law, 77-79
  compared with medicine, 77-79
  defined, 71-72
  Peanuts cartoon about school and, 8
Educational philosophy, 164
Education and schooling, 71-74
  distinction between, 72-74
Elementary teachers: in vignettes, 63-64, 87, 129-31, 132-34
Emergent values. *See* Value change
End values. *See* Intrinsic values
English teaching: and values, 169-70
Esthetic education: Peanuts cartoon about, 90
Esthetics
  emotive experience versus analysis in, 90-91
  and "lasting significance," 92*n*
  movies related to, 91
  the nonrationale in, 90-91
  pop music related to, 91
  rock music related to, 25, 84, 90, 92
  social-political dimension of, 25-26
  superior art forms in, 92-93
Esthetic values, 24-26, 89-95
  and connoisseurs, 24-25, 31*n*
  definition of, 24, 89
  in esthetic courses, 24, 89-93
  inculcation of, 115
  in mathematics, 7, 93-94
  and moral judgments, 24
  and nonesthetic courses, 93-94
  Peanuts cartoon about, 90
  and performance values, 26*n*
  as personal taste, 31-32
  school's role in promoting, 89-95
  in science, 94
  shift to moral values from, 25, 31, 92, 93, 96
  social-political dimension of, 25-26
  take on moral tones, 25, 31, 92
  and teacher's commitment, 89-90
  teacher-student relations and, 93
  and value conflict, 35, 94-95
  vignette on, 42-43
  See also Esthetics; Nonmoral values
Ethical decisions, 121, 125
  definition of, 21

Fairness
  as children's value, 110, 158
  vignette on, 128-29
Feiffer, J., cartoon by, 109
Foxfire, 169-70
Frame of reference, 8-9, 33, 71, 76, 164, 168
  of parents, 83
Freedom of press: illustrated by Zenger case, 115-16
Funky Winkerbean cartoon, 122

Gallop Poll, 11
Generation gap, 32-33
Geography teaching, 169-70
Goss v. Lopez, 121

Hair styles, 19, 25, 28
Handicapped student: in vignette, 132-34
Health courses, 170
Hidden curriculum, 6, 64, 68, 73, 74
  basic moral values and, 119-24
  definition of, 1
  J. Dewey and, 119, 120
  and esthetic values, 93
  instrumental teaching values and, 96, 98
  Peanuts cartoon about, 8
  and political action by teachers, 81
  positive effects of, 123-24
  Supreme Court and, 120-21
  vignettes on, 11-14, 15-16
Honesty, 32, 33, 95, 118
Human dignity, 31, 48, 61-62, 78, 83, 118
  and authoritarianism, 143
  and decisions, 113

Human dignity *(continued)*
  democratic schools and, 124
  and equal consideration, 48n
  and esthetic values, 89, 91, 93
  as guiding ideal for teachers, 79
  historical roots of, 59
  and intelligence, 51–52, 88–89, 108, 113
  and rationality, 51–52, 88–89, 108, 113
  and relativism, 143
  and the right to choose, 51
  and teachers as professionals, 79
  and teaching students to think, 51–52
  value development beyond home and, 118–19
  value inculcation and, 114–17
Human worth and dignity. *See* Human dignity

Inculcation. *See* Value inculcation
Indoctrination, 3, 80, 114, 115
  analytic frame and, 114
  in vignette, 161–62
  See also Value inculcation
Inservice education: vignette on, 102–04
Instrumental teaching values, 95–99
  definition of, 95
  may be esthetic, performance, or moral, 95
  Campus Clatter cartoon on, and ethics, 97
  importance of scrutinizing, 95–99
  and teacher authenticity, 99
  See also Instrumental values
Instrumental values, 21, 28–29, 30, 31
  shift to intrinsic values from, 31, 96
  Value Exploration on, 106
  vignette on, 43–45
  See also Instrumental teaching values
Intelligence and feeling, 51
Intrinsic values, 21, 28, 29, 30
  definition of, 28
  vignette on, 104–06

Just community schools, 152

Ku Klux Klan: in vignette, 85–87

Lau v. Nichols, 119–20
Law: compared with teaching, 77–79

Literature teaching
  and esthetic values, 7, 24, 89, 93
  and values clarification approach, 142

Majority rule, 47–48, 50
  in conflict with minority rights, 47–48, 50, 50n
  in vignette, 63–64
Manual arts, teaching of: in vignette, 15–16
Manual skills and esthetic values, 24
Mathematics teaching
  and equal opportunity, 166
  and esthetics, 7, 93–94
  and esthetic values in vignette, 100–02
  in Value Exploration, 14
Medicine: comparison with teaching, 77–79
Melting pot, 54–55
Middle level values, 23–24
Mills v. D.C. Board of Education, 120
Mindlessness, 78, 98
Minority rights
  and the courts, 50n
  protecting, in a democracy, 47–48
  in vignette, 63–64
Minorities: in vignettes, 66–67, 69–70, 87, 128–29, 131–32
Moral dilemma discussions: vignette on, 161–62
Moral stages approach. *See* Cognitive moral development approach
Moral values, 21–24, 30
  basic, 21, 22–24, 30–31, 48–49
  on a continuum, 21, 22–24
  inculcation of, 115–17
  levels of, 21, 22–24
  middle level, 23–24
  personal, 21, 22–24
  Value Exploration on, 45
  vignette on, 41–47
  See also Basic moral values
Moral values education
  affective aspects of, 114–17, 124, 125
  cognitive aspects of, 108–13, 125
  taken in logical sequence versus sequence based on psychological effect, 125
Multi-cultural context, 54, 68
Music. *See* Pop music; Rock music
Music teaching and esthetic values, 7, 24, 28, 89–93

SUBJECT INDEX

National Assessment of Educational Progress, 54
National Council for the Social Studies, 83
National Education Association. *See* NEA
Nature and esthetic values, 24
NEA, 83
Neatness
  Peanuts cartoon on, 25
  in Value Exploration, 84
  in vignette, 11–14
Nonmoral values, 21, 24–28
  esthetic, 21, 24–26
  performance, 21, 26–28
  shift to moral values from, 2, 26–28, 30, 31, 92, 93, 96

Parents
  and playing devil's advocate, 64–65
  and subversion, 81–82
  and teacher stand in the classroom, 114
  and values, 10
Parents' demands on schools: in Value Exploration, 83–84
Patriotism: in vignettes, 64–65, 126–28, 131–32
Peanuts cartoons, 8, 25, 90
Performance standards for teachers: in vignette, 102–04
Performance values, 21, 26–28
  defined, 26
  and esthetic values, 26n
  inculcation of, 115
  take on moral tones, 26–28, 30, 31, 96
  See also Nonmoral values
Personal appearance and esthetic values, 24
Personal preferences, 22n
Philosopher, definition of, 163
Philosophy
  educational, 164
  and experience, 164, 165–66, 168
  rationale-building as, 164
Physical education
  and esthetic values, 89
  and performance values, 26, 28
  in Value Exploration, 14
  vignette on, 104–06
Physical fitness and esthetics, 28
Pledge of Allegiance: vignette on, 131–32

Pluralism, 52–58
  benefits of, 53–55
  and conflict, 55–56
  and democracy, 52–57
  protection of, 52–53
  and value development beyond home, 118–19
Political involvement by teachers, 81
Pop music, 91
Prayer in schools, 47, 50, 56, 57
Preferential admissions policies
  court case on, 50–51
  vignette on, 128–29
Preschool: vignette about, 11–14
Privacy: vignette on, 155–57
Punctuality, 26–27, 95, 96

Qualified decisions
  use by teachers of, in taking a stand, 114
  Value Exploration on, 131
  See also Rational valuing

Rationale, 9–10, 55, 65, 71, 73, 74, 78, 79, 82, 107, 117, 153
  development of, 10, 164–65
  other school personnel and, 121
  parents and, 79, 125
Rationale-building, 9–10
  like education, 165
  and experience, 164, 165–66, 168
  lifelong commitment to, 165
  as philosophy, 164
Rationale-building approach: evaluation of, 163
Rational valuing, 159
  examining consequences of, 110–11, 113, 124
  parents and, 117–19
  and qualified decisions, 112
  and value clarification, 108–09, 115, 124
  and value conflict recognition, 111–12, 124
  and value conflict resolution, 111–12, 115, 124
  and value identification, 108, 115, 124
  and value label generalization, 109–10, 124
  and value labels, 109–10

SUBJECT INDEX

Reading instruction: in Value Exploration, 14
Reflective thinking and rationale-building, 164
Relativism
  value conflict and, 113–14
  values clarification approach and, 143–44
Responsibility for values: Value Exploration on, 83–84
Responsibility of schools to society, 46, 75
  J. Dewey and, 119
  Supreme Court and, 119–21
Rock music, 25, 84, 90, 92
Rules, 106, 171

School and education: Peanuts cartoon about, 8
Schooling. *See* Education
Schools: limited role of, 72–73
Science teaching
  and student thinking, 170
  and values, 3–6, 93–94
  vignettes on, and values, 38–40, 129–31
Self-confrontation
  cultivation of, 168–71
  of Elliot Wigginton, 169–70
  and value and behavior change in a classroom, 170
  and value change in student teachers, 168
  without crisis, 170–71
  See also Self-dissatisfaction
Self-dissatisfaction
  value change and, 167–68
  See also Self-confrontation
Serna v. Portales Municipal Schools, 120
Sex education, 141–42
Sexual behavior, 154
Sexual standards, 5–6, 24
Shared values
  and meaningful arguments, 58
  in vignette, 67–68
Social studies program: in Value Exploration, 14
Social studies teaching
  and student thinking, 170
  values in, 7
  and vignettes, 64–65, 69–70, 126–28, 128–29

Socio-economic status and work demands on students, 171
Solitude, 30, 32
Struggle and progress, 53
Student code of conduct: Funky Winkerbean cartoon about, 122
Student government, 122
Student interests: J. Dewey and, 122–23
Subversion, 79, 81–82, 117

Taking a stand
  and frame for analyzing issues, 114
  risk of, 82–82, 114
  teacher, in the classroom, 80, 113–14
  Value Exploration on, 131
Teacher authenticity, 80, 81
  instrumental teaching values and, 99
Teachers as agents, 46, 74–76
Teachers as citizens, 80–81
Teachers as philosophers, 163–71
  J. Dewey on, 164–66
Teachers as professionals, 75–76
  and democratic schools in vignette, 85–87
  inquiry into values and, 118
  and parents, 82
  in vignette, 84–85
Teaching. *See* Art teaching; Biology teaching; Chemistry teaching; Education; Education and schooling; English teaching; Geography teaching; Manual arts, teaching of; Mathematics teaching; Physical education; Science teaching; Social studies teaching; Values implied in teaching
Teaching as a profession, 76–79
  and basic moral values, 79–82
  and law, 77–79
  and medicine, 77–79
  and a rationale, 78–79
Teasing: vignette on, 132–34
Terminal values. *See* Intrinsic values
Thinking and parents: vignette about, 64–65
Thinking skills: teaching of, 108–13, 125, 170–71
Tinker v. Des Moines, 120, 123

Value analysis in the classroom: vignette on, 129–31

SUBJECT INDEX

Value change, 32–33, 62
   Value Exploration on, 45
Value clarification, 108–109, 115
Value conflict, 32–36
   and basic moral values, 34–35, 61
   and esthetic values, 35, 94–95
   inherent nature of, 32
   interpersonal, 33, 55
   intrapersonal, 33
   and irrationality, 32
   and moral and nonmoral values, 35
   and performance values, 35
   recognition of, 111–12, 124
   and relativism, 113–14
   resolution of, 111–12, 115, 124
   values clarification approach and, 140–41, 143
   in vignette, 85–87
Value identification, 108, 115
Value inculcation, 114–19
   and choice between conflicting values, 116
   and elementary school teaching, 116
   and esthetic and instrumental teaching values, 115
   and moral values, 115–17
   as opposed to inculcation of value judgments, 116–17
   parents and, 117–19
   as red herring, 116
   and reinforcement of basic moral values, 116
   and value definitions, 116
   See also Indoctrination
Value judgments, 17–18, 20, 28*n*
   implicit, 18
   Value Exploration on, 36–38
   vignette on, 131–32
Value label generalization, 109–10
Value labels, 109–10
Values
   and action, 34, 61
   and affective commitment, 57
   and affective domain, 18
   and attitudes, 19–20, 167–68
   and attitudes in rationale-building, 166–68
   and cognitive domain, 18–19
   defined by courts, 56

   defining, 56
   definition of, 1, 17, 139
   as determinants of attitudes and behavior, 167–68
   and emotions and controversy with parents and administrators, 125
   as feelings, 18
   as ideals, 50, 61
   in mathematics, 7, 93–94
   relations among types of, 30–32
   in science, 4–6
   in science and society, 5–6
   in social science, 5–6
   types of, 20–30
   vagueness in descriptive meaning of, 56
   and valued objects, 29
   and value judgments, 17–18
   See also Esthetic values; Instrumental values; Intrinsic values; Moral values; Nonmoral values; Performance values
Values clarification approach, 135–44
   and avoidance of moralizing, 136, 143–44
   and choosing values to discuss, 141
   and definition of value, 139–41
   and failure to distinguish types of values, 141, 144
   parents' objections to, 141–42
   privacy and, 142, 155–57
   as psychological therapy, 142–43
   purpose of, 136
   research on, 138
   reservations about, 138–44
   strategies and activities in a, 136–37
   value conflict and, 140–41, 143
   vignette on, 155–57
Values implied in teaching, 1–7, 166
   in Value Exploration, 14
   vignette on, 67–68
Valuing. *See* Rational valuing
Violence: teaching about, 79–80
Vocational arts and esthetic values, 24, 89

Water pollution: vignette on, 84–85
West Virginia State Board of Education v. Barnette, 120
Writing instruction: in Value Exploration, 14

NAME INDEX

Allen, D., 77
Anyon, J., 171

Beard, C. A., 9, 164
Bennett, W. J., 141, 150
Berlak, H., 17
Beyers, B. K., 151–52
Bloom, B. S., 18
Bowe, F., 62
Britton, D. D., 136
Bronowski, J., 4
Broudy, H. S., 31n
Butts, R. F., 58n

Clement, D. C., 27, 54–55
Combs, A. W., 78
Coombs, J. R., 111
Copernicus, 5

Dahl, R. A., 50n
Davis, J. U., 150
Davis, O. L., Jr., 107n
Delattre, E. J., 141, 150
De Vries, T., 93
Dewey, J., 51, 119–23, 164–71
Dickins, C., 20
Douglas, W. O., 53–54
Douglass, F., 53

Edel, A., 60
Edel, M., 59–60
Elkind, D., 145n

Feiffer, J., 109
Fenton, E., 158n
Fielding, J. D., 138, 145, 152
Fields, C. M., 51
Fraenkel, J. R., xi–xii, 111, 152n
Frankena, W. K., 26

Galbraith, R. E., 151
Galileo, 5
Gallup, G., 11
Gibran, K., 118–19
Gillespie, J. A., 81n
Gilligan, C., 146, 147n
Glasser, W., 99
Greenstein, T., 168

Hall, R. I., 150
Hamilton, A., 115–16
Hamingson, D., 142
Harmin, M., 135–44
Hawley, R. C., 136
Helburn, S. W., 107n
Hersh, R. H., 138–39, 145–46, 151–52, 163
Himes, C., 61

NAME INDEX

Hitchcock, R., 3n
Hogan, R., 6n
Howe, L. W., 137–39

Jensen, A. R., 5
Johnson, J. A., Jr., 27, 54–55
Johnson, P. A., 27, 54–55
Johnson, V., 6n
Jones, M., 151
Judson, H. F., 94

King, M. L., Jr., 61–62
Kinsey, A., 5–6
Kirschenbaum, H., 138–39, 143
Kleinfield, S., 62
Knight, R. S., 123n, 159
Kohlberg, L., 144–55
Krathwohl, D. R., 18
Kroll, J., 92

Larkins, A. G., 17, 112n, 125n
Lockwood, A. L., 138, 142–43, 151

Masia, B. B., 18
Maslow, A. H., 23
Massialas, B. G., 116
Masters, W. H., 6n
May, R., 94
McGough, K. A., 141, 154
Meux, M. O., 111
Miller, E., 93
Miller, J. P., 138, 145, 152
Muson, H., 150–51, 153
Myrdal, G., 32n, 34–35, 57–59

Newmann, F. M., 113
Nichols, R. C., 5n
Nimnicht, G. P., 27, 54–55

Oliver, D. W., 17, 48n, 58n, 113n, 116, 152
Orth, M., 91, 92

Patrick, J. J., 81n
Piaget, J., 144–55
Postman, N., 72, 73

Raths, L. E., 135–44, 150
Ravitch, D., 116, 117
Rescher, N., 17n, 28
Rest, J., 152n
Rice, B., 5n
Rice, D., 93
Robinson, P. A., 6
Rokeach, M., 19, 28, 166–68
Roosevelt, F. D., 49
Russell, G. K., 4

Schmidt, J. A., 4
Schroeder, D., 6n
Scriven, J., 6n, 48n
Selman, R. L., 158n
Shaftel, F. R., 158n
Shaftel, G., 158n
Shaver, J. P., 17, 48n, 50n, 107n, 112n, 113–14, 125n, 152
Silberman, C. E., 98
Simon, S. B., 135–44, 150
Simpson, E. G., 150
Simpson, G. G., 4
Steiner, E., 3n
Stephens, J. M., 71–72
Steward, J. S., 138
Strong, W. J., 11n

Taylor, H., 77
Tovatt, A., 93
Twain, M., 72

Wadsworth, B. J., 145, 147n
Weingartner, C., 72, 73
Wigginton, E., 169–70

Zenger, J. P., 115–16
Zimmerman, P. D., 91